ONCE UPON A FAR HILLSIDE

ONCE UPON A FAR
❧ HILLSIDE ❧

The Life and Times of an Indian Village

Brenda Kidman

CENTURY PUBLISHING

LONDON

First published in Great Britain in 1985
by Century Publishing Co. Ltd,
Portland House,
12–13 Greek Street, London WIV 5LE

British Library Cataloguing in Publication Data

Kidman, Brenda
  Once upon a far hillside: the life and times
  of an Indian village.
  1. Borli Panchaton (India)—Social life
  and customs
  I. Title
  954'.792   DS486.B7/
  ISBN 0 7126 0707 2

Map by John FitzMaurice
Photographs by Brenda Kidman

Printed and bound in Great Britain
by Anchor Brendon Ltd, Tiptree, Colchester, Essex

To my eldest son Lawrence
who always gives his love
and encouragement . . .

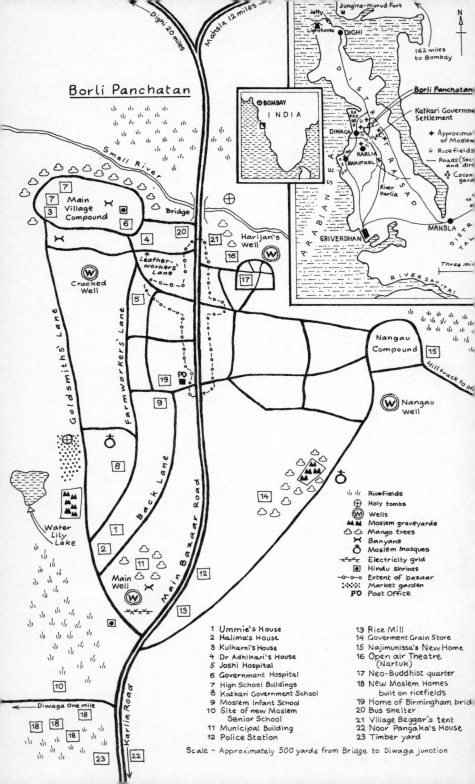

Borli Panchatan

Map Legend

1 Ummie's House
2 Halima's House
3 Kulkarni's House
4 Dr Adhikari's House
5 Joshi Hospital
6 Government Hospital
7 High School Buildings
8 Katkari Government School
9 Moslem Infant School
10 Site of new Moslem Senior School
11 Municipal Building
12 Police Station
13 Rice Mill
14 Goverment Grain Store
15 Najimunissa's New Home
16 Open air Theatre (Nartuk)
17 Neo-Buddhist quarter
18 New Moslem Homes built on ricefields
19 Home of Birmingham bride
20 Bus shelter
21 Village Beggar's tent
22 Noor Pangaka's House
23 Timber yard

Symbols
Ricefields
Holy tombs
Wells
Moslem graveyards
Mango trees
Banyans
Moslem mosques
Electricity grid
Hindu shrines
Extent of bazaar
Market garden
PO Post Office

Scale – Approximately 500 yards from Bridge to Diwaga junction

Dighi 20 miles
Mahsla 12 miles
Small River
Bridge
Main Village Compound
Cracked Well
Leather workers' Lane
Farmworkers' Lane
Goldsmiths' Lane
Back Lane
Main Bazaar Road
Harijan's Well
Nangau Compound
Nangau Well
Hill track to o...
Water Lily Lake
Main Well
Diwaga One mile
Karlia Road

Inset map
Jungira–Murud Fort
Jetty
Lighthouse
DIGHI
162 miles to Bombay
Borli Panchatan
Katkari Governme Settlement
Approxima of Moslem
Ricefields
Roads (Sec and dirt
Coco gard
DIWAGA
KARLIA
BARUTKOL
River Karlia
ARABIAN SEA
DISTRICT RAJASAD
SRIVERDHAN
MAHSLA
DIST TAL
RIVER SAVITRI
Thre miles

Bombay inset
BOMBAY
INDIA

✍ INTRODUCTION ✍

I HAVE OFTEN been asked why I chose the village of Borli Panchatan as the subject for this book. After all, there are some six hundred thousand villages in India and, like Borli, two thousand are situated on the nation's coastline. So why this particular village? The answer is simple. I didn't choose Borli Panchatan; the village chose me after a somewhat bizarre series of events which began in 1972.

At that time I was living with my family in Tunbridge Wells and as a hobby occasionally contributed to BBC 'Woman's Hour' and other Radio 4 programmes. Then, in November of that year, my country suddenly became the sanctuary for twenty-eight thousand Asian refugees from Uganda, victims of racial persecution by Idi Amin. These Asian people had lived for many years in Uganda, going there from India when that part of Africa was still under British rule. It was only natural that those who still held British passports should turn to Britain for protection when they were forcibly exiled. Initially the refugees were sent to sixteen reception centres across the south of England until they could be gradually dispersed to other parts of the country and settled in local authority accommodation.

In November 1972, two Uganda-Asian families arrived in my home-town where our council had hurriedly converted a large and dilapidated Victorian house into two flats. The largest family consisted of Mahommed and Badrunissa Hussein and their eight children. The eldest son was eighteen and the youngest daughter not two years old.

During the next few months, as I made recordings with this family for 'Woman's Hour' about their resettlement, I came to know them quite well. Although the parents spoke hardly any English, the older children had been educated in English-speaking schools in Kampala so they spoke it fluently. The completed programme was broadcast early in April 1973. In it the Asian father mentioned that his old mother was seriously ill in India and he wished he could visit her. Within minutes, a listener in Brighton had telephoned the BBC offering to donate the air-fare to make this possible. After an absence of twenty-five years, Mahommed Hussein and his wife were able to return to their birthplace in an isolated village on the coast of Maharashtra just south of Bombay. In order to document this fresh twist to their story, at the last moment I decided to go with them. The next four weeks were a revelation for a middle-aged suburban housewife whose knowledge of the Third World had previously been confined to flag-days for Oxfam! Being plummeted from the niceties of Tunbridge Wells into the heat and squalor of Bombay administered a severe culture shock, which was exacerbated by the fact that during May India was in the grip of severe drought and food shortages. But once we reached the village of Borli Panchatan, I began to relax and enjoy myself. To me the village represented an idyllic place, set against a mountain backdrop and facing the palm-fringed shoreline of the Arabian Sea. Moreover, I had the strangest feeling that I'd been there before!

The Husseins' sick mother lived at the top of the Nangau compound in a small whitewashed mud hut with overhanging roof. In the same house lived her youngest son, his wife Najimunissa and their newborn daughter, as well as several older relatives. Once the Husseins joined the household, even by Indian standards, three low-raftered rooms were considered overcrowded. Consequently, I was sent to the other end of the village to stay with Kerima, one of Mahommed's sisters who occupied an equally primitive dwelling opposite the kindergarten school. So it was that I first met the old Muslim woman called Ummie who happened to live a few doors down on the same side of the lane.

Having originated from South Africa, Ummie (or Jainub Undre to give her proper name) was one of the few people in the village who spoke passable English. We soon struck up an acquaintance which, during the next month as Ummie became my guide and interpreter around the village, turned into a firm friendship.

This brief introduction to Borli Panchatan left a deep impression. Although it was obviously a poor and primitive place, I was struck by the happiness of the people and the honest simplicity of their lives. I resolved that one day I would return to find out more about the origins of this strangely captivating

8

corner of the Indian subcontinent. As it happened, a full decade passed before this became possible.

During the intervening years I was divorced and went with my youngest son to share a country cottage in Nottinghamshire with my widowed mother. At forty-six, I began a career as a professional broadcaster and writer and was just getting well established when my mother became ill with senile dementia, a protracted illness which ended in her death in 1976. A year later my own health broke down and the possibility that I would ever again set eyes on my beloved Indian village faded from my mind. Yet during those difficult years I continued to correspond with my old Muslim friend Jainub Undre, who kept me in touch with all the joys and vicissitudes of village life through her quaintly phrased but delightfully descriptive letters.

In the winter of 1983/84 I once again travelled the five thousand miles to Borli Panchatan to be reunited with the village I'd fallen in love with ten years before, also with my good friend Ummie, her widowed daughter Halima and Reshma, the adopted granddaughter—a babe-in-arms when I first saw her. While staying with them—in a room in Halima's house set aside for me so I could work in privacy—Ummie and her daughter responded with commendable patience and good humour to my endless queries about village life. For hours at a time, Ummie sat down with me to record accounts of her early days in South Africa and the extraordinary circumstances which surrounded her arrival in Borli, relating with typical charm the story of courage and resourcefulness which forms one essential theme of this book.

I also made a number of new Hindu friends in Borli, many of whom spoke excellent English. Certainly without their help I should have found it difficult to obtain the necessary information. As the villagers speak four distinct languages, I should have needed the services of more than one interpreter!

The local regional dialect is Konkani (pronounced 'cokney') which ninety-nine per cent of the villagers use. A handful of well-educated Hindus speak Marathi, which is also the language now used in the High School. Then there are Muslims who speak Urdu; and there is also a language spoken by the once-nomadic Katkari, a tribe of diminutive aboriginals who have recently been settled in government housing on the southern outskirts of Borli. Nobody understands a word they say! Therefore, when I was living in Borli Panchatan, I had no other recourse but to rely on my English-speaking Hindu friends, who, despite my insatiable curiosity concerning every aspect of local life, treated me with inexhaustible courtesy. (I have since wondered about the reaction of my Nottinghamshire villagers should an Indian writer suddenly appear with a similar project in mind!)

Considering the help and kindness this stranger received in Panchatan, it would be remiss of me not to express my thanks to Borli's most respected citizens. First my gratitude goes to octogenarian Nana Sahib Kulkarni, Brahman patriarch of Borli whose ancestors first settled in the area two hundred years ago. Nana was able to supply extensive information about social developments in the village as handled by the village *panchayat* (council), as well as express his views on the advantages and disadvantages which have resulted from the village's exposure to the influence of mainstream India brought about by modern communications.

My heartfelt thanks also to Ravi Kulkarni, Nana's farming son. Ravi is an example of a new breed of college-educated agriculturists keen to introduce modern cultivation methods in an attempt to raise the living standards of subsistence farmers. Again, with consummate patience, Ravi sat down to record the interviews which largely comprise the chapter on the growing of rice, coconuts and mangoes.

Then there was Madhusudan Adhikari, the first doctor trained in Western medicine to arrive in Borli in the 1930s and who is still practising at the age of eighty-three. It was this doctor who over a number of interviews traced the development of health care in the village. As a prominent member of the village *panchayat*, Dr Adhikari could also relate in some detail the struggle the village elders have always had in trying to introduce social reforms to a largely illiterate peasant community.

My thanks to Gumpoo Bapat who lives in the coconut gardens at Diwaga. This Hindu gentleman made available books which helped clarify certain religious traditions associated with the tiny region of Maharashtra, once called Jungira.

Last, but by no means least, I am indebted to Dr Vasudha Joshi and her husband Dr Nilkanth Joshi, a couple who exemplify the dedication necessary to devote a whole professional lifetime to country people. Their generous friendship enabled me to witness certain private Hindu festivities, which, as an outsider, I might otherwise have missed. And I shall always remember their gift of a Christian Christmas cake given to me as a gesture of Hindu goodwill!

Returning to Borli Panchatan for a second and longer visit

after an interval of ten years undoubtedly provided me with a valuable basis from which to make comparisons. I was able to observe at first hand the changes which have resulted in commercial links with mainland India, the way prosperity amongst the Muslim villagers has markedly changed the architectural appearance of Borli and to see for myself how a young generation of educated villagers are turning away from the traditions of family life in their eagerness to become Westernised.

Should I go back to Borli in 1994, I doubt that I should find more than a trace of the rural lifestyle which for centuries has bonded the villagers to the soil, the seasons and their religious cultures. Therefore, this book is a tribute to a vanishing corner of India. It is composed from legends, anecdotes, hearsay and fragments of gossip, together with personal research and observations made during my four delightful months in Borli Panchatan. I trust that it is an unbiased and representative account of the life and times of my hillside friends.

BK
Norwell
December 1984

❧ PART ONE ❧

How it was . . .

✦ CHAPTER ONE ✦

Mystical Beginnings

Time and many twilight tellings
Richly weave the tales of history's dawn
So who can ever truly say
Where dreaming ends and truth is born?

Shortly before nightfall the Katkari tribe reached a jungle clearing above the birthing place. While the men went to empty snares, the women lit fires.

Tali sat against a sesum *tree and watched. Occasionally, when her belly hardened, she arched her back and uttered a low ululating cry to make sure Ayana had not forgotten her. Busy at the fireside, from time to time the old woman nodded reassuringly in the girl's direction. Later she brought a gourd of oil and aromatic herbs to rub on Tali's breasts and stomach and into the aching void between her thighs.*

Soothed, the girl slept. From her lair in the rocks overlooking the campsite, chita *caught the scent of Katkari and took her cubs to hunt on another hillside.*

Near dawn, Tali awoke and groaned. Ayana's exploring hand knew it was time. She roused Dutta and between them the older women hoisted Tali to her feet and started down the track to the river. In winter the Karlia was a shallow band of water hemmed by wide beaches of shale. A mile westwards, the river crossed salt marshes and deposited an elbow of dark silt before merging with the sea.

The women waded knee deep. Dutta held Tali beneath the arms so that she floated with the icy current. Presently, as daybreak tinted ribbons of groundmist lemon yellow, the nomad child was born into the flowing river. Draping the infant across Tali's stomach, Ayana wound cotton thread round the umbilicus. Then she searched the shallows for two stones, one flat and the other sharply edged. Placing the first behind the cord, she deftly severed it with the other. Next she bound the baby against the mother's ribs with a length of coloured cloth.

At the estuary, Channakia the vulture landed clumsily on a sandbank, snatched the placenta in her talons and, swiftly airborne again, flew back to her brood.

* * *

At daybreak Kabutari climbed to a rocky ledge above the campsite. He saw three go down to the river and four return. His people would now remain in the clearing for a second night in order to perform the sacrificial rites necessary to acquaint the great spirits with the latest member of the tribe. Then, looking out to sea, Kabutari's keen eyes saw something to change his mind. No larger than sparrow wings, two sails topped the horizon. A deep uneasiness warned Kabutari that they were not Koli fishing boats blown off course. Memory recreated the stench of hot blood in his nostrils. He knew the tribe must move inland to a place of safety.

In Kabutari's youth, the Katkari tribe numbered a hundred or more, travelling the thickly-forested hills which formed the backbone of the tiny hook-shaped peninsula. Some thirty miles long and twelve miles at its widest point, this land was bordered on the west by the Arabian Sea and on the east by a watery arm of the great Rajpuri creek at Murud, which, extending due south, all but severed the little promontory from the wild mountainous regions of the interior.

Small of stature and placid by nature, the Katkari hunted with spears, bows and arrows and traps, never taking more meat than they needed for daily sustenance, never staying long enough in one place to alter the fine balance of decay and renewal which existed between man, beast and vegetation. In this way, all signs of their passing were soon obliterated. During their wanderings the men went ahead to mark the path. In straggling groups, women and children followed, carrying on their heads shallow baskets for cooking pots, woven cotton blankets, machettes for cutting firewood and little else. The smallest children rode perched on someone else's hips, the babies strapped to their mothers' backs. Behind— often far behind and leaning heavily on thumb-sticks—came the long-in-tooth.

When the nomad approached the end of his walking days, the other men would escort him to the threshold of a large cave in the escarpment which crowned the peninsula's highest point. There the old one would wait out his last hours. Soaring on warm thermals, the ever-vigilant Channakia would also wait.

It was in the winter of his initiation to manhood that Kabutari had been called upon to perform the final service for his own father. While the rest of the tribe continued towards the coast, tradition obliged him to sit within calling distance of the old man, attend to any needs he may have and witness his going. The waiting was always soon over. Intuitively the old one knew when the moment of liberation was near.

There was a full moon that night. Squatting in the shadows, a few

16

paces from the entrance to the cave, Kabutari heard his father's voice, scarcely louder than a fall of leaves, as it whispered on and on. Kabutari listened carefully. Turned to white stone by the moonlight, the dying man continued far into the night, softly intoning the ancient wisdoms which generation upon generation of the tribe had used as the formula for survival.

When his father died, Kabutari removed the talisman from around his neck and transferred it to his own. Then, going to the back of the cave, he searched the ledge until he found a crude stone-headed hammer and an iron spike. Chanting farewells, Kabutari placed the spike against his father's forehead at a point just above the bridge of his nose. With one forceful blow of the hammer, he punched an opening in the bone so that the old Katkari's spirit could escape. After replacing the ritual implements, Kabutari left the sacred burial-place and set off in pursuit of the tribe. He had failed to notice that Channakia, who since daybreak had patiently circled the hilltop, was flying at speed towards the marshes.

*   *   *

In the fifteenth century the peninsula supported a scattering of peasant settlements as well as the Katkari. The Koli people had established fishing communities in rocky coves along the seashore; and on terraces cut in the lower slopes of the hills Hindu farmers cultivated rice. The nomads had little contact with the settlers. Occasionally the older men would go to a village ironworker to exchange medicinal herbs for knives and metal tips for their hunting weapons. Otherwise they kept away. If the villagers were reluctant to venture into the jungle and forage plants for themselves, the nomads were equally apprehensive of habitations plagued by mysterious spirits which could cause healthy men to spit blood and die. So the relationship between nomad and settler was amicable but tenuous.

Which was why the young Kabutari, running to catch up with his tribe, felt spasms of uneasiness as he realised the track his people had taken led him out of the forest and on to the open hillside.

Standing in the shadow of the bluff, he had searched the landscape for a sight of them. There was none. Cupping his hands to his mouth, he uttered a series of birdlike calls. He listened. No answering call came back. Cautiously Kabutari followed a path which led to a vantage point overlooking the marshes. Simultaneously his gaze took in the Koli village shrouded in smoke and the presence of two sailing vessels anchored in the bay.

Then Kabutari saw his people.

Once a year the Katkari braved the leeches to wade in marsh

17

ponds gathering *cutchera*. What puzzled the young nomad was why a simple liking for water chestnuts should have resulted in the carnage he now perceived. Where each butchered Katkari lay, the dark marsh waters had turned to crimson.

Ten old people had stayed at the edge of the forest and had survived; also four men who had gone to set traps. Two young boys, a girl named Tali and three women had managed to scramble to safety when the black assassins plunged through the reeds, curved swords swinging in a frenzy of savage decimation.

Ten years later, as Kabutari's people hurriedly turned their backs on the coastline and sought sanctuary in virgin jungle, they had no way of knowing that this time their fears were groundless.

* * *

Out on the point, diving for oysters, Javan the Koli was also aware that the approaching ships might signify death and destruction, as he tried to decide which was his quickest way back to the village.

Secreted in the coconut and *kiora* palms behind the dunes, the Koli had excavated underground shelters, concealment being the only means of protection against the fanatical brutality of the fuzzy-headed barbarians.

The Arab seamen always came during the months when the prevailing westerly trade winds enabled their narrow craft to skim the waves with the speed of sea-serpents. Once in the shallow waters of the bay, the crew would furl the single main-sail, drop anchor and man the longboats. They stayed to ran-sack the Koli settlement before setting fire to the huts. As flames flushed the remaining occupants into the open, the Arabs singled out the women and girls for taking captive.

The Koli did not lack courage. At first they had vigorously defended themselves against the marauders. However, primitive weapons were scarcely a match for cutlass and pistol wielded with pitiless accuracy. The death or permanent disablement of a fisherman was not a sacrifice likely to insure the survival of his progeny. So, among the palms at Diwaga, the Koli dug bolt-holes, lined with stones and skilfully roofed with foliage to render them invisible. Unfortunately, safety for the coastal Koli meant trouble for their inland neighbours. Thwarted in one place, the Arab slavers crossed the marshes behind Diwaga to terrorise rice farmers, cutting down all those unfortunate enough to get in their way.

Javan had heard tell that, some fifteen miles to the north, a fisherman called Ram Raj Koli had organised resistance against Arab aggressors. Even as a young boy, Ram Raj had been renowned for his extraordinary strength. Muscular and fearless, Ram Raj was able to fish single-handed in waters shunned by his more timorous neighbours.

At a point some six miles off the tip of the peninsula, a rocky island jutted high out of the sea. Known then as Jaldurga, it was equidistant from the city of Murud to the north and, directly behind, from the entrance to Rajpuri creek. A plateau of grass and palms, altogether some fifteen hectares, extended across the summit of the island. There was also a good freshwater spring.

Ram Raj Koli realised that the island could, if properly reinforced, protect local fishing and farming communities from seagoing predators. So he recruited a small band of men and under his supervision they erected palisades and bastions around the island's perimeter. Within this compound, Ram Raj organised the construction of a village with a granary and stone storage tanks for water, thus creating a self-supporting fortress for the defenders and their families.

From now on, alien ships when trying to navigate the narrows between Jaldurga and the mainland would be exposed to a barrage of sling-shot and arrows.

Thus, Ram Raj Koli the fisherman became protector of Jaldurga. With many bitter memories of foreign molestation, the coastal people welcomed his protection, and when Ram Raj demanded that every village contribute towards it, none objected.

*   *   *

Javan had gone pearl fishing at low tide when refracted sunlight dappled the sea-bed and simplified his task. Working selectively and taking only the oldest oysters, he soon accumulated a sizeable heap. Then hoisting himself out of the water, he sat with his back to the waves and began the search. Deftly the tip of his knife penetrated each shell, cutting the ligament which bound the two halves together. After a quick examination of the fleshy contents, the remains were tossed to the gulls.

At the moment Javan found the third and largest pearl, he sensed danger. Brushing hair from his face, he looked over his shoulder. Two Arab vessels had sailed round the headland and were preparing to anchor in the bay. With rivulets of sweat streaking his salt-encrusted body, Javan leaped from rock to rock, skirting deeper pools, splashing through others, fear not exertion causing his heart to pound in his ears like angry surf.

He doubted if anyone in the village had noticed the ships. At daybreak the other men had gone to the creek behind Diwaga to dig for shellfish, their view of the open sea obscured by the palms. The women, he knew, were busy preparing the betrothal feast for Azad. The pearls in Javan's pouch would complete the price asked by the family of the girl chosen to be his brother's wife. If he could get back to the beach before the longboats, Javan believed there would still be time to warn the others and go into hiding.

In years to come, whenever Javan told the story to his children's children, he could never quite remember whether he slipped before or after he caught sight of his children. Even at some distance, Javan had no difficulty recognising Mitha and Shama amongst the group of children who emerged from the dune cactus. The pain from his foot, firmly wedged in a crevice, was nothing compared to the anguish Javan felt at having to watch helplessly as the Arab *dhows* spawned two long-boats which rapidly approached the shore.

* * *

The voyage from Abyssinia had taken longer than the crew had been given to expect. For one on board, it proved too long. As the crew pulled for the land, three white-robed figures in the prow of the first boat sat huddled over the corpse of a fourth.

When, twelve days out of Masqat, one of his four passengers had died, Captain Nure Repeer ordered the body to be thrown overboard. Patiently the dead man's companions insisted that Sheik Ahmoud's remains deserved more than an unmarked grave in the Arabian ocean. Repeer laughed in their faces. Once the body began to stink, he said, they would be glad enough to forget such nonsense.

It was another twenty days before they sighted land. In death, as in life, the holy sheik remained incorruptible. This phenomenon had a profound effect on Repeer. At first he refused to believe the evidence of his own eyes and nose. Several times daily he would visit the cramped quarters astern which had been assigned to the holy men. Reverentially they would fold back the burnouse covering the corpse so that the captain could once more ascertain that no signs of decompo-sition marred the serenity of the stone-cold face, that his nose was assailed by nothing stronger than the reek of sandalwood incense.

After thirty years roaming the hostile oceans which divided his desert country from the wild jungle regions of Konkana,

Captain Repeer could not remember anything having affected him so deeply as the indestructibility of Sheik Ahmoud's mortal remains.

The captain was no stranger to death, an ever-present reality woven into the fabric of his seafaring life. He neither feared death for himself nor hesitated to inflict it upon others, whether they happened to be idol-worshipping savages or any of his countrymen foolish enough to challenge his authority. But death which was not death was like a fishbone in the craw: he could neither swallow it nor could he spit it out and forget it. For the rest of the journey, the captain frequently lapsed into periods of brooding silence when his lips moved as if in argument with an unseen inquisitor. Spurning the rough ship's fare of salted meat and biscuits, he ate sparingly of dried figs and almonds given to him by the oldest of his three remaining passengers, Shah Walli.

It was he who had approached Captain Repeer when he put into Masqat, the last port of call before heading out to sea on the most arduous part of the crossing. Shah Walli was wearing the white robes and black cloak of a *peshmam* (priest). He requested passage to Konkana for himself and his three fellow priests. Captain Repeer was on the point of elbowing him out of the way when he caught the glint of rosary beads round the old man's throat. The payment offered in silver coins was meagre enough, but the prospect of acquiring four gold rosary beads prompted the captain to take the priests on board, thus unwittingly fulfilling the final stages of a prophesy long known to his four passengers.

The night before he set sail, another vessel had moored alongside Captain Repeer's. Finding that they were both bound for the Konkana coast, the captains struck up an acquaintance.

In Repeer, Captain Malik Muhammad recognised a man who enjoyed violence for its own sake, and he sought to gain his support for the venture with which he hoped to ingratiate himself with his fellow merchant Siddi Perimkhan.

One of the first Arab merchants to recognise the advantages of colonising the Konkana coast, Perimkhan had encountered scant opposition from the indigenous Hindu population when, between 1460 and the end of the century, he established a series of Abyssinian strongholds in the coastal area surrounding Murud. At first these were trading posts where Arab ships could stock up with provisions and barter for pearls, spices and hardwoods. Then, realising the potential value of territory so much more fertile than the arid deserts of their homeland, many stayed to join Perimkhan in a campaign to annex peasant settlements further inland.

The largest of the immigrant landowners assumed the title of *nawab*. Under their tutelage, local labourers were used to construct Moorish-style homes for the nawabs and their families. Eventually Hindu girls were enticed into their harems, thus founding a hybrid Muslim dynasty which lasted for more than four hundred years.

On previous voyages to Konkana, Malik Muhammad had seen for himself the problems posed by the impregnable fort of Jaldurga, a perpetual thorn in the side of Perimkhan and all those seeking a safe passage to the Rajpuri creek. The steep rock sides to the west of the island were washed by dangerous rip currents. Elsewhere the wooden barricades were well guarded against surprise attack. The only accessible point was the inlet used by garrison boats when bringing supplies. A steep and irregular flight of stone steps led directly up to the great door, flanked by wooden towers manned by the pick of Ram Raj Koli's warriors.

Captain Muhammad believed he had devised a strategy to bring about the downfall of Jaldurga, and when Repeer learned that the conquerors of this island fortress would be well rewarded by Perimkhan, he was quick to promise his support. Captain Repeer had, of course, reckoned without the demise of one of his four passengers and the mystical effect it had had upon him.

* * *

None of Repeer's crewmen would touch Sheik Ahmoud's body. Between them the priests dragged it out of the longboat and away from the water's edge. Then, turning towards Mecca, they fell to their knees in worship.

Meanwhile, the crew from Muhammad's vessel had landed further down the beach and were unloading empty water kegs. Then they joined forces with Repeer's men. While some stayed to collect driftwood, the rest headed inland to forage for food and water. The rigours of the voyage had left no man unmarked. Salt sores and lice, frugal rations and close confinement had made the mariners hollow-eyed and irascible. Had they seen the women and children, they would certainly have slain them like so many cockroaches. The fact that they did not was yet another manifestation of the mystical forces which surrounded the arrival of the Muslim priests at Diwaga.

Armed with cutlass and pistol, the foraging party found the

sandy track which crossed an expanse of scrub cactus and grass before disappearing into the palm groves. Urged on by hunger, the sailors hurried along it, knowing it would lead them to habitation and eager to satisfy their appetites for violence and food at one and the same time. In a clearing close to a pool of fresh water, they came across five goats tethered to stakes in the ground. Without the need to look further, the sailors filled their kegs, shouldered the live beasts and returned to the beach.

Nure Repeer, stricken by a strange sense of inertia, sat apart from the others, as if in a dream, watching Malik Muhammad ritually slaughter the five goats according to the Muslim law of *halal*. Twisting the first animal on to its haunches, Malik clamped it between his knees, intoning the prescribed prayers. Then forcing its head backwards, he severed the animal's jugular. At each killing, Repeer trembled as he saw the goat's head change into the face of one of the priests. As Malik Muhammad's knife sacrificed the fifth and last goat, Repeer felt his body drenched by icy sweat.

For one fleeting moment the face which became transmogrified was his own.

* * *

Lying amongst the rocks at the southern end of the bay, Javan the fisherman had seen the foraging party leave the beach. Tensely he waited for the distressing sounds which would indicate that they had reached the village. Instead the sailors reappeared, thin columns of smoke spiralled up from their fires and Javan smelled roasting meat.

Javan calculated that once their hunger had been appeased the strangers would stretch out on the hot sand to sleep. Then, trusting that his foot would bear his weight, he planned to run to the children and quickly lead them to concealment behind the mudbanks. From there it would be an easy matter to reach the village by way of the riverbed and, even if the Arabs did raise the alarm, Javan felt sure that they would be too slow to muster an effective pursuit.

Waiting for the right moment to make his escape, Javan was unprepared for the children's next move. Seduced by the appetising aroma of hot meat, they forgot their original fear of the strangers and began to whisper. Presently Mitha and Shama were prodded out of the group towards the nearest figures squatting on the beach.

Shah Walli extended a hand and touched his companions, first Kwaja Shabbudin then Kobulla Husseine. Nodding assent, the priests got to their feet, intercepted the small girls and gently herded them back to their companions. Kwaja Shabbudin, who possessed the gift of tongues, told the Koli children to go home by way of the Karlia riverbed. The children obeyed meekly, only once pausing to look back before being waved on again by the holy man.

Kobulla Husseine then appeared on the rocks in front of Javan and motioned him to follow the young ones. Not until he had reached the safety of the village hideouts did Javan begin to wonder why it was that although the escape had been made in full view of the seamen, none had paid the slightest attention. To add to his puzzlement, examination of his foot, which had been badly lacerated when he fell, failed to show any trace of injury.

* * *

On the following morning Malik Muhammad made preparations to sail on the high tide. Two of his ship's company had to remain behind, stricken by a fever which caused violent shaking and delirium. When he approached Captain Repeer to make arrangements for their departure, at first he suspected the captain was also down with the fever. Then he saw that Repeer's brow was cool. Only his eyes burned with a peculiar unfocusing intensity. From his salivating lips, Muhammad heard what could have been muttered passages from the Koran. Then again, quite possibly it was no more than the incoherent babble of a lunatic. Leaving Repeer to his fate, Malik Muhammad rejoined his men and set sail for the north.

Ram Raj Koli's lookout on the western end of Jaldurga sighted Malik Muhammad's vessel as it tacked up-wind towards Murud. Two days later the same man recognised the ship in convoy with two others and holding a course which would bring them close to the fort's entrance.

The sun was dipping into the horizon as the sound of the alarm drums rolled across the coppered waters and echoed in the hills. In two of the three vessels sailors dipped rags into the kegs of oil they had brought with them and tied these to their arrows. The third vessel, captained by Muhammad, dropped to the rear, waiting until the first bombardment had set fire to the immense timber doorway. Anticipating that Ram Raj Koli would be forced to concentrate his main defences at the gate, Muhammad planned to slip round the eastern tip of the island and attack the garrison in its flank.

It was a bold plan, but destined to failure. The women in the fort were ready with great pots of water which they poured over the battlements to extinguish any fires before they got a hold on the fort's structure. Ram Raj Koli's marksmen from their elevated positions were able to discharge a rain of burning arrows which fell across the first two boats. Leaping overboard, the sailors made a desperate attempt to swim to safety but, as their boats sank, burning oil fanned out on the water engulfing them. The creek resounded with their agonised cries mingled with the triumphant shouting of Ram Raj Koli's men. Once more, the fortress of Jaldurga had proved invincible. Captain Malik Muhammad, commanding the only ship to escape, beat an ignominious retreat.

Jaldurga was never conquered by force. After his death, for a few years Ram Raj Koli's successor, Aitbarrao Koli, ruled this miniature kingdom with equal bravado, but its days were already numbered.

By 1490 the land known as Konkana, a narrow strip of coastal hills and valleys between the Arabian Sea and the Western Ghats of India, was playing host to numerous colonies of Arab origin. Having once established their autocracy, the nawabs proved tolerable overlords, especially since the Hindu peasantry were by and large adaptable people, wanting only to pursue their simple lives as farmers and fishermen. However, this meant that Jaldurga's need for self-sufficiency became increasingly important as Aitbarrao's levies on the peasants were now paid to their new lieges. But somehow the fortress of Jaldurga survived, a reminder to Siddi Perimkhan and the nawabs that they were not yet the masters of all they surveyed. When it came, the downfall of Jaldurga was accomplished not by direct assault but by trickery.

One May evening in 1490, as Aitbarrao was watching storm clouds thickening on the horizon, out of the west he saw an Arab merchantship running before the wind. When still some distance from the island it dropped anchor and a small boat began making slow headway on the choppy seas. When it finally reached the cove at the foot of the stone steps, Aitbarrao and an armed guard were there to receive it.

The merchant said he had been on his way from Goa to Surat with a cargo of wine, silks and ivory when the storm had forced him off course. He requested a night's sanctuary for himself and his crew, and by way of inducement he presented Aitbarrao with a purse of gold dinars and a keg of wine. Aitbarrao agreed to shelter the merchant, his personal servants and such valuables as he cared to bring into the fort for safe keeping.

Otherwise, the rest of the crew would have to weather the storm on board their vessel.

The ship having been anchored close to the steps, the merchant and his men carried into the fort a quantity of large chests, which they left in the courtyard on the other side of the gateway. All but a handful of the men then returned to their ship and the great door of Jaldurga was shut and barred.

In the next few hours the visitors generously distributed wine to Aitbarrao and his guards until one by one they collapsed in a drunken stupor. At a pre-arranged signal, armed warriors emerged from the merchant's 'treasure chests', massacred the gateway guards and, as the door swung open, the remainder of the assault force swarmed into the fort. Before the garrison realised what was happening most lay dead or dying.

The name of this shrewd merchantman was Siddi Perimkhan. His second-in-command was Malik Muhammad.

Soon after the fall of Jaldurga, the fortress was handed over to Siddi Ramdu Niek, who renamed it Janjira Mehroob. In due course, the sparsely-populated peninsula to the south of the fortress also came under the heel of the nawabs. First known as Habasan, or 'home of the dark ones', a century or so later this same territory became the state of Janjira. From then on, despite attempts to dislodge them, an unbroken lineage of nawabs governed there until Indian independence in 1947.

* * *

On the beach at Diwaga, Nure Repeer was locked in conflict. Since the expedient of surrender was impossible, Repeer's tormented soul sought refuge in insanity. Convinced that their captain was bewitched, Repeer's crew hurriedly elected a new leader, rowed back to their ship and hoisted sail.

Once the Koli lookout had reported the departure of the Arab *dhows*, from his position high in a palm tree, the fisherfolk emerged from hiding and returned to their homes. When a small group of strangers was sighted still on the beach, an armed party set out to investigate.

As the fishermen reached the dune cactus, the three *peshmam* calmly positioned themselves between the Koli and the figures of Repeer and the other two sailors slumped on the sand. The body of the dead priest also lay close by.

Uttering shouts of defiance, the Koli launched their spears with all the force and accuracy usually reserved for hunting sharks. The slender shafts hurtled through the air with a sighing sound, but just before impact they miraculously dissolved into a flock of black ibis. Wheeling sharply to avoid the priests, the birds flapped away towards the headland.

There followed a brief interval of silence. Then, falling over themselves in their eagerness to escape, the terrified Koli fled from the beach. All but Javan. Something kept him standing there, within yards of the dark strangers who had once again demonstrated their supernatural powers. 'Do not fear us, we intend no harm to anyone in this place.' The words Javan heard and understood came from the lips of Kwaja Shabbudin. 'We ask for shelter for these sick men and burial for our friend. Go to the village and tell your people what I've said.'

It was some hours before Javan succeeded in convincing the village council that the men on the beach posed no threat. Reinforcing his argument with details of his miraculous escape with the children, he reminded them that the Arab sailors had also not ransacked the village when they first arrived. Finally there was the incredible business of the spears. 'They are few, we are many,' Javan said to the elders. 'Let us make them welcome to our village and in return ask the old men to use their magic powers to protect us from sea attacks.'

So the matter was resolved. Shortly before nightfall a party of bearers with bamboo litters, accompanied by villagers carrying torches, returned to the seashore to bring the Arabs to Diwaga. The two sick sailors were carried to Javan's family dwelling, where his women began the long task of nursing them back to health. The three priests chose to spend the night squatting beside their dead fellow priest beneath the *banyan* tree which was also the village shrine. Nure Repeer, who had stumbled after the procession when it left the beach, took up his position nearby, his strange behaviour soon attracting the attention traditionally accorded to those possessed by evil spirits. After scratching symbolic patterns on the earth with pointed sticks, the elders put garlands of flowers round Repeer's neck and gently fed him with rice and pieces of fruit. Repeer accepted these ministrations in silence before curling up like a dog to sleep.

* * *

For a few hours each day the three-mile-long ridge of coconut and banana palms behind the dunes became an island. High tides filled the creek which curved round the northern end of Diwaga and overflowed into the marshes. At the opposite end of the bay, waves swept into the Karlia estuary and, breaching the low banks, completed the watery encirclement.

27

For three-quarters of the year the connection between Diwaga and the foothill villages inland could be made on foot. Once the tide receded, the sun rapidly dried all but the deepest pools to reveal a zig-zag track between the reeds. During the monsoon months of June, July and August not only was Diwaga isolated from the mainland by a mile-wide expanse of choppy water, but it was also periodically swamped by rogue waves which broke over the dunes and contaminated fresh-water supplies.

The monsoon was a time of extreme hardship for the Koli. Reduced to a diet of dried fish and rice, obliged to drink rain-water, the people had little resistance to the diseases spawned by extreme heat and humidity. Even the snake-bone charms they wore sewn into little leather pouches round their necks, or bunches of spiky *gohana* (wild herb) hung over hut doorways, often failed to protect them from the ravages of malaria and tuberculosis.

But the disease feared above all was leprosy. Those unfortunate enough to develop this affliction were twice cursed. Not only did they suffer the miseries of gradual disfigurement, but they were also driven from their homes and condemned to live as outcasts. Most lepers fell prey to wild animals or died of starvation long before the disease itself would have killed them. One exception was a Koli leper called Bakha.

As a boy, he remembered the shame and horror which accompanied his grandmother's banishment from the village, even though he was one of the youngsters who brandished sticks to chase the old woman away whenever she tried to return. Some years afterwards, when Bakha found tell-tale blotches of white skin on his legs, he neither expected nor received any other kind of treatment.

The monsoon storms had been particularly bad that year and, had he not been a strong swimmer, Bakha would have been drowned. Instead, with the last of his strength, he reached a spit of rock-strewn land which jutted out into the creek on the other side of the marshes. In a shallow cave, Bakha made his shelter. At first, the leper not only longed for death, but also sought to hasten its arrival. He walked heedlessly into the jungle, waiting for the snarling leap of *chita* or the fatal embrace of *aar* the python. But it seemed even these predators declined to feed on leprous meat.

As the years passed, Bakha learned to accept his solitary existence and was especially comforted by his vivid and recurrent dreams. Sometimes these were so real that Bakha would run outside to look across the marshes to Diwaga, always puzzled when the only movement was that of flying foxes against a starlit sky. But he never doubted that eventually his dream figure would materialise. When it did, he, Bakha the leper, would be waiting.

One morning, when the wild mango was in blossom, the leper saw a strange procession on the winding path across the marshes. At first he mistook it for a hunting party with a dead pig suspended from a carrying pole. Then, as the figures came nearer, Bakha saw that the two men who carried the pole came from his village and the elongated shape swinging beneath it was no pig. Following the bearers came three men in long robes and, some distance behind, the last member of the party, who repeatedly stumbled and fell before staggering on again, as if he had been drinking too freely of palm toddy.

Bakha felt his heart constrict with joy when he recognised Nure Repeer as the man he had seen so often in his dreams. Where the land began to rise, the party stopped. Bakha could just hear their voices as they argued. The men from his village kept pointing in Bakha's direction, but when the robed figures urged them on, they lowered their burden to the ground and made off.

Bakha watched two of the robed men shoulder the pole and, picking their way through the rocks, walk up the hill towards him. The leper attempted to cry out a welcome to the strangers, but without lips or tongue only succeeded in making incomprehensible noises. Nor did his gaping mouth convey the smile that was in his heart when Kobulla Husseine placed a strong hand on his head. Never expecting to be touched again by another human, this contact sent waves of happiness coursing through Bakha's malformed body.

The Arab priests carried Sheik Ahmoud's corpse into the cave. Turning westwards and bowing their heads to the ground, they spent some time in prayer. Afterwards they laboured until sunset, rolling boulders into the cave entrance and sealing the cracks with smaller stones.

So the first of the five holy men from Arabia found a final resting place on a foreign hillside.

* * *

When Nure Repeer recovered his senses, the past had been wiped from his memory like chalk from a slate. So he questioned neither his surroundings nor the presence of the holy men and the perpetually yawning Bakha.

29

As confirmation of his rebirth, the priests took Repeer to a pool of springwater set in a declivity of rocks. Stripping off his filthy garments, they made Repeer kneel in the water while they scrubbed him with handfuls of grass and seeds from the Ritti tree (natural soap). Then Kwaja Shabbudin honed his knife on a stone, shaved the captain's matted hair and beard and finally, removing his own long black coat, put it on him.

Bakha watched this with the attention of one who has already seen it all before. When the last fragment of Repeer's woolly hair fell into the pool the leper, springing forward to retrieve it, placed it in the cavity which was his mouth and swallowed.

A strange tingling sensation spread through Bakha's body. The scene tilted and spun until he fell in a deep faint. When he regained consciousness, the first sound Bakha heard was that of his own voice, speaking clearly. With increasing excitement he examined his hands. They were intact. Similarly, he fingered his face and felt only healthy flesh and normal features. As predicted so often in his dreams, every trace of disease had vanished.

Bakha demonstrated his gratitude in practical ways. On a level piece of ground, near the pool, he built the priests a hut, laying a heavy thatch of palm leaves on the roof to protect them from the fast-approaching rainy season. He gathered wild fruits from the forest behind the hillside and cut a store of firewood. He fished in the creek and put the gutted fish on long poles to dry in the sun. Then, shortly before the rains set in to isolate Diwaga, Bakha ventured back to his village.

Having no idea of the events which surrounded the arrival of the Arabs, he approached his people with apprehension. Because none had witnessed the worst effects of his disease, Bakha feared that they would drive him away again before he had a chance to describe his miraculous recovery. He need not have worried. Many years had elapsed since he left. With no more attention than an occasional glance of curiosity, he walked unmolested to the hut where his family lived. They talked long into the night. Next day the entire village assembled under the *banyan* tree to listen while Bakha repeated the account of his cure so accurately foretold in his dreams.

But it was the unfulfilled conclusion to these dreams that had brought Bakha to Diwaga. 'In my dreams,' he told the people, 'just before waking I would see on the hillside behind my cave a ball of glistening light. Clustered round it I saw huts tall as the *jumblum* tree and coloured like the sea and the sky and the feathers of parakeets. I saw plenty of people,' Bakha continued. 'They were fat and smiling people with many children and old ones too. I saw crops of rice heavy with grain, fine herds of buffalo and goats. In the air I heard voices.'

When the elders urged him to remember what the voices said, Bakha shook his head and admitted that this was where his dreams always ended. 'I only know that they were calling me to that place,' he said. 'I have come to see who will go with me.'

Reluctant to exchange known for unknown discomforts, at first Bakha only succeeded in attracting a handful of Koli to live on the other side of the marshes. Javan and his family went, taking with them the two Arab sailors. Realising that life in a new place could be no worse than the privations of widowhood in the village, four women with their broods were also amongst the founding population of Bakha's once-deserted hillside. They cut a clearing in the jungle, built huts and on virgin soil raised crops of rice, vegetables and *thil* (sesame) for cooking oil. Some of this produce they bartered with other settlements for domestic animals, and soon there were several flourishing herds of oxen and goats.

Bakha's people also flourished, apparently impervious to the sicknesses which annually decimated the inhabitants of neighbouring communities. Taking the Koli widows for their wives, the Arab seamen eventually founded a breed of children who did not worship at the *banyan* tree, but went instead to sit at the feet of Kwaja Shabbudin and listen to his teachings. This Muslim priest chose to live below the northern slope of the hill close by a stream. Kobulla Husseine took up his abode on high ground to the west of the village, and Shah Walli went south to the other side of the Karlia, where in wild territory renowned for its lions, he lived out his life as a hermit.

As for Nure Repeer, the fifth holy man, he remained in the hut Bakha had originally built beside the rock pool, and five times each day Bakha heard his strong and melodious voice intoning the words of his dreams:

> 'Allah is great
> Come to pray
> Mahomet is Allah's apostle
> Come to pray
> Allah is great . . .'

* * *

The ancient historical landscape of India is studded with myths and legends, peopled with saints and mystics, heroes and

31

villains, the delineation between fact and fantasy blurred both by time and the telling.

Exactly how the Abyssinian priests came to be interred on this remote hillside has been lost in the mists of might-have-been. But the tombs are still there, as is the village above Diwaga which all those centuries ago became known as Place of the Five Holy Graves, or Borli Panchatan.

❧ CHAPTER TWO ❧

INDIA HAS ALWAYS been a land of villages. During the early days of the British raj, Sir Charles Metcalfe, a government official in charge of land revenue reform, described the typical Indian village as akin to 'a little republic' and went on to say:

> The union of the village community, each forming a separate little state in itself, contributed more than any other factor to the preservation of the people of India through all the revolutions and changes which they have suffered. The village is in a high degree conducive to their happiness and to the enjoyment of a great portion of freedom and independence. I dread anything that has a tendency to break them up.

In 1818 Sir Charles Metcalfe was expressing fears which were soon to become a reality. Under British rule, administrators with less insight into the values of village life, began to erode an existence which for centuries had supported eighty per cent of the entire population of India, in rural communities where all economic needs were met within the village itself.

The carpenter, the blacksmith, the weaver, the potter and the basket-maker—as well as other artisans—worked for one another, bartering their skills and services for raw materials, food and clothing, their livelihoods protected by the nature of the Hindu caste system which bonded specialist occupations into a kind of 'closed shop'. The peasant born into a family of weavers, for instance, would spend his working life in this trade and in no other. Inherited skills were safe from rivalry within the village or from competition outside it. In the village each citizen was a valued contributor to the welfare of the whole community, living in a mini-democracy presided over by a council of respected elders (the *panchayat*), with personal grievances or cases of anti-social behaviour resolved according to local justice.

The size of the villages varied enormously. In some, the population numbered perhaps one or two hundred; elsewhere, the village would have several thousand inhabitants. But always the governing principles were the same. The people depended upon agriculture and handicrafts for their survival and paid taxes levied by their local landlords in crops, goods or labour. The village landlord might be a Hindu prince or a Muslim sultan, depending upon who was ruling the district during that period of Indian history.

Originally the Moguls came to northern India from central Asia, Persia and Arabia, first to plunder and pillage, then to establish military outposts and finally, between 1200 and 1580, to settle down and adopt India as their homeland.

During centuries of political upheaval, it was the fragmented nature of Indian village life which prevented any form of unified resistance to foreign conquest. It was the same characteristic that ensured the survival of the Hindu people, who were able to shelter within the independent stability of their 'little republics'. Like corks in a troubled sea, the villages were able to remain afloat when larger vessels became submerged.

The Muslim conquest of India differed in many respects from the invasion of earlier races such as the Greeks, the Scythians and the Parthians. These invaders had been absorbed by eclectic Hindu culture, not so much a religion as a way of life which honoured every man's right to seek his own spiritual path to perfection even when this involved the mystical deification of animals and the elements.

The monotheistic devotees of Allah strenuously resisted assimilation into Hindu society. In fact, they sought to force Hindu conversion to the Muslim faith. Only when the followers of Muhammad became a permanent force in central and northern India did the cultural and religious differences between the two races find a common meeting ground. Hindu philosophy advocated universal brotherhood, which the Muslims recognised as one of the essential teachings of their own holy scriptures. From this common spiritual belief evolved the new Hindu sect of Sikhism, a synthesis of the mystical ideas of both Hinduism and Islam.

But the practical fusion of the two cultures was strengthened by the enlightened reign of Akbar in the late sixteenth century. The great Muslim warrior removed the fear Hindus had of forcible conversion to Islam, and appointed Hindus to positions of responsibility. He also encouraged cross-culture marriage between Muslim and Hindu nobility. To unite further the common interests of both races, Akbar made Persian the language of the people, founding universities to promote Persian scholarship.

At the height of Mogul rule in India, Muslim influences on Hindu culture were far-reaching and beneficial. The classical form of vocal and instrumental music, known as *ragas*, even today a celebrated attribute of Indian art, was originally introduced by Tansen, the great Muslim musician at the time of Akbar and Akbar's successor Shah Jahan.

The Muslim conquest also left an indelible mark on Indian architecture in every city from Kabul in the north to the Assam borders in the east, to Gujarat in the west and as far south as Bombay State. They built fine mosques, palaces, forts, tombs for their famous and, of course, created one of the greatest monuments of all time, the Taj Mahal—to this day as much associated with the word India as elephants and *ashrams*.

The steady influence of Muslim rule penetrated into every corner of Hindu life, right down to food and fashions. So the seeds of resentment lay dormant for three centuries until, when Shah Jahan's son Aurangzeb seized power in 1658, the Mogul dynasty entered a period of decadence.

Over the centuries, prominent Hindus in the Muslim administration had been rewarded with gifts of land. Many 'little kingdoms' sprung up across India. Some were governed by nawabs and nazims, the titles given to Muslim noblemen in charge of civilian and military affairs. The title of *peshwas* was given to Hindu governors. However, the existence of so many autonomous little states proved an unwieldy empire, difficult to control from the central sultanate in Delhi, especially since Aurangzeb was more interested in self-aggrandisement than in state affairs.

Aurangzeb was notorious for the extravagance and corruption he brought to the palaces of Delhi. He also encouraged the deliberate religious persecution of his Hindu subjects. So the glorious empire built up by the wise and liberal Akbar went into a sharp decline. It was the propitious moment for the Hindu people to rise up and overthrow the Moguls.

The legendary exploits of Chatrapatti Shivaji, today a much

revered national hero, are chronicled elsewhere. The fight for Hindu independence begun by Shivaji continued well into the eighteenth century. During these turbulent times, the strongholds built to protect the 'little kingdoms' changed hands many times as the fortunes of war flowed first one way and then another. Only one fortress remained inviolate. That was the island fortress in the tiny Konkana kingdom known as Jungira.

* * *

With the Mogul empire in chaos, the Marathas—the indigenous Hindu hillsmen—might well have restored Hindu rule in India had it not been for the appearance of yet another foreign power.

Decimated by civil war in the north and bitter skirmishes between minor states, the Muslim potentates were already fast losing control when the first Europeans came to India, initially to establish trade routes, ultimately to gain territorial footholds. The Portuguese annexed Goa, the French settled in Pondicherry and the British, under the auspices of the East India Company, bargained for trade concessions in Surat and Bombay on the west coast and Calcutta on the east.

The next hundred years were riddled with bloodshed and strife as various political factions struggled for supremacy. Maratha forces continued to fight the Moguls but with decreasing success. By the latter part of the eighteenth century, Maratha strongholds had been reduced to Indore, in the north, and Pune in the high mountains of central Maharashtra. The last Maratha energies were used in a heroic attempt to drive the English out of western India, but this only resulted in the annexation of the Maratha territories in Pune by superior English military forces.

Between 1757 and 1850, either by military conquest or political manipulation, the East India Company increased its holdings in India. In return for cash payments from state governors, the Company organised military protection in the feuds which raged between one 'little kingdom' and another. In this way the East India Company gradually extended its frontiers, building armies of occupation manned by local recruits and forcing local rulers to pay for their maintenance.

The demoralising effect this had was soon reflected in the growing disregard for the welfare of the people displayed by the displaced nizams and nawabs, who extracted heavy taxes in order to meet the financial demands of their new 'protectors'.

Eventually disheartened Indian rulers yielded authority to the English, thus facilitating the scope of British colonising activities.

In 1857 smouldering resentment at the domination of foreign powers erupted in the bloody events of the Indian Mutiny. Aided by Sikh forces, the military superiority of the British soon quelled this final defiant bid by the Hindu people for possession of their country. A year later a proclamation by Queen Victoria transferred administrative powers from the East India Company to the British Crown.

As it happened, it was also only a matter of time before the villages of India, having survived centuries of political upheaval, found their freedom and independence threatened by a revolution taking place more than five thousand miles from their homeland. This was, of course, the Industrial Revolution in Europe.

*   *   *

Before the advent of the East India Company, which paved the way for the British empire builders, Indian handicrafts were renowned for their high quality. Utilitarian goods supplied the needs of ordinary people, luxury articles satisfied the more opulent requirements of noble households. In overseas markets India was famous for the skill of her craftsmen, many working within village communities.

Well into the seventeenth century, fine muslins from Dacca, silks from Murshidabad, flowered brocades from Benares and Ahmedabad, carpets and woollen shawls from Kashmir, brass statuary from Bombay, enamelled jewellery and intricately carved furniture inlaid with mother-of-pearl and brass were among the merchandise coveted by free-trade markets in Africa, Arabia and Europe.

Then came the development of industrial mechanisation in the West, especially the growth of the textile industry in the English Midlands. England, a country which until the nineteenth century had been largely agricultural, began to build up heavy industries. People who had relied on agriculture for their livelihoods flocked to the cities to work in the factories.

Since the importation of Indian calicoes, silks and chintzes was in direct competition with markets for English textiles, the governments of the time imposed heavy tariffs to discourage trading between India and England. But, as the East India Company gained power in India, it was able to flood the market there with cheap British goods. Inevitably, this had a disastrous effect on the Indian economy.

Indians who for generations had spent their working lives within independent and self-supporting communities found that foreign competition and factory capitalism had devalued the worth of the individual craftsman. British policies directed towards disinheritance of the noble houses of India also meant that even on the home markets there was small demand for their skills.

But this was not all. Village autonomy was also threatened by the construction of road and rail communications and by land reforms which had catastrophic repercussions on the rural masses. Traditionally tenant farmers paid taxes in kind or by working for one day out of every eight for the local landlord. In 1896 British legislation, totally ignoring age-old barter systems, demanded that in future land taxes be paid in money. The peasant smallholder was thus forced to grow and sell his produce outside the village. At best this provided him with an uncertain income, since food prices began to fluctuate according to supply and demand over a wide area. The peasant farmer was ill-equipped to understand the commercial stratagems which obliged him to grow crops for money instead of to feed his family and to pay his neighbours for help with sowing and reaping.

Having disrupted the self-supporting nature of village life, the British failed to provide alternative employment, either by using taxes to develop industrial India or in any other way. As a result, displaced villagers were forced to go looking for work as coolies on road and railway construction or to try and find employment as farm labourers. In fact, agriculture was quite unable to support this surplus of casual labour.

Between 1860 and 1908 there were twenty years of famine in India. The British allocated food to distressed areas, but the people were too poor to buy it. In the seven years up to the turn of the century the Famine Commission reported the death of 19 million people from starvation. It also reported that these deaths had, for a time at least, restored the balance between food production and the growth of the population.

By the end of the nineteenth century the entire structure of village life had changed. The citizens of Charles Metcalfe's 'little republics' had been irreparably impoverished by the commercial exploitation of their new rulers. It was not difficult, therefore, for the British to recruit Indian labour, faced with starvation or immigration, for its colonial activities in South Africa.

The Dutch, who were the first to settle in South Africa, brought their slave labour from Malaya, Java and other Pacific Islands. British imperialists arrived much later and, failing to persuade the Negroes to work on their sugar cane, tea and coffee plantations, made arrangements for shipments of indentured labourers from India. The Indians in South Africa were not called slaves but 'serfs'. The first Indian immigrant families in Natal were put to work on the land or in mining and paid wages of 10s a month and their keep.

As well as indentured labour, thousands of free Indians went to South Africa over the next decades to escape widespread unemployment in their homeland. Intent on establishing themselves in business, these workers often trekked into remote parts of the interior, where white traders would not go, in order to sell goods to the natives. Eventually many of these enterprising Indians found prosperity in their new country. The fate of the indentured workers was not so fortunate.

At the end of a five-year contract, these workers were given the choice of being deported or agreeing to a life of serfdom in South Africa. There was also a third choice. Once the five-year period expired, a worker could opt for free citizenship— provided he paid an annual tax of £3, as well as a similar amount for each of his dependants. The immigrants were caught between the devil and the deep blue sea. Even though these people were as much the subjects of Queen Victoria as the white and black populations of the Cape colonies, they were regarded as 'semi-barbarous Asiatics', refused the vote and forced to live in slum ghettos.

It was the plight of Indian immigrants which in 1893 inspired an Indian lawyer called Mohandas Karamchand Gandhi to embark upon a long struggle to win racial equality for his fellow countrymen in South Africa. Deploring any form of violence, for the first time but by no means the last, Gandhi exercised the ingenious political weapon of *satyagraha*, or civil disobedience, which by 1908 had become a popular mass movement in the Transvaal. Many were imprisoned along with Gandhi in Johannesburg jails, where coloured inmates were forced to wear white caps. The white cap subsequently became the Gandhi cap, symbol of Indian nationalism.

But it was not until 1920 that the twenty thousand immigrant workers in South Africa were given free and equal citizenship and Mahatma (literally 'great-souled') Gandhi returned to his homeland to mastermind the passive struggle for *purna swaraj*, or complete freedom for India. In the process, the Mahatma also became champion of the oppressed and an indefatigable campaigner for the revival of village independence.

* * *

Momentous historical events on mainland India scarcely penetrated to the tiny kingdom of Jungira. The ridge of mountains and forests called the Western Ghats formed a natural barrier between the villages on the peninsula and the interior; communication with other parts was almost entirely restricted to sea traffic to and from the jetty at Dighi on the northern tip of the promontory.

By the end of the eighteenth century the hillside village of Borli Panchatan had become a sizeable community. Some three thousand Hindus and Muslims and a scattering of Jews lived in clusters of simple mud and palm thatch *bungala* shaded by a leafy canopy of tall trees.

By all accounts, the independent nawab rulers of Jungira were tolerant overlords. In the royal household all military concerns were under the control of Muslims, the appointment of Hindus being restricted to insignificant posts.

One octogenarian inhabitant of Borli, Nana Kulkarni, is able to trace his Brahman ancestry in Borli Panchatan back to the eighteenth century. He outlined the development of the village during his father's lifetime.

The people round here were easy-going. We were not much aware of the fact that our state was governed by the nawab's sweet will and that Hindus had no say in the administration of the area. In olden days the people in all the villages hereabouts were mainly agricultural. They toiled hard all day and their only recreation was *bhajans* (worship) in our Hindu temples and *azaan* (Muslim prayers) in the mosque.

Though the people of this village professed different religions, there was always tolerance amongst them and no religious scuffles of importance. Our main disturbances came from the outside, from robbers called *ganguls*. These thugs roamed the countryside and were attracted to big houses where they could steal plentiful stores of grain and other valuables. They always came stealthily at night and, as there were no lights in the village, after dark people stayed home, afraid to go out.

My father tried to unite the people to protect the village with vigilantes, but this could not be arranged. People didn't have any idea of social order in those days. But that is why my family always lived in modest mud and thatch houses. For three centuries we were the most prominent landowners in this place, but we lived in a simple way so we wouldn't attract the attention of the *ganguls*.

As there were no good roads, travelling in the old days was always tedious. There was just one good track running between Shriverdhan, some fifteen miles south of here, through Borli and on to Dighi, ten miles to the north on the end of our peninsula. Ordinary people went everywhere on foot. Just a few families travelled by bullock-carts or on horseback. We also used *dholies* (sedan chairs) with side-curtains to carry sick persons and Muhammedan ladies, who were not permitted to be observed in public. And we always travelled by day and if we couldn't finish the journey, we would stop at a village for the night because in those days the jungles around here were full of wild animals.

When I was a child, I can remember hearing tigers roaming near the house, although they never came down to the village. Once, when my father took me on the cart to Shriverdhan, as we climbed one big hill, ahead of us on the road we saw a tiger. He looked at us and we said our prayers. Then he got up and walked off into the jungle. So, in the old days, nobody went far from the village unless they had to.

Poor roads meant that marriages were usually settled within our village. Child marriage amongst Hindu people was quite usual, the age of the bridegroom and bride being perhaps twelve and ten respectively. Muslims married a little later and their religion permitted a man to take as many as seven wives, although I think two or three was more the custom.

As for traffic from Borli to Bombay, during the fair season this was carried on by small steamships, passengers having to go from this village by bullock-cart ten miles to Dighi, then across the Dighi creek in a small sailboat to board the steamer at Jungira-Murud. There was a land route to Bombay, but even in the fair season this took several days. The way was over the steep Ghats, which in those days were covered by thick jungle full of wild animals. And there were no bridges over the six wide creeks between here and Bombay. Few people made that journey if they could avoid doing so.

Our village economy was largely self-supporting. The few goods we needed from outside were brought to Dighi by *machava* (a small cargo vessel)—things such as jaggary (raw cane sugar), salt and sweet oil. Local village traders had to store these for the monsoon days, but from May to August there was always a scarcity of perishable foods such as onions and potatoes.

In the rainy season our village was almost cut off from other places. Sea travel had to be suspended and going by land was very treacherous. There was no telegraph office either. Our postal service was by letter bag carried by a runner to the post office at Jungira-Murud. If someone wanted to send a telegram that man had to go on foot to Dighi, then cross the creek and get the message telegraphed from Jungira-Murud. In the monsoon this was very dangerous for him as the creek was all rough water.

40

Borli is very fortunate that the seashore is only two kilo-metres away at Diwaga. In the hot season we get cool breezes and even when there is a scarcity of other foods, the villagers have been able to get fresh fish. Borli has always been the market-place for fish and produce brought in from villages within a radius of seven or eight miles. Most of our other needs were met within the village.

We had craftsmen who were the shoemakers. They tanned local hides and prepared good *chappals* from them. These village sandals were very nice and had a good market in and around this area. Then there were the *kumbhars* who made clay pots and also mud bricks used in the better class of building. As for weavers, in the old days there were at least twenty in Borli who made *kurta* (long-sleeved shirts) and *dhoties* (volumin-ous sarongs caught up between the legs) for the men, and saris for the ladies from yarn brought by sea from Bombay state. I have to admit, we have always had a big class of *bhandari*, the people at Diwaga who climb palm trees and tap juice from the coconut flowers to make into strong toddy. All the Hindu people round here drank it, but who can criticise this habit? After toiling all day in the wet ricefields, palm toddy put some warmth back into their bones. I'm not saying that sometimes it didn't overheat their brains too, but you must understand that the poor working people had very little enjoyment in their lives.

Now in the past there were a few Jewish families in the village, although they've all gone back to Israel now. These people operated old wooden oil-presses worked by bullock-power to crush edible seeds like sesame for cooking oil and non-edible seeds for lamps. There was no other form of lighting in Borli Panchatan until we got electricity in 1963.

Consequently, in the old days nobody went out after dark. Then all the doors of the *bungala* were closed for the night. Simple houses in the village were built very close together with large sloping roofs. This gave collective protection from the heavy monsoon storms, as well as plenty of shade during the hot season. Living close together also gave the people a sense of protection in times when jungle animals such as lions and jackals prowled close to the village at night.

Concerning the health of villagers, they did not suffer much from serious sicknesses. There were sometimes outbreaks of cholera and typhoid, and overcrowding in the homes spread these diseases. There was no medical help, but if a person recovered he got a good immunity.

My father and his father before him were Ayurvedic prac-titioners, using local herbs and plants for medicines. They held early morning dispensaries on our front veranda and people walked in for miles around to wait in the courtyard for treatment although mostly their problems were minor ones, sore eyes, boils and diarrhoea. Both my father and my grandfather were experienced *vaidya* and had studied ancient books on natural remedies. They mixed medicines for the needy sick, but never made any charge. Of course, there were also several old-type medicine men in the village, *ghoti* wallas who could charm away snake and scorpion bites and cure some types of nervous disorders. But mostly the illnesses my father treated were the result of poor diet or lack of clean water.

There was always an acute water shortage in our village every year during April and May when the rivers dried up. Dada Sahib Kulkarni, my father, worked for the good of the village for more than sixty years, and during this time persuaded the Jungira local board to dig drinking-water wells in Borli. There were eight of them altogether, but one had to be reserved for the untouchables. These people could not drink from the same wells as we high-class Hindus. But Dada Sahib made great efforts to persuade our villagers that untouchables should be given equal rights. He was a liberal person and made sure he employed many of these unfortunate people in our ricefields.

My father also took over the great task of draining the marshes between Borli and Diwaga – some four hundred acres in all. He organised the construction of an earthen dam across the creek to keep the sea out, and spent many years bringing this land under cultivation. This extra rice gave a very big boost to food stocks in the village. It also helped rid the village of malaria. Up until 1914, malaria was a serious health problem for the people of Borli because the marshes were a good breeding ground for mosquitoes. When this land was brought under cultivation, the mosquitoes largely disappeared and so did the incidence of malaria.

Dada Sahib was also a keen educationalist. In the last century there were only vernacular schools in the village teaching up to seventh grade (twelve-year-olds). Muslim students wishing to have an English education could study at the high school boarding establishment founded by the nawab at Murud, but Hindu students had no similar opportunity until 1930. Well-to-do families had to send their sons to Pune for their education.

In the village, less than ten per cent of the population of three thousand attended school; most were illiterate. Children worked with their parents in the ricefields from an early age. Then, when the British government introduced the Land Settlement Survey in 1897 and landlords had to find taxes in cash, many workers were thrown off the land. It was the start of three very terrible years for this village.

First unemployment for our poor and then, in 1898, the outbreak of an illness which we had never seen before. People got large purple swellings in their necks and groins and had a high fever. Whole families died of this plague, which we think was brought by rats which came ashore from foreign boats. We had no medicines for this sickness and it spread from person to person. So, in some ways, it was a good thing when the worst disaster of all struck this village in 1899.

Nobody knows for certain what started the fire. Rumour had it that one night a family on the bazaar road had been drinking toddy and began fighting. An oil lamp was tipped over and nothing could stop the flames spreading to other *bungala*. People ran into the ricefields and escaped, but many more perished most dreadfully. The lanes between the houses were narrow, the breeze fanned the flames from one hut to another, and by morning only my family house at the top of the hill and a few of my neighbours' homes that had tiled roofs were left standing. The rest of the village was reduced to ashes.

As you can imagine, on top of all their troubles, the people of Borli were in great difficulties. There was no help to come from anywhere. That year many Muhammadans decided to leave our village and go to South Africa to try and do business there. Some called their families to follow, some left them behind and sent money for their support.

Following the fire we had some hard years, but in time we rebuilt the village. My father and the *panchayat* planned it so that the lanes were wider and there was more space between the houses. I am proud that my father was highly respected in his lifetime by all who lived in Jungira state, regardless of caste, creed or station in life. In 1937 the British government of India wanted to present coronation medals for outstanding service to the community. Our nawab only recommended two people in this district and one was my dear father, Dada Sahib Kulkarni.

* * *

Among the Muslims who left Borli Panchatan at the turn of the century to seek prosperity in South Africa was a young man of twenty called Haji Mahmoud Undre. Haji had married his first wife at the age of sixteen, but when, at the end of two years, she failed to present him with any children, he took a second. This wife gave birth first to a daughter and then, despite their fervent prayers for a son, another.

Haji Undre's family survived both the plague and the fire, only to find themselves heavily in debt to the local money-lender. When his father ordered Haji to go and join his uncles in Cape Town, the young man did not protest. Once he had recouped the money he had to borrow to pay the steamship passage, he would work hard and save enough to return to

Borli Panchatan and buy himself a third wife. The law of luck and averages, he believed, would then get him the sons he needed to keep him in his old age.

One November morning in 1900, just before dawn, Haji Undre went out into the yard behind his parents' *bungala* and, with more care than usual, performed his morning ablutions. Then, donning snow-white tunic and *pyjama*, he pressed his lace skullcap on to his wiry head and joined his father for the walk to the mosque. Half an hour later, while Haji located his sandals from amongst the many pairs left at the entrance to the mosque and embraced his neighbours in a last farewell, his father fetched the bullock-cart. The two yolked beasts hauled the creaking vehicle up the bazaar road. As it passed his home, Haji heard the loud wailing of his mother and two wives. Little did he realise that he would not set foot again in his village for more than forty years. Haji Mahmoud Undre landed in Cape Town and went to work for his two uncles in their small general store, in a suburb of the city.

Nine years later, also in Cape Town, twin baby girls were born to a Dutch Afrikaner couple called George and Sarah Williams. The mother's labour was long and difficult. Within an hour of the birth both the mother and one of the infants had died. The midwife swaddled the surviving twin in cloth soaked in olive oil and put her in a shoebox. The remaining twin was baptised Jainub in a Christian church and taken to the home of a maternal aunt. George Williams was a regular soldier with a regiment of the Transvaal Scottish. He sent maintenance for his daughter, but seldom visited her. In the third year of the Great War he was posted to France with the South African Overseas Forces, and in 1917 his sister-in-law received War Office notification that he had been killed in action.

A year later a virulent form of influenza swept through Cape Town. It was thought to have been brought by soldiers returning from the insanitary conditions of European battlefields. For Jainub, who was nine years old, it formed one of her earliest memories.

> My aunty got it. One day she was all right, next day she was delirious with a high fever. My uncle ran for the doctor, but he couldn't come. Many doctors were also ill and the others had no time to see to everybody who was sick. Anyway, there were no medicines which made any difference.
>
> I got a slight fever but was soon over it. My aunty was ill for three days and then she died. I remember the truck stopping at our door. On the back were piled up bodies wrapped in

44

blankets. The trucks came down our road every day because all our neighbours was dying like flies. The scouts in charge used to break down the doors to some houses and find all the family dead inside. Sometimes they'd discover a small baby crying, with nobody to take care of it.

It was a terrible scourge. The authorities dug huge trenches outside the city and used to take truckloads of bodies to tip in there. White people, black people, my aunty and everybody got buried there together, without any prayers or anything like that. We saw in the newspapers that more people died from that influenza than was killed in the whole four years of the war.

Jainub's widowed uncle re-married and the little Afrikaner orphan's new 'aunty' gave the child a good upbringing. Jainub was sent to a Christian church school, where she learned to speak and write English.

I also learned the piano and had singing lessons. I had a sweet voice and won prizes for singing in Sunday school concerts. My favourite hymn was 'All things bright and beautiful' and the Christmas carol 'Once in royal David's city'.

My new aunty looked very nicely after me. She worked as a cook in the house of a Scottish family called McKenzie. Professor McKenzie wore a long black gown and a mortar-board hat. He was a very important person at the university. The McKenzies lived in a big house and had five small children; two boys and three daughters. When I was about twelve, Mrs McKenzie asked my aunty if I would like to go and help with the housework and taking care of their smallest baby. So I left school to work in the big house. I got three shillings a week and my dinners.

During the next two years, Jainub grew into a buxom young woman with a mop of soft brown hair tinged with auburn. Her happy friendly disposition made her a favourite both with the McKenzies and the rest of the domestic staff.

As they came from Scotland, my madam liked European food. So that is what I learned to cook. Every meal started with broth. We used to get sheep lungs from the butcher and put them in a big pot with vegetables to cook on the range. Then, before serving, we'd take out the lungs and feed them to the cats. I learned how to lay the table in the family dining-room with a starched linen tablecloth, crystal glasses and real silver cutlery, with a special spoon for soup. After soup, the family had meat with two vegetables, then stewed fruit and custard, then cheese and black coffee sweetened with little crystals of coloured sugar.

Once or twice every year, my madam and Professor McKen-

zie took all the children to Simonstown to stay in a seaside
hotel. Then we servants could have the run of the house. When
I cleaned the sitting room, sometimes I would lie on the sofa
and think how it would feel to be the madam of such a rich
place.

There was this young fellow who worked in the vegetable
garden. He used to pinch strawberries off the patch and give
them to me and little posies of lavender. I was going on fifteen
when I got pregnant. We called my little girl Florina and my
madam was very kind. She let me stay on at the house and
look after my baby along with hers.

One of my jobs was to attend to the ordering of the weekly
groceries. There was a general store not far from the McKenzie
residence, run by Muslim people from India. The shop boy used
to call at the back door for madam's weekly list and bring back
the groceries the same day. But sometimes things got left out.
Then my madam would tell me to bicycle down to the shop
and fetch what was missing.

The old man who owned the store used to tease me, in a
friendly sort of way. Often he'd slip presents into my overall
pocket—not much, perhaps a small bar of chocolate or some
cachous (sweetmeat made of cashew-nut). For a whole year it
went on like this, but I didn't mention it to my aunty. Then
one day, while I was at the store, that Indian gave me a letter.
It said: 'You can go where you like in the whole wide world,
but I will marry with you.'

The name of that person was Haji Mahmoud Undre.

The secret courtship of Jainub continued for nearly a year.
The grocery shop proprietor had fallen in love with the young
Afrikaner girl. Even after such a lengthy absence from his
homeland, Haji Undre remained a dutiful son. He wrote to his
parents asking for their consent to marry a Christian. In due
course he received a stern reply forbidding him to do so.

After much soul-searching Haji came to a conclusion. Having
obtained a marriage licence, he and Jainub were married in a
Cape Town registry office in 1926. He was in his forty-sixth
year; Jainub was seventeen.

Haji owned a nice house next to the store. There was furniture in all the rooms, plush curtains at the windows and across
the doors, plenty of coconut matting on the polished floorboards.
In the kitchen I had a gas stove and the bathroom was modern
with a proper flush toilet and geyser over the bathtub.

I started to have very good times with Haji and he was also
very kind to my daughter Florrie. Whatever I wanted that
good old man did give it to me—all there was to eat and drink,
whatever I did wish to wear. Cape coloured girls came every

46

day for housework and the laundry and in my husband's home I was the madam. There was only one small difficulty. At the McKenzie place I ate the proper way with a knife and fork. But my Haji used his fingers and made me do the same.

Haji Undre also insisted that his wife take religious instruction from a Muslim priest so she could be converted to Islam.

I didn't mind giving up my Christian faith. I loved my husband and only wanted to make him happy. We had been married one year when I became a Muslim and our first son, Ahmed, was born.

For the next sixteen years Jainub Undre enjoyed a full and busy life. She learned to help Haji in the store, rising before daylight to organise the daily delivery of fresh bread. She assisted with stock-taking, with the dispatch of orders given over the new telephone Haji had installed, and at the end of each working day totalled the money in the brass embossed till and entered the figures in leather-bound ledgers. And all this time their family steadily increased.

After Ahmed came three daughters; Karimunissa, Halima and Aisha. Then another son named Adam, and after Adam three more girls; Amina, Kadija and the last we named Howabi. All my confinements were at home, attended by a live-in nurse, and each one cost Haji ten rands for the whole week. But he never minded because by then the business was doing well.

In the 1930s everybody in Cape Town had money to spend. Our children went to a Muslim school where they were taught English. They were all good students and a credit to their father and me. As for Florrie, when she was sixteen she took a clerical course and went to work in an office at the university. A year later she found herself a nice boy and they got married.

I can't tell you how good life was for us, specially on Fridays when we didn't open the store. Often Haji would go to the mosque and then come back, hitch our mare Nelly to the trap and take us all off on a family picnic to the seaside.

One Friday, when we were driving home, Haji suddenly got a bad pain in his chest. I had such a big fright I whipped that horse and made her legs go so fast all the children start to laugh! They think it's a big joke because they don't understand. The doctor come to give Haji an injection and say it is nothing serious. Just asthma. But in the next few years my poor husband get several more bad attacks, which force him to stay in bed and let me do everything for him. In the end our Doctor Futtuq advised my husband that if he went back to India the change in climate might help improve his health.

47

So that was the big decision. At first I told Haji to leave us and go alone to India because I was already pregnant with my tenth child. But my husband refused point blank. Then he suggest we go for a six-month holiday just to see how we like it. If we don't, no harm done and we can turn round and come straight home again. So what can I do, except to start with that packing?

It was 1942. The blitz of London was at its worst, the armies of Rommel and Montgomery were fighting in the north African deserts and, in the Far East, Singapore had fallen into the hands of the Japanese. Yet these distant events were of little consequence to the ordinary people of Cape Town, more concerned with day-to-day domestic trivia. So it was that when Jainub and Haji Undre left Cape Town on a coastal steamer to sail round the Cape of Good Hope and north to Durban, they were not encumbered by any sense of impending danger.

Having sold their house and furniture, Haji Undre put the store in the safe keeping of a Muslim relative and purchased steerage class tickets for his large family. On board they had to split up, Jainub and the girls occupying one cramped cabin amidships, while Haji and the two boys slept in an airless dormitory one deck lower.

On the first stretch of the journey they all suffered from sea-sickness; Haji, his asthma aggravated by the claustrophobic nature of the accommodation, was too ill to leave his bunk. The passage to Durban took ten days. There the family transferred to the SS *Karanja*, an ocean-going liner which was to make a last port of call at Mombasa before heading out into the Arabian Sea for the three-week crossing to Bombay.

Me and the children stayed on deck most of the time so we could get some fresh air. It was too hot down inside that big ship. We were all suffocating, but my poor Haji suffered the worst. And all the time the children keep asking: 'Why do we have to leave our home? Why must we go away from all our friends?'

I tell them to trust in our Almighty Father. What else can I say? I have so many doubts about what we are doing but I am a good Muslim wife and must obey my husband's wishes.

As the *Karanja* approached Mombasa, the passengers crowded to the rails to watch the docking. Instead they heard the rattle of anchor chains and felt the uneasy bucking motion of the vessel as it lay hove-to in the harbour entrance.

That night a series of violent explosions sent shudders through the liner. Woken from sleep, the passengers reacted

48

with understandable panic. Earlier that day the purser's some-
what vague explanations for the delay had started a series of
wild speculations. Some believed Japanese planes were attacking
Mombasa; others thought the British were trying to torpedo
German gunboats. The most plausible conjecture was that a
German E-Boat in the vicinity was being depth-charged by
British minesweepers, but in the confusion nobody really knew
what was happening, least of all the Undre family.

When those bombs go off everybody is screaming and shouting. I start to pray. Then the officers order us to stay in our
cabins and that was worse. They are chucking those bombs in
the sea all round and I thought we would die down there like
rats. We stayed five days anchored in that harbour. Then one
morning the engine start up again and they take us to the
dockside.

I beg Haji to let us all get off and go home again, but he
tells me not to be so foolish. The tickets are paid for, arrangements have been made for his family to meet us in Bombay and
we must go on. So then I keep quiet and make the best of it.
But for the first time in my whole married life, there is much
unhappiness in my heart.

Three weeks later the SS *Karanja* reached Bombay. Poor food
and inadequate sanitation had left their mark on the dishevelled
steerage class passengers lining up to disembark. And their
ordeal was not yet over. Regulations required that before going
ashore every man, woman and child be subjected to a medical
examination.

Hours after docking, Jainub and Haji marshalled their
children down the gangplank and, pushing their way through
the crowds thronging the reception area behind the customs
shed, they were immediately overwhelmed by a large party of
Haji's relatives.

Such heat, such flies, I was near to fainting, but all my
husband's family pressed round us crying and wailing like
hungry cats. The women were all covered up in long black
robes, so only their wet eyes were showing. They hung flowers
on our necks and jabber, jabber in my ear, although I didn't
understand one word they said. My Haji told me his family were
honouring me as a new bride because this was the first time I'd
set foot in India. I felt more like I was dying and they had
brought wreaths for my funeral!

After that they get three of those *tongas* (carriages) pulled by
horses so thin they looked like bags of bones. Our boxes were
piled into one *tonga*. Haji, me and the children got in the next
and the relations clip-clopped off in another one to lead the way.

I could hardly bear to look at all those dirty streets crowded with poor people. I put a hanky over my face to stop from breathing so many bad smells at once.

They took us to some sort of hostel. It was dark inside and we had to climb so many stairs to reach this tiny room, without one single piece of furniture in it. My husband's people unrolled mats and told us to sit down. We was so tired and hungry we just flopped on to the floor. The relations fetched chappatis and tea and told us we need only spend one night in the hostel because next morning we would be going to the village.

I didn't sleep hardly a wink, only stood looking out of that small window to see such sights below! So many black and broken buildings and people living down there on the dirty streets, cooking on little fires, washing their naked bodies, passing urine and emptying their bowels in the gutters and then going to sleep wrapped up in rags. I'd never seen such things before and woke Haji to ask if all India was like that.

He told me not to worry. In the village everything would be fine. So I trust him. What else can I do?

Early the next day, after a breakfast of sweet tea and bananas the family and the relatives returned to the dockside to board a small coastal steamer bound for the port of Jungira-Murud some eighty kilometres to the south. During the leisurely journey, Jainub sat on deck, dozing in the sunshine. She breathed the fragrance of fresh rice-straw wafted on off-shore breezes and through half-closed eyes watched the coastal scenery glide past.

Against a milky-blue sky distant mountain escarpments rose dramatically from expanses of dense blue-green forest. Elsewhere crescents of pale sand were fringed with coconut palms. Then again the landscape changed to open country, where saffron-coloured humpy hills sat in mosaics of golden rice stubble. Signs of habitation were few and far between, here and there a village nestling in a rocky cove, the occasional fishing boat anchored motionless in the calm deep magenta seas.

As the tensions of the past weeks gradually subsided, Jainub's innate optimism returned. Perhaps after all Haji was not wrong to bring them so far from home and, anyway, was six months really such a long time? Thus comforted, Jainub's thoughts turned to more practical matters. The new baby was due in December, less than two months away. Under her breath the young mother began to murmur suitable names for her next daughter, never for a single moment doubting the gender of the child now lying beneath her ribs.

At noon the steamer altered course, turning across the mouth of the Rajpuri creek to tie up at the town jetty of Murud. On the cliffs, overshadowing the busy little port, stood the sombre ruins of a medieval castle.

Coolies swarmed on to the steamer and hoisting the family's belongings up on their heads set off for the opposite side of the harbour, where a large rowing boat was moored under some wooden steps. Once the luggage had been stowed and everybody had taken their seats, the ferry-boat's gunwales were no more than a few inches above the waterline. Fortunately the sea was calm as the two oarsmen began the six-mile row across the creek, skirting the western flank of the steep-sided island of Jungira on the way.

At Dighi the boat was tied up to a long pole sticking out of some rocks. The ferry was bobbing up and down so we had to wait our chance to jump one by one on to a flat rock. Haji's cousin-brothers carried our three youngest safely ashore.

Some men were waiting for us with big wooden box-like things fixed under long poles. Haji told me and the children to climb in those *dholies* so the men could carry us across the sands to the houses. But I felt scared of those half-naked fellows with their blood-red teeth. To me they looked altogether fierce and I told Haji: 'You take the children if you like, but I'm not going with those people. They may stop and cut me to pieces!'

My husband got cross then because his relatives were waiting for him to put me in my place. But I still refused to get in those boxes. So Haji pushed the children into one and, before I could do anything, those human horses put the poles on their shoulders and ran off with all my children screaming: 'Mummy, Mummy, where are they taking us?'

In the village of Dighi, Haji's relations had quite a nice house and once we had arrived everybody was talking and crying and all I could do was nod and smile. Then they put a big dish of rice and curry on the floor and all the men sat down to pick from this side and that. My children had to wait with us women until the men finished. Then, when they had gone outside, the rest of us were permitted to sit down on the mats and eat. But next minute all the children were crying and holding their throats. So I shout for Haji and told him we couldn't swallow such hot curry and he'd better ask for some plain rice with sugar on it. But before we have a chance to finish this, Haji comes running to say that lorry has arrived to take us to his village.

The children were very excited to know that our long journey was nearly over. When all the luggage was again loaded up, the truck honked its horn and we started up a steep stony track behind Dighi. I sat in front with Howabi and Kadija on my lap. The lorry bumped along and soon I felt so sick and uncomfortable because of my tight corselets. Higher and higher into the mountains we went and sometimes, through the trees, we could see the sea a long way below us. And I thought to myself, how many jungles must we pass before we reach our destination?

At one place the lorry had to stop because black smoke was pouring out of the engine. All round were thick cactus and tall trees which hid the sky and we could hear the sound of strange animals calling in there. The children stopped singing and started to talk in whispers.

After two hours, the old lorry lumbered on to flat, open ground chequered with ricefields. Ahead, on the other side of a wooden bridge across a shallow river, the road made a gentle ascent to where, beneath a canopy of mango trees, the blue dome of a mosque was just visible.

Haji pointed up the hill and said to me: 'This is Borli Pan-chatan, the village where I was born.' We passed mud and straw huts and I thought they must be for cattle until I saw people creep out and children too with no clothes on. Then I say to myself, 'O my God, where in the world has my husband brought me?'

The lorry stops at the gate to the mosque and Haji tells us to wait while he visits his father's grave and says prayers. So we sit and sit in that hot sun and soon children with wild tangled hair and dirty noses come out of the huts to stare at us. When Haji comes back, he is crying like a baby so I must comfort him. Then the lorry turns round and takes us up a dusty lane until we get to a white *bungala* with a tiled roof and two goats tied up on the front veranda. This is the home of my husband's mother where we are going to stay. I have to bend to get through the front door and after the strong sunlight it is quite dark inside.

Haji starts crying again and so do all the relations. My children keep tight by my side and don't know whether to laugh or cry. None of them can understand what is going on.

I sit on a bed and the children sit there with me until all that crying dies down. Then I called Haji and spoke sternly to him because I was very tired. 'No more crying now. Tell these people we must have hot water so we can wash and change our clothes.' So they brought large copper pots of hot water from the kitchen and we went into a small side room. When all the children had washed and combed their hair, I took off my clothes and had a good rinse. But before I could dress again, two women came in and started to force me into first a petti-coat, then a cotton blouse and on top put a long piece of sari material all tucked and folded.

Again I had to call my husband. 'Please tell these women I have plenty of my own clothes to wear. I'll not wear this stupid stuff.' And once more he got angry with me. 'You keep the sari on and don't give insult to my people.' So I waited until those two women had gone off to get tea and cakes for us, then dressed again in my own clothes.

That evening so many people called to see us, it was very late before Haji took us into the small room to sleep. There were two narrow beds, so the older children slept on the mud floor. But they were so tired, this didn't matter. The hard string bed didn't worry me either and in two flicks of a billy goat's tail I was fast asleep.

But later I woke up and found my husband gone. I shouted 'Haji, Sahib, where are you?' When there was no answer I got really frightened to be all alone in that strange place and woke Ahmed and told him to go and find his Daddy. Presently he came back and spoke very quietly to me. 'You go to sleep again, Mummy. Our Daddy is quite safe. He said tell you tonight he must sleep with our other mothers.'

Which was how Jainub, after sixteen years of marriage, learned that Haji Mahmoud Undre already had two other wives in the village of Borli Panchatan, each one fully entitled by Muslim law to claim his love and protection.

❧ CHAPTER THREE ❧

THE FOOTPRINTS ON the dusty lanes were real enough and witnessed by many villagers. None, however, had ever caught a glimpse of the lion, despite the full moon which always accompanied its strange nocturnal pilgrimage. People only knew that it came from Mahsla-side and went first to the tomb of Kwaja Shabbudin on the northern extremity of the village. The firm imprint of its paws could then be seen on the bazaar road, before turning west to circle the final resting-place of Sheik Ahmoud in the rocks facing Diwaga. Thereafter the tracks continued south to Karlia and the grave of Shah Walli,

before turning east, along paths left by goatherds, to encompass
the tombs of Kobulla Husseine and Nure Repeer. At this point
the lion's spoor vanished into the mountains. Some said it was
the ghostly reincarnation of one of the five holy men; others
believed it to be the embodiment of a tormented soul seeking
absolution. One way or another, when the full moon of December was due, well before nightfall, Hindus and Muslims alike
retreated to the safety of their homes.

The night Jainub's labour pains began was the night of the
December lion. Ahmed was sent to get help from his step-
mothers, but returned without them. None would venture out,
especially not on account of the Afrikaner woman who had
rejected all offers of friendship.

The humiliating discovery that she was the third wife of Haji
Mahmoud Undre and stepmother to three middle-aged
daughters, had shocked Jainub into a state of grief. For
days she lay on the string bed, a cover pulled over her head
to shut out the incomprehensible chatter of the relatives.
Whenever Haji tried to explain, she drowned his voice with
loud weeping.

Jainub's next reaction was to escape from the house at every
possible opportunity, taking the children on long walks down
the road to the Karlia river. In 1942 the way was still hemmed
in by jungle thickets, home of black monkeys, shrill-voiced
parakeets and other more fearsome creatures.

The relatives all shout after me, saying where is that silly
woman going? Muslim women cannot walk outside in this
village, showing their faces in such a rude way. But I had to be
on my own to think. As for the dangers of snakes and wild
animals, how could I worry about such things when I didn't
know they were there!

My Haji told the relatives not to try and stop me going.
Perhaps he liked it better than having me crying inside the
house all day. In that three-roomed *bungala* there wasn't space
to swing a cat. There were my husband's two wives and his old
mother, as well as Haji and me and our eight children.

The wives cooked on wood-fire stoves on the back veranda.
Water was fetched from a rainwater well near the house, and
washing had to be done in the yard under the *shoga* ('drum-
stick' or 'aspargus') trees. The spiced food and unclean water
didn't agree with us. We all suffered from diarrhoea and
vomiting. Haji got some men to dig a latrine in the corner of
the yard and fence it round with woven palm leaves, but after
our comfortable life in Cape Town all this was a terrible come-
down. I just couldn't get used to so many people in one small

space with nothing much to do all day. And I refuse point blank to make friends with Haji's other wives.

Along the lane was an empty house. Haji found the owner who agreed to rent it to us. It was only three rooms with thick mud walls, wooden bars at the windows and cow-dung floors, but once I'd brushed it out and taken my children and all our belongings there, I began to feel altogether better.

Haji went to Bombay on the steamer and after about ten days brought back a load of second-hand furniture, which he put on a truck to bring to Borli. So from then on we managed to make some kind of family life for the children in that strange place. I learned how to blow down a copper pipe to get a hot fire going in the little clay oven on the back *stoep*, and cooked plain rice and vegetables for our meals. The children started to pick up the Konkani language and teach me a few words so I can go shopping in the bazaar. But still I cannot settle happily. After our busy life in a modern city, in Borli there was nothing to do all day and nowhere to go without small Hindu boys chucking stones and shouting. We can't even visit the seashore unless Haji takes us, and my old husband doesn't like to walk far because of his asthma. Anyway, we soon found out that the sea was only for fishing people. In this village people don't play. They just work from dawn to dusk to earn their bread.

So after some weeks I tell Haji, I'm sorry but please take us home again, and, with hand on heart, he promises that before the rainy season sets in he will book return tickets on the liner.

Then came that night of my delivery. I got no help with the birth except for some old Hindu woman with broken red teeth and dirt under her finger-nails. I wouldn't let her put a hand on me even though I was in great difficulty. I sent her packing and all my children apart from Karimunissa and Halima. I thought they were old enough to help, but when they became frightened at all the noises I was making, I told them to run off and see to their small brothers and sisters. While they were gone the baby arrived. It was a hard birth. The long sea journey and poor food, as well as so much misery for me, didn't give my new daughter a chance.

She breathed for one hour. Then she passed away.

* * *

The winter months between November and February in Borli were hot by day and cool enough at night for people to rummage in tin storage trunks for the patchwork quilts they had stitched from pieces of old saris during the rainy season. At sun-up these colourful blankets appeared draped over veranda rails or laid flat on the lanes in front of the *bungala*,

55

creating the impression that under cover of darkness the dusty red earth had sprouted dozens of rectangular flower gardens.

In November, nature too was ready with genuine surprises. Normally unremarkable trees and shrubs blossomed with spectacular abundance. Soaring *shoga* trees sported white heads of froth, oleanders cascaded over sienna walls in fountains of purple and red and every back yard came to life with white roses and clumps of periwinkle. Between the houses smelly ditches propagated orange lilies, the gnarled twisted limbs of *chaffa* trees became encrusted with wax-pale flowers. In the ricefields the thorny fingers of silk cotton (kapoc) trees sprouted waxen trumpets of coral pink. Perhaps the most surprising revelation was the nocturnal flowering of the *ratkirani* bush. Pale as moonlight, this blossom bathed the night air in a fragrance so powerful that, in its vicinity, even the stench of excrement failed to monopolise the olfactory senses!

The villagers' delight at such natural profusion was much in evidence. Every female wore flowers in the hair, every farmer adorned his favourite oxen with garlands. Impassive temple gods sat on carpets of freshly-picked flowers and corpses being carried to the Hindu cremation field were smothered with colourful blossoms.

Prudent housewives bottled the scented *chaffa* flowers in brine for use at future wedding ceremonies, and in the bazaar the *paan* – a mixture of betel nut, tobacco, lime and *kath* (*catachou* bark) wrapped in betel leaf – vendor's stall outside the fish-market sold fresh *chaffa* blooms for the fastidious to hold to their nostrils while haggling over the price of fish.

But as blossom precedes fruit, so frivolous preoccupation with fresh flowers soon turned to more essential matters. After the rice harvest in October, when the rice was tied in bundles and stacked on stilt platforms to protect it from rats, preparation for the threshing began.

Women with baskets of cow-dung under their arms and carrying pots of water on their heads, went into the ricefields to spread a thick layer of dung over an area of stubble. Once sunbaked, this provided a clean hard work-surface.

Male workers dismantled the ricks and, with a rice bundle in each hand, flailed the dried heads against wooden trestles. Afterwards they took rattan shovels and tossed the grain to separate the chaff, which was carefully swept up and stored in baskets for use as fuel in clay *shagri*, the slow-burning portable fires used to warm homes during the rainy season.

Nothing was wasted in the cyclical communion between the

villagers, their animals and the land. Rice straw, re-stacked on the ground, went for cattle fodder. In due course, this was returned to the soil in the form of dung as oxen ploughed the stubble in readiness for a quick crop of chillies or water-melons, before being ploughed once more in readiness for the rice-grain in April.

Success or failure depended upon the weather. Gentle showers in May were imperative if the emerald rice seedlings were to be ready for planting out once June cloudbursts, trapped by the low mud parapets surrounding every small field, transformed the landscape below the hillside village into a mosaic of mirrors. If the rains were late, or inadequate of strength and duration, the crops suffered. So did the people, rice and rain being inseparable components for their survival.

In Borli the winter season was also the traditional time for marriages—and for house repairs.

* * *

Since Haji Undre had spent so many years abroad, his wives were in no doubt that he was a man of wealth. For the sake of family esteem, Haji saw no good reason to deny this exaggerated assumption, even though he was soon called upon to prove it.

Feasts paid for by Haji when the family first arrived were obligatory. So were gifts of saris and household utensils, such as copper *hundas* (pots) for his two village wives and the extensive family network which had flourished in his absence. Then came more substantial requests. Haji's brother came asking for money to settle long-standing debts to the village money-lender; then a deputation from the mosque begged for funds to repaint the dome. On each occasion Haji responded with gracious generosity. Needless to say, such largess only confirmed his reputation as a man of substance and generated the expectation that before long he would demonstrate this in a more substantial way.

Haji's mother, by then approaching eighty, knew exactly how this could be achieved. She began by pointing out the inadequacies of her small *bungala* and the constant expense of repairs. Then she raised the delicate subject of filial responsibility. How was it that the widowed mother of such a prosperous son should be living in such humble circumstances? And, as a devout Muslim, was it not his duty to make certain that she spent the remainder of her days in comfort? Simultaneously shamed and flattered, Haji ordered the laying of foundations for a brand new house.

Where the back lane sloped to join the main bazaar road,

on the south side of the village, was a triangle of land covered in scrub cactus. Within a week builders had cleared it and with pegs and string delineated the groundplan of a large rectangular dwelling. In another week deep trenches had been dug in the soft red earth and cartloads of granite rocks brought from an inland quarry. All day the sound of chipping echoed in the lane as stonemasons roughly shaped blocks for the foundation walls. Then followed a period of waiting until, early in January 1943, supplies of cement arrived from Bombay.

Struggling to recover her health after the difficult confinement, Jainub was completely unaware that Haji had embarked upon this extraordinary display of extravagance. One evening he came to ask if she would make sure that Ahmed and Adam were up early and dressed in their best suits for the foundation ceremony next day.

Soon after daybreak, before invited male members of the Undre family, the guests assembled on the top of the granite foundation walls which lined the open trenches. The priest chanted prayers of blessing, and Haji went to each corner of the new house and into the cavity dropped a gold rand. Dates and fresh coconut slices were distributed to the guests, and a succession of girl labourers, carrying pans of dirt on their heads, began the task of levelling the excavations.

One month later the shell of the house was finished. There were dividing walls between the rooms inside, and over all there was an enormous barnlike roof of unhewn timbers and thick pipe-tiling. Digging deep into his savings, Haji had just enough to pay carpenters to fit window frames and doors. Then he went to his mother to admit that his funds were exhausted. She offered no recriminations. Poverty was a condition every villager understood, and anyway she had the house she wanted.

Jainub, once she discovered how Haji's latest display of prodigality had ruined their chances of going home, was heartbroken. On the surface at least, however, she remained an obedient Muslim wife; when Haji ordered her and the children to occupy half of the new house alongside his other wives and his mother, she quietly complied.

Since its original plan allowed for the house to be on two floors, it was one of the largest in the village at that time. When the money ran out before the rough walls could be plastered or ceilings boarded over, eight open-topped brick boxes were left under a cavernous roof, which amplified the smallest sound made by those living beneath it. The house was divided in half.

Each had a storage room in the middle without windows and two rooms with windows to the side, accessible from a central front veranda. Across the back of the building were two kitchens with doors to the yard. Hardened dung slurry surfaced the floors, the windows were barred and shuttered and there was neither electricity nor plumbing. The nearest approach to modern amenities were concreted sumps in the corners of the two side rooms, intended for washing clothes, for bathing and for use as urinals.

Haji Undre continued to divide his attentions between Jainub and his other wives. For her part, Jainub stubbornly avoided them. But in a house without ceilings, there was little chance of privacy. Even though Jainub could not understand much of what was said, she was able to recognise the sound of angry arguments echoing through the roof space as Haji's older wives voiced grievances, the result of forty years of what they considered gross neglect. They also complained about Jainub's behaviour. She continued to go out and about in the village as she had been accustomed to doing in Cape Town, where emancipated Muslim women did not subscribe to the *purdah* observed by their cousins in India.

Weary of constant bickering, Haji soon began to spend more time with Jainub.

My husband told me that the other wives were jealous because I was young and had so many fine children. I told him what chance will our fine children have if they remain in this poor village? And by-and-by Haji comes to see the sense of my words and admits that bringing us to Borli was a big mistake. He also confesses that he still has enough money left in his box for two steamship tickets. I ask him what good is that? He says: 'You and me will go back to Cape Town and leave the children with my other wives. When we have saved enough money, we can send for them.'

I am so shocked I nearly spit in his face. Instead I cry and cry until my eyes is redder than two tomatoes and tell him I will die before I leave my children. Then Haji comes to a decision. He will go back alone, work hard in the shop and then send the money for me and the children to follow. So this is the arrangement we agree to.

In February 1943 Haji Undre turned his back on Borli Panchatan for the second time. Before leaving, he gave Jainub a string threaded with twenty gold pieces, the remnants of his 'wealth', and told her to tie them round her neck for safety.

59

After he'd gone we waited patiently in that house and manage very nicely with what my husband has left for us. At the end of March, a long letter comes saying my husband has reached safeside and, although he was again very ill on the ship with his asthma, he is back in the grocery business and working hard. His letter ended with the words: 'If God helps me, I shall fetch you all home very soon. Do not worry.'

A week later, Jainub and Halima were sitting on the back doorstep shelling peas, when a frightful wailing broke out at the other end of the house. Halima, who had become quite proficient at Konkani, went to find out what was happening. Presently the girl came back, white-faced and trembling, able only to stammer that two men who spoke a little English were coming with a message.

As soon as I saw them my insides turned to water. Then they said: 'Be calm now. We have bad news. A wire has arrived from Cape Town. Your husband has passed away.'

Haji Mahmoud Undre had died of a heart attack while on his prayer mat in the mosque, leaving in the village of Borli Panchatan three widows. The youngest, with eight children to support, was just thirty-four years old—and, once again, Jainub was pregnant.

* * *

In a male-dominated society, for a young woman to survive her husband was often a compound tragedy. Not only did she lose her protector and provider, but also whatever social prestige she enjoyed at his side. Forbidden by religious custom to remarry, the young widow had to rely on the charity of her husband's family. Since this invariably imposed an economic burden it could ill afford, her treatment was less than kind.

In the old days Vedic scriptures, which are a source of divine guidance for Hindus, actually sanctioned the practice of suicide, or *sati*, the ancient assumption being that the ideal wife would not want to remain alive once her husband was dead. If she voluntarily chose to be burned on the funeral pyre with him, she could thereafter be declared a *sati*, or divine goddess, and worshipped as a family deity.

In the eighteenth and nineteenth centuries, when the economic welfare of the people deteriorated under British domination, the obligation of keeping a widow and her children posed a direct threat to family survival. In some

60

northern provinces of India there were eye-witness accounts of widows being forcibly tied to their husband's funeral pyre and kept there with bamboo sticks until they expired, the elevation of widows to the status of divine goddesses in the next world thus enabling the family to gain ownership of their possessions in this!

Over the decades, Indian reformers urged the British to abolish the act of *sati*, but the raj, reluctant to interfere with religious customs and risk provoking open hostility, prevaricated. So the practice of widow-burning was not officially declared illegal until 1829, and even to this day, cases of newly-bereaved women committing ritual suicide occasionally appear in the national newspapers.

In the village of Borli, nothing so drastic happened to the widows of Haji Undre. Nevertheless, there were certain Muslim formalities to be observed. The day after Haji's demise was announced, the two older widows were visited by female relatives. With much wailing and weeping, the glass bangles on their arms were tugged off and smashed to smithereens. Their gold marriage ornaments were removed and stored away, never to be worn again. After that, the relatives left the two distraught women who, drawing their *dupattas* (muslin scarves) over their heads, settled down to observe forty days of mourning.

Jainub was left alone with her children to get over her bereavement as best she could.

> For three days I am crying. Then my children was getting hungry, so I put my troubles to one side and make food for them. What good is crying? I have to accept that gone is gone. It was the will of Allah.'

When Jainub was stranded in Borli Panchatan, her eldest son Ahmed was fifteen. In Cape Town he would have had no difficulty finding work, but in a poor agricultural community, where the inhabitants had a hard enough time scratching a living, a city boy had little chance of finding employment. The few gold rands which Haji had left her relieved Jainub of immediate money worries, but she harboured no illusions about what lay ahead for herself and the children unless Ahmed was able to support them. So she turned for advice to the *jammut*.

The *jammut* was the local branch of the Muslim Society, a national network created to safeguard Muslim religious interests throughout India. In Borli, every Muslim family contributed a few rupees each month towards the work of an elected committee of elders; they provided religious instruction for small children, arranged burials, marriages and other ceremonial occasions and generally supervised the moral conduct of members.

Having already demonstrated her liberal attitudes, Jainub's request for the *jammut*'s help met with a cold reception. Before even considering the question of assistance, the young widow was reminded of her religious obligations as a Muslim mother. The elders pointed out that going around without first covering herself in the *bourka* (black habit) was bad enough, but had she considered the effect of such behaviour on her oldest daughters? If they continued to flout their faces in public, what chances would they have on the marriage market when the time came? Finally, the elders insisted that unless Jainub accepted the strict rules laid down in the Koran for the proper conduct of Muhammadan women, they would not feel disposed to offer their assistance.

There was no denying the gravity of her position. Even so, the narrow-minded attitude of the village elders kindled a stubborn streak in Jainub's nature. She could not see that the wearing of the *bourka* would affect either her devotion to Allah or her ability to bring up her daughters to be virtuous Muslims. What she did see was Muslim men free to come and go as they pleased, while Muslim women, once they reached puberty, were forced into *purdah*. Remembering her own free and happy childhood, Jainub had no intention of inflicting this religious restriction upon Karimunissa and Halima, who were then aged thirteen and eleven. Instead Jainub tried to appease the *jammut* with a compromise.

> My eldest daughters could understand what the elders were asking, so I told them that I would never wear the *bourka*, but that from then on I would wear long dresses to hide my legs and put a muslin *dupatta* over my head. Karimunissa and Halima could wear saris and the *bourka*, if they wanted, but I would never force them to keep *purdah*.

Karimunissa, who was already approaching marriageable age, decided she would comply with the local customs. Halima, who had not yet started to menstruate, had more time to consider whether or not to follow her sister's example. But as she was already mixing with schoolgirls of her own age and religion, she also decided that she would want to be like them.

Satisfied with this compromise, the *jammut* agreed to help Jainub with the problem of employment for Ahmed.

They told me that a man from Durban was visiting the village and would take Ahmed back to work in his shop for £12 a month and keep. Out of this, the cost of the journey must be repaid. Then my son's wages would be sent to keep the rest of us going. Rice was cheap then, only Rs 10 for 50 lbs. With vegetables and sometimes a little fish, this would last us one whole month. We manage nicely on Rs 10 for food every week (about 50p). Then we need to buy firewood and kerosene and, except for clothes, which I sew myself, that is all. So £2 or £3 a week is plenty for us to live.

Well, my son didn't want to leave, but eventually sees the sense of the arrangement. If he stays in the village, we might all end up starving. But it was a sad day when Ahmed got on that boneshaker bus for Dighi. As we walked home, it came on to rain very hard so nobody could see how much we are crying. But I try to be strong after that for the sake of my other children. And that's how it has to be for a mother. When the child is in the stomach, it kicks in the ribs. When the child is born, it kicks in the lap. And when children grow up, they are kicking in your heart.

*　*　*

By 1943, having reached national adulthood, India was ready to kick free of its imperialist mother. However, it was a leave-taking fraught with complications.

Gandhi's wish for the freedom of a united India was in direct opposition to the policies of Mohammed Ali Jinnah, leader of the Muslim League. Jinnah was urging the British to partition the northern provinces from the rest of India and so to create an exclusive home for Muslims once India was granted independence.

There were 100 million Muslims and 300 million Hindus in India at that time. Jinnah believed that, once the British handed over to an Indian democracy, minority Muslim factions would be persecuted by Hindus. In his campaign to arouse Muslim fervour for the idea of a separate identity from the rest of India, Jinnah incensed the majority of the Hindu people. Like Gandhi, Hindus wanted to retain a united nation, and the deep resentments which had festered over centuries of foreign occupation finally boiled over to bring the northern provinces of India, where there were 60 million Muslims, to the brink of bloody revolution.

After five wearisome years of war, the British were in no position to try and combat the troubles in India. Major outbreaks of discontent in larger cities quickly developed into widespread atrocities as Muslims embarked upon a spate of religious barbarism. Hindu men and women were forcibly converted to the faith of Islam. The women had their marriage bangles broken and *tikka* (happiness marks) on their foreheads publicly obliterated. Hindu men were cruelly circumcised, forced to grow beards, recite the Koran and, worst of all, made to slaughter sacred cows and eat the meat. This last violation of the ancient Vedic laws ensured that they could never again return to the Hindu faith.

Gandhi made supreme efforts to pacify the people. He toured the northern provinces to preach continual messages of non-violence, religious tolerance and universal brotherhood, but with little success. Once ignited, like forest fires, religious hatred between Muslims and Hindus spread out of control. Hindus no longer wanted to try and love Muslims, Muslims did not love Hindus at all, and Gandhi was caught between the two. Hindus resented Gandhi's accusation that they adopted a patronising attitude towards Muslims. Muslims disliked being referred to as religious fanatics and challenged Gandhi's teachings of the brotherhood of man, insisting that the idea originated in the Muslim holy scriptures. Hindus retorted that the only brotherhood Muslims understood was for them-selves.

In this climate of religious bickering, where once Hindus and Muslims had amicably coexisted, the smallest incident sparked off ferocious reprisals. Even a quarrel between two small children of opposite faiths was enough to set off a horrendous orgy of killing throughout a whole neighbourhood. Then, probing the soft belly of the political chaos, came communist delegates from Russia and China, urging India to join the Asian Union. Hoping to fend off Marxist political manoeuvring and stem what the viceroy Lord Louis Mountbatten described as 'this terrible pendulum of massacres swinging wider and wider', the British government hastily concluded negotiations for Home Rule, which sanctioned the partition of Pakistan.

On 15 August 1947, India achieved freedom. Bloody carnage ensued as Muslims seeking safety in Pakistan were assassinated by Hindus, and Hindus fleeing from heavily populated Muslim areas met with a similar fate at the hands of Muslims. Muslim mosques were burned, Hindu shrines desecrated and, as millions fled from their homes to seek sanctuary elsewhere, the countryside was flooded by starving refugees.

Without telegraph facilities or radio sets, news of these momentous happenings only filtered slowly into the village of Borli Panchatan.

Nana Kulkarni, representing the oldest and most respected Hindu landowning family in the area, recalled that in the years just before independence, when the Gandhi movement of *swaraj* began to inspire Hindu nationalism, the nawab of Jungira issued a strict ban on all political meetings in the state.

Nobody was permitted to speak or write on political matters. I think this managed to prevent any open displays of animosity amongst the Muslim and Hindu people of our village. But secretly our leaders were planning to cast off the yoke of the nawab.

Then in 1947, soon after independence, Mr Nehru's government compelled our nawab to establish a small council of ministers to control local administration. My father was one member of it. Thus, for the first time, three Hindu ministers managed the affairs of this territory. Then, after ten months, the state of Jungira was annexed into the Indian Union and re-named Kolaba. The nawab was forced into exile near Pune and at long last we Hindus were able to take charge of our own district.

So, after five centuries, Muslim rule in the village of Borli Panchatan came to an end.

* * *

Over the next three years Jainub Undre also had to learn the harsh realities of independence. Calculating that the first money from Ahmed would begin to arrive after the rainy season, whenever necessary she went to the village money-lender to exchange another gold rand for rupees. She enrolled Halima, Aisha, Amina and Adam for lessons at the free government school, a short distance up the lane from where they lived. Karimunissa was already too old for the top class; Kadija and Howabi, not yet seven, were too young to start lessons. Jainub was determined that their family misfortunes should not deprive the children of an education, even though the standards achieved in the village school were modest. In an agricultural community, little value was placed upon academic performance and, since schooling was not then compulsory, only a small proportion of village children attended classes, most of those being boys.

Jainub's insistence upon schooling her children infuriated the old widows. It seemed to them yet another attempt to impress them with her superior city ways. So the animosity between them deepened. And had it not been for her dead husband's brother, Jainub would doubtless never have been told of her entitlement to a small ricefield on the outskirts of Borli. The one-acre field on the Karlia side of the village was one of many on a stretch of land lying between the roadway and the steeply-rising hills. In one corner of the field stood a silk cotton tree with a large stone wedged in its roots and decorated with marigolds to please the earth gods, a shrine put there by the old Hindu couple who worked the land.

Haji's brother informed Jainub that half the rice crop must be paid to the couple for cultivating the field. In a good year, she could then expect the other half to feed herself and the children for six months. Jainub was also advised to invest in some goats and chickens, so that, with rice, milk and eggs, her family need never starve. Jainub, therefore, cashed another gold coin and bought a nanny-goat, a billy and half a dozen bantam hens lorded over by a prancing rooster with tail feathers of iridescent green and bronze.

As her new life began to take shape, for the first time since Haji's death, Jainub allowed herself the luxury of optimism. Then came the rains and with them three tedious months of extreme heat and humidity.

In the monsoon months of June, July and August, the wisdom of building the village on a tree-clad hillside became apparent. Just as the trees and closely-positioned homes with big sloping rooftops protected the inhabitants from winter heatwaves, so they also provided maximum shelter from summer rains. After each cloudburst the narrow lanes between the *bungala* turned to muddy streams, but the water quickly drained to lower land and huts built on raised foundations escaped flooding.

After nine dry months, when the deluge came it was like the bursting rush of amniotic fluid before a birth. Suddenly parched land was alive again, overnight sproutings of grass and weeds and slender succulent cactus shoots celebrating the renaissance in a glory of wetness. Small children danced naked in puddles, large black umbrellas blossomed on the lanes as their barefoot owners laughingly hurried for more permanent shelter. At dawn, women workers sang as they splashed down the hill to the paddyfields to work all day planting out rice seedlings, the rattan covers on their back transforming them into human tortoises.

But initial relief was quickly followed by the grim business of survival under almost impossible conditions. Rough seas prevented the passage of steamships, landslips on the unpaved inland road turned any journey into a hazardous undertaking.

Three times weekly the State Transport (ST) bus, if it could get through, made the day-long trip from Bombay. Otherwise, during the monsoon, the little peninsula practically lost touch with the outside world. But this was normal.

As the wet season was an unavoidable component of the village life-cycle, everybody planned for the rainy months. Stocks of firewood for cooking stoves were stored indoors, rice from the previous harvest was put aside in covered bins and mud-daubed baskets, and fish, dried during the winter, was stored in airtight jars, safe from the ravages of pests which infested every *bungala* once the humidity set in.

During the rainy season there were always food shortages. In the bazaar, people could buy kerosene for their lamps and cereals such as millet, wheat and rice, curry spices and chillies, but little in the way of fresh vegetables. Onions and potatoes were always scarce and expensive. The villagers relied on what they managed to produce in their back yards: marrows, cucumbers and brinjal (fruit of the egg plant), patches of cress-like *meti*, goat's milk and eggs. Only water was plentiful, swirling between the *bungala*, pounding the rooftops, filling the village wells to capacity—a wealth of wetness which brought both blessing and blight to the villagers. Steady rains assured good rice crops, but they also cultivated a lush breeding ground for physical complaints.

Jainub was completely unprepared for that first monsoon in Borli. With her pregnancy six months advanced and not yet acclimatised, the oppressive atmosphere sapped her energy. It was like trying to breathe through a wet blanket. The children also suffered, developing eye and throat infections. Karimunissa especially was troubled by a persistent cough that refused to go away. All through the rainy months, dampness permeated clothes and bedding and they had no *shagri* (earthenware fires) to dry them. At night the family slept huddled together in one room, Jainub and the three youngest on the big canopied *palang* (wooden bed with canopy), Karimunissa, Halima and the two other sisters on *charpoys* (simple wood-framed bed) pushed close alongside it, each rolled up in a cotton cover as protection from mosquitoes.

Lizards clambered on the rough brickwork, cockroaches emerged from every nook and cranny and under the cavernous roof mice scampered on the exposed rafters. But it was the poisonous snakes and scorpions which kept Jainub in constant fear for the safety of her children. As it happened, she herself became the first victim.

67

One morning, before daylight, I have to get up to pass water. I quietly get down from the bed so as not to disturb my children, but when my foot touches the floor, oh such a red hot pain shoots into my leg! The children is so shocked to see me rolling on the floor and crying louder than loud. Halima runs to get help from the other mothers and they come to see. I think I am dying. Never has my body suffered such pain.

The old widows tell Halima, 'Don't worry. The scorpion has bit before sun-up so your mother will surely live. Go quickly to the *muntera* (Muslim medicine man) who lives on the bazaar road because this man has the knowledge to cure poisonous bites.' I don't know how I get there, but with the help of my big daughters we reach that person's house. He comes out and crossly shouts: 'Shut your mouth, keep quiet and stay on the veranda.'

We wait for such a long time I think he's forgotten us. Then the *muntera* comes back and orders me to pull up my dress. First he makes prayers, then seven times he chucks ashes over my legs. After that he sends us home, telling me to lie on the floor for one whole day. I must drink plenty of water but not eat any food. Next morning, at the moment the scorpion did bite, the pain will go.

That magic man was right. All day I suffered. My leg was like a balloon and I was frightened because at that time there was only one Hindu doctor in Borli and how could a Muslim expect help from him? Anyway, just as the *muntera* said, before dawn next morning the pain went and by the grace of Almighty Allah, I feel altogether better.

The monsoon months brought Jainub to the limits of endurance. She had no provisions for the rainy season and had to buy rice in the bazaar at exorbitant prices. The children collected firewood from the outskirts of the village but, when they came back with thorn scratches, these quickly turned to open sores which took days to heal.

Feeding her children became a daily struggle. Fortunately the goats proved a wise investment. Tethered by one foot on the front veranda, these animals thrived on armfuls of fodder which the children cut from the lush undergrowth on the Diwaga side of the house. Morning and night Jainub milked the nanny, and the four pints of rich milk formed their principal source of nourishment.

Unfortunately, the poultry were not a success because Jainub did not realise that they had to be shut up in baskets every night. One by one the bantams were lost either to rats or to thieving neighbours, until only the rooster remained. Then, one morning, this also vanished, only a scattering of wet tail feathers in the cactus hedge marking its going.

Thereafter Jainub had to buy eggs, although, as her savings dwindled, she and the children lived mostly on boiled rice, rice chappatis and little else. But through these difficult weeks, Jainub was sustained by the prospect of a regular income from her son Ahmed. The man who had taken him to Durban wrote to say the boy was well and settling down nicely to his work. The first payments were promised for the end of September.

Towards the end of August the rains began to ease. The intervals between cloudbursts lengthened and the sodden countryside steamed in the sunshine. Water in the ricefields gradually subsided and, swayed this way and that by stiff sea breezes, the crops dried and ripened to the colour of tussore silk. On the lanes where the Hindu farm-workers lived, the men sat honing the long harvest knives, testing the edges with their thumbs, swinging them experimentally as they summoned strength for the heavy work to come. Village Muslims got ready to observe the month-long fast of Ramadan.

As a pregnant woman, Jainub did not have to keep this holy fast. Nor did she see the sense in forcing her children to refrain from eating and drinking during the hours between dawn and darkness. Jainub considered they had suffered enough. Each of her children had lost weight, but Karimunissa was arousing most of Jainub's concern. Sometimes when the girl put her hand to her mouth to stifle a cough, her palm came away stained with blood.

* * *

Although there was no open hostility between Hindu and Muslim villagers, their totally different outlook on life and religion created insurmountable social and physical barriers. The Hindus, comprising more than two thirds of the total population of Borli Panchatan, lived mostly at the top of the hill to the north. Muslim homes occupied the southern slopes to the south, the dividing line marked by the turquoise dome of the mosque, which rose above the trees to dominate the skyline.

Within the Hindu section of the village were smaller subdivisions created according to caste and occupation. Agricultural workers lived on one lane, tanners on another, metalsmiths, potmakers and goldsmiths elsewhere, each forming a specialist enclave within the larger community. The Muslims, on the other hand, owned most of the ramshackle shops in the bazaar. In essence, it was Hindus who worked the land and supplied local crafts and Muslims who controlled village trade and commerce.

But, of course, the differences which gave Hindu and Muslim separate identities went deeper. Hindu people were small of stature, lean and energetic by nature, quick to display humour and equally quick to flare up in anger. They also possessed a tremendous capacity for back-breaking work. Muslims were more passive introverted people, especially the women, who retired into *purdah* once they reached puberty. Muslims of both sexes who led largely sedentary lives had a tendency to run to fat.

Hindu worship was loosely defined and heterogeneous, as much devotion offered to rocks, animals, elements and ancestors as to the more formal, but grotesque, statuary in the village temple. Muslims, on the other hand, strictly regulated their entire existence around the mosque and believed that Allah was the only true God.

So it was that in the village Hindus and Muslims co-existed like oil and water in the same pot, each side keeping themselves to themselves. Moreover, within each separate community, families that had lived in Borli for many generations were linked back and forth by marriage, so the term 'cousin brother' was often a precise statement of fact!

In the Muslim community there were comings and goings as men went abroad to work in South African and Arab countries. But their links with Borli were seldom entirely severed. This was not the case with the handful of Brahman families in Borli who sent their sons to be educated in Pune. Once qualified in one or other of the professions, they tended to turn their backs on a backward rural life, and to marry and set up home in either Pune or Bombay.

One boy who 'made good' and did return to Borli was Madhusudan Adhikari, son of a Hindu clerk employed in the nawab's palace at Jungira in the early 1900s. By the time Madhusudan had reached the top class in the village school, he was showing such academic promise that his father scraped together the cost of further tuition at the high school of Jungira-Murud. There his education would have ended, because although by then an outstanding scholar, the Adhikari family did not have the means to send him on to university.

Each year the nawab awarded state scholarships for further education, most of which went to Muslim candidates. However, Madhusudan was allowed to sit the examination and in 1920, to his delight, he won a place at medical school in Pune, on condition that once qualified he must either work for the state government for fifteen years or repay the whole cost of his training.

Once my fellow students qualified, most of them set up practice in Bombay, where they could make a lot of money. I was in no position to repay the nawab and in any case, I wanted to go back to practise in Borli. But first I had to spend the first four years in a remote part of Mahsla-Taluka, near Pune. There were no proper roads in the 1930s. I had to travel from village to village on foot, carrying my medicines with me. News of my arrival used to go ahead, so people were always gathered waiting. To begin with not many came for treatment even though it was free. In those days people felt a great loyalty to their local *fakirs* (country folk doctors). They didn't trust me. But I learned a lot during those first years. Mostly I became famous for treating roundworm and malaria!

Then, in 1935, I asked to be transferred here to Borli. My wish was granted. I was the first doctor in this area of about thirty villages and I made my home beside my dispensary, here at the top of the hill, where I am now fifty years later!

As well as treating people, I saw my job as a teacher. People were very ignorant about cleanliness in their homes and didn't understand how they got illnesses like typhoid and cholera. In those days when people got ill they turned to country medicines such as roots, leaves and herbal remedies. But I soon realised that these were not to be scorned. I had one patient with advanced diabetes which had caused a deep gangrenous ulcer on his wrist. You could see the bones. My advice was to amputate the hand to save the man's life but he was not willing. First he wanted to try the *fakir* who at that time lived at Karlia.

The *fakir* crushed some leaves and put the juice on the diabetic's ulcer. He also gave the man the same juice to drink. Seven days later that patient came to me and showed me his arm. It was almost completely healed. So I went to that *fakir* and told him that if he took the formula to the Bombay Medical Institute they would give his ulcer remedy a proper trial. If it proved effective, he would get a good name and, if he wanted, money as well. But he shook his head and sent me away. He refused to tell his secrets.

That was always the way with nature-cure doctors. They acquired their skills by knowing the habits of the people they treated and by understanding the health properties of roots and plants growing in the area. Simple country doctors always gave the patient the sense that someone cared about him and believed he might be cured. This gave the patient the will to recover which, I have always said, is as important as any medicine we give.

Of course, as a trained doctor, I could not use remedies which had not been officially investigated, but I came to learn that I must not destroy the people's faith in traditional treatments which were mostly quite harmless and inexpensive. If they didn't work, then the people could come to me for modern medicines, although in the early days I had no antibiotics—only sulphur drugs and diuretics.

I often consulted with the local Ayurvedic doctor Dada Kulkarni, especially when we got an outbreak of typhoid in the villages. We used to put people on a liquid diet, giving only water and glucose by mouth. In bad cases of dehydration I used to give coconut water by intravenous drip. This was sterile and full of nourishment. But on the whole Hindu people had excellent resistance to such illnesses. What they ate was altogether sensible food, only rough rice which was full of vitamins; and as they worked in the fields, they got plenty of vitamin D from the sunshine.

Once a woman who had eleven children and was due to give birth to the next came to my dispensary. She had walked from Diwaga with a 50-kg bag of rice on her head to sell in the market. She was quite alright. I questioned her about her diet and she said she never ate *ghee* (butterfat) or milk. In the morning she had fermented porridge before going to work all day in the fields; in the evening she made a meal of rice, chutney and fish.

In the old days the main problems were diarrhoea, coughs and colds and sore eyes. Infant diarrhoea was a big problem once people got the notion of bottle feeding their babies. When they used a spoon and cup this never happened, but glass feeding bottles came to the shop in the bazaar and they were cheap. It was much easier for a woman working in the fields to give her baby a bottle to suck, but she didn't keep this properly clean. This caused much ill health amongst the babies.

Another big problem which I often saw was tuberculosis. Of course, this illness began because there were famine years when people did not eat enough good food. But it was also due to poor conditions in the homes. Muslims especially suffered because their womenfolk were kept in *purdah* and didn't get enough fresh air and sunlight. Tuberculosis sometimes spread in a family because of the habit of sleeping close together and of spitting on the floor.

When patients could afford it, I sent them to Bombay for treatment at the free government hospital. Otherwise all I could do was to educate them about a good diet and hygiene. But it was always an uphill battle to persuade simple village people to take notice of what I was saying. They strongly believed sickness was caused by evil spirits or the anger of their gods. They didn't believe me when I told them it was because they drank bad water and did not take care where they deposited faecal matter. And how could one doctor do anything about poverty and ignorance? If the people didn't have enough to eat, my treatments were no good.

I remember one day a Muslim woman came to my dispensary with her daughter. The girl had been ailing for some time, but the woman had not brought her before. I took sputum samples and sent them to Bombay and it was as I suspected. The girl had consumption. I told that lady she must take her daughter to Bombay for treatment. She said she had no money. I told her to borrow it and she said she would try to do this. I also advised her to give her daughter plenty of nourishing food and fresh air.

I didn't see that woman again for nearly a year when one of her other children came to call me to their house. The young girl had suffered a bad bleed. It was altogether too late for me to do anything to save her. That foolish mother had not followed my advice.

Jainub was that foolish mother, Karimunissa the girl.

✍ CHAPTER FOUR ✍

ONCE A YEAR, early in May, a holy man came to Borli Panchatan to celebrate the Hindu festival of Yattra. Soon after the dawn *muezzin* the sound of pipes and drums announced the arrival of the *yogi* and his two attendants from Mahsla, as the procession crossed the bridge at the bottom of the bazaar road and then turned right up the hill to the village compound.

There the *yogi* made *puja* (prayer) at the temple, offering coconut and rice to the statue of Lord Krishna. Then, trailed by a growing number of small boys, the cavalcade wound its way back to the bazaar road and downhill to the temple near the main village well. Once again the holy man went inside to ring the bell suspended from the low roof and to announce his presence to the gods. This done, the musicians and the *yogi* set off for Diwaga along the well-worn track topping the earth-works thrown up twenty years previously, when the marshes were brought under rice cultivation.

By mid-morning a steady stream of villagers was heading for the Diwaga coconut groves. They were mostly Hindus enjoying a holiday from work, but there was also a substantial number of Muslims unable to resist witnessing the awesome spectacle which always concluded the festival. The clearing surrounding a very ancient banyan tree was soon crowded, people squatting on the ground, lively conversations punctuated by crimson jets of betel juice ejected in streams of spittle on to the dust between their feet. *Char* vendors on the edge of the crowd presided over small wood fires, selling glasses of sweet tea; the *paan*walla's dextrous fingers parcelled fragments of tobacco, areca nut and lime into betel leaves; and the lanky-legged sweatmeat man, stepping carefully through the seated people, resembled a wading bird as he peddled rings of brittle toffee impaled on the long stick resting on his shoulder.

Preparations for the climax to the festival had been in progress for several days. A gang of workmen climbed into the banyan and lashed a strong pole into position so that it pro-truded some twenty feet above the topmost branches. A metal fixing secured a crossbar to the summit of the pole so that it could pivot, and from one end of the crossbar, a long loop of rope dangled to a wooden platform built at ground level. When completed, the contraption resembled a gibbet, the only difference being that, instead of a noose, at the end of the rope was a large curved meathook.

The *yogi*'s last place of worship was the Diwaga temple, located deep in the palm groves more than a mile from where the crowds patiently waited. A path of marigold blossoms led to the dark inner sanctum where, lit only by the soft flicker of candles, stood the chocolate-brown statue of Lord Krishna. Clasped in one of the god's two right hands was the sacred *chanko* (seashell) which when sounded was supposed to arouse every last Hindu in the land to unite in prayer. In the other was the *padma* (lotus flower), symbol of mankind's many-layered dimensions of existence. The god's two left hands held the *gaddah* (truncheon) used solely for purposes of defence and the *chakra* (a disc-like weapon which the legendary warrior Krishna was reputed to have used with consummate accuracy in mythical battles with celestial enemies).

74

Once more the holy man prostrated himself in homage. Some minutes afterwards he lit a bundle of joss-sticks and placed them with those already smouldering in a jar. Then, stooping to kiss the idol's feet, he backed away, repeatedly touching prayerful hands to his forehead, his lips and his breast.

As the drum and pipe music drew nearer, the crowd under the banyan fell silent. Only the crows kept up their irreverent cawing as the *yogi* and his two attendants slowly walked to the platform. Then, to the sonorous beat of the drum, the *yogi* stripped off his long saffron robe and stood naked except for a flimsy loincloth, his bush of thick hair streaked with henna and heavy-lidded eyes sternly fixed on the spectators as if to mesmerise them to rapt attention. The crowd held its breath, knowing what was coming next.

One of the attendants seized the rope, the other took hold of the rapier-sharp hook. The *yogi* sat with his legs in the lotus position, his head bent forward. In full view of the people, the attendant inserted the point of the hook into the flesh of the holy man's back, just beneath the right shoulder blade and, pushing hard, forced it out beneath the left. A huge sigh fluttered through the crowd. The holy man remained motionless.

Then, aided by several others, the attendants began to haul on the rope. Higher and higher went the *yogi*, his body hanging limp, eyes closed, a chunk of human meat suspended more than forty feet above the ground. In the summit of the tree helpers waited to support the *yogi*, while others quickly coiled the loose end of rope round a sack of sand to act as a counterweight. Then, given a strenuous push, the bar began to pivot, *yogi* and sack circling the banyan tree like some gruesome toy mobile.

One hour later the procedure was reversed, the *yogi* descended and the crowd closed in round the platform. As his inert body slid to rest on the planking, once again their excited chatter subsided. The holy man lay face down with his eyes closed, the tip of his tongue showing between froth-covered lips. Momentarily the spectator's view was obscured as attendants leaned over the body. In the next instant the hook was swinging free and the *yogi* was on his feet, drinking greedily at a small bowl of water. The crowd gasped. The only visible signs of the holy man's impalement were two patches of darkened skin where the hook had penetrated.

At the back of the crowd, Jainub's six youngest children had watched in silence, scarcely able to believe that what they were seeing was not a hideous dream. Then, when the people surged forward to witness the holy man's release from the hook, they turned to walk back to Borli.

They were hot, tired and very thirsty. The water they had brought with them in a glass bottle had long since been finished by eight-month-old Kudbadeen, last addition to the family, riding perched on Aisha's hip. Scuffing their feet in the dust, the children trudged along the track, keeping well to the edge to avoid bullock-carts and bicycles. Half way home, Adam caught the flash of bright orange in a corner of a nearby paddy field, and clambering down the embankment, gathered the lilies before hurrying to catch up with the others.

Glad of an excuse, Jainub had sent the children out of the house much earlier in the day, keeping only Halima behind to help nurse Karimunissa. The sick girl lay on the *charpoy*, thin and comatose, her shallow breathing scarcely perceptible. All day mother and daughter took turns to bathe the girl's face and hands, often their lips moving in silent prayer as they watched life slip quietly away. When the children clattered into the house, proudly bearing the lilies, they were only in time to lay them on the closely-wrapped corpse of their eldest sister.

* * *

The money from Ahmed never came. Jainub wrote letters which went unanswered. Then, shortly before Karimunissa died, a letter arrived from Durban. It was brief and to the point. Ahmed had run away and nobody knew where he had gone.

The *jammut* arranged the burial on the day Karimunissa died. She was interred in the graveyard behind the mosque. Muslim burials and Hindu cremations were undertaken within hours of death, a sanitary imperative in a climate which grossly accelerated all forms of decomposition.

The loss left Jainub numb with grief. She spent sleepless nights, the ceaseless chatter of grasshoppers orchestrating the frantic thoughts which churned over and over in her mind. How could she safeguard the survival of her children in this godforsaken place? It required no great stretch of the imagination for Jainub to foresee even harder times ahead unless she could find a way to support her family. Of the gold pieces that Haji had left her, only two remained, worth about Rs 120 (£4). Whatever happened, Jainub intended to keep this intact as a last buffer against destitution. Kudbadeen's birth in September, as well as Karimunissa's long illness, had left their mark on the young widow. Dresses which had hugged her well-rounded

76

figure now hung loosely and a frosting of white had appeared in Jainub's frizzy auburn hair.

The children had little difficulty in acquiring a good working knowledge of the local language. With their help and encouragement, Jainub also began to converse more easily with her neighbours. She struck up a friendship with a tailor in the bazaar who rented her an old Singer sewing machine for Rs 5 a month, enabling Jainub to start stitching sari blouses and children's clothes. But orders were few and far between since most of her neighbours were scarcely any better off than she was. Then, as if in answer to prayer, her son Adam was offered a job.

The tailor knew a man who was ticket-collector on one of the old buses which went every day from Dighi to Shriverdhan. He got Adam work cleaning the inside of those buses at a wage of one rupee a day.

When he started that job, my son was ten years old. Each morning he was up before six to catch the first bus from Dighi and travel on it fifteen miles to the depot. He worked all day there, cleaning buses when they stopped to refuel and turn round. It was dirty work. In the rainy season all the seats got soaked and Adam had to dry them. And often those bumpy mountain roads made people sick.

Adam would get back home at six in the evening and eat whatever we had to give him. Sometimes we were waiting for his wage so we could go to the bazaar and buy food. It made me unhappy when some days I could not send him with a piece of bread in his pocket for later.

That second year in Borli was a difficult time for us. Sad to say, some days I had to sink my pride and take the children from door to door asking our neighbours to give us a little rice. But nobody had much to spare. In this place every person had to look out for himself. In bad years the village beggars couldn't come to our doors twice a week, but only once. The first year when I was going to get rice from my field, strong storms beat it into the mud. It was fit for nothing but the crows.

Then our luck changed a little bit. One evening the children come running to say a bullock-cart has stopped outside and Adam is on it with a strange Muslim man. I asked that person into the house, thinking he was going to make complaint about my son. But he entered smiling and in a kind voice say he is the bus inspector at Shriverdhan. Earlier that same day Adam came to his office to ask for a drink of water. My son looked so ill that the inspector asked if he was hungry. Adam had to nod his head. Then that good man takes my boy to his home and lets him eat with his family. His wife made Adam tell her about himself and then she strongly suggest her husband bring Adam back to Borli to see if what he spoke was really true. Before that man leaves, he fetches a bag of rice and another of onions from his cart and puts them on my kitchen table. When my own husband's family at the other end of this same house would not lift a finger to help, strangers took pity on us.

Sometimes after that the bus inspector used to send that bullock-cart and take me and all my children to Shriverdhan, keeping us with them for three or four days at a time and feeding us well. Then, when the cart bring us back again, always we had presents of rice and vegetables. With that good man and his wife, I did not have to hold out my hand to beg. They took my hand in friendship.

The hardship that Jainub and her family were enduring did not escape the notice of the *jammut*. One function of this council was to reserve funds to assist its most needy members. But before doing this, in a village where poverty was widespread, the *jammut* made sure that all avenues of help within the family had first been exhausted.

In order to satisfy these conditions, Jainub wrote to her married daughter in Cape Town, begging Florina to try and find her brother and persuade him to honour his filial obligations. Weeks later Florina replied. She had located Ahmed. He was in good health and working elsewhere in Cape Colony. Once properly settled, he would start to send regular money orders. However, to Jainub's consternation, her daughter made no mention of a forwarding address or how long it might be before Ahmed began payments. All she could do was wait and hope. But once again the *jammut* intervened to suggest that where her first son had failed, Adam might prove a better investment. Since the boy was already working, they reasoned, surely it made sense to give him an opportunity to earn more substantial wages in South Africa.

Jainub was horrified at the idea of sacrificing Adam as a solution to her predicament. Instead she dipped into the last of her already depleted savings, confident that before these were finally spent she would hear from Ahmed. But she did not. Furthermore, Jainub's intransigence had again offended the *jammut*, unused as it was to having a woman challenge the male authority invested in it by the teachings of Islam.

* * *

The word 'Islam' is an Arabic word meaning submission, surrender and obedience. Only total self-negation, it is claimed, enables the individual to achieve peace in body, mind and spirit. In turn, unceasing effort by every individual creates a peaceful society. Contrary to popular belief, the religion of Islam does not owe its origins to the Prophet Muhammad any more than Jesus Christ was the founder of Christianity. The Prophet was the last messenger of God, chosen to convey to Islamic people the Divine Revelation. Drawing on the earlier teachings of Zoroaster, Jesus of Nazareth and the Gautama Buddha, Muhammad was the creator of a cultural blueprint for what is claimed to be a totally harmonious and enriched existence. Yet, unlike Jesus, the Prophet's early life gave no indication that one day he was to provide the inspiration for the largest religious body in the world.

Muhammad was born about AD 570, the son of Bedouin parents. He spent his boyhood shepherding sheep and goats in the desert outside Mecca, a district peopled by nomadic tribes isolated from other emerging civilisations by vast oceans of sand. Illiterate and riddled with superstition, the Bedouins were fond of engaging in bloody battles with one another. It is said that although Muhammad lived and worked amongst these rough tribes, he gained a reputation for honesty, chivalry and a profound dislike of the lawless activities which delighted his contemporaries.

In his fortieth year, Muhammad retreated to the hills. How long he remained in solitude is not recorded, only that when he finally reappeared among his people, he had undergone a miraculous transformation. Henceforth, his charisma as a preacher held audiences spellbound. Wherever Muhammad travelled, crowds gathered to listen as he preached the divine message of total submission to the will of Allah. Before he died, Muhammad had dictated his revelations in the Muslim holy scriptures known as the Koran, giving not only a full account of his life, but also a practical manifesto to guide the faithful towards physical and spiritual fulfilment.

This unique book has never been subjected to any form of abridgement or revision; to this day the Arabic text remains intact. Moreover, most Muslims learn to read the text in its original form.

The Koranic groundrules for living appear, beside more liberal theosophies, unashamedly dogmatic. Certainly the followers of Islam do not keep their religion for Sunday—or more precisely, for Friday, this being the Muslim holy day. Five times each and every day, Muslims turn towards Mecca to perform *salat*, or prayers of obeisance. The first *azaan* (call) is at dawn, the second at ten in the morning and the third around one o'clock, before the midday meal. The fourth is at three, the *muezzin*'s tremulous call shimmering on the afternoon heat-haze. The fifth and last call is as sunset speeds flocks of noisy crows to roost in trees silhouetted against a vivid orange sky.

On every occasion, worshippers will not pray until they have cleansed their faces, hands and feet—either at home or in the small stone washing chamber provided in the courtyard of the local mosque. Then, either attending the mosque or unrolling a prayer mat in the home or place of work, the worshipper kneels to recite texts from the Koran, intermittently prostrating himself by touching palms and forehead to the ground. Muslim women never attend the mosque, praying instead at home.

In this way, five times a day the Muslim devotee reaffirms his covenant with Allah, recharges his spiritual batteries and brings the teachings of the Prophet into every corner of his daily existence. Most important of all is the influence religion has upon his family life, where Islam has established strict divisions of duty.

The husband is always the head of the household, entitled to unquestioning obedience from his womenfolk. In return, he provides for the needs of his wife (or wives) and children and is a constant source of protection. The Muslim woman devotes herself to household management, raises an unlimited number of children (contraception being a sin against God) and concentrates all her energies on seeing to the comfort of her own family and that of her in-laws, with whom she lives. In order to avoid distractions from these tasks, the Muslim woman remains in *purdah*, which means literally to 'hide from sight', and whenever venturing out of the home, she goes closely veiled.

Relationships between the sexes are again circumscribed by strict religious protocol. Beyond the family circle, neither men nor women seek each other's company. In this way, the Koran insists, they will develop modesty, moral purity and respectful attitudes towards one another. Children also learn the art of submission to their elders and especially the law which assigns to adult sons the responsibility for the support of parents. So within the well-disciplined Islamic family attention to detail carefully eliminates the possibility of controversy and creates what is claimed to be a shining example for society at large.

From the womb to the grave, the devout Muslim is in no doubt about what he may or may not do. He is well aware that suicide, theft, bribery, forgery, cheating and gambling are forbidden, that he is not permitted to drink alcohol, hoard wealth or luxuriate in social aggrandisement, adultery, fornication or any form of behaviour liable to threaten family life or the welfare of others. Not that Islam believes in the suppression of sexual desires any more than it frowns upon legal polygamy; it is merely that such intimacies must always be sought within marriage, not outside it, strictures which undoubtedly account for the high incidence of early marriage among Muslims.

By the time a Muslim girl is fifteen she is usually married, very probably to one of her relations. Connections between families have always been encouraged on the grounds that partners with similar habits and customs are much more likely to form happy liaisons. And there is another advantage. In large families intermarriage creates a protective network in times of adversity, especially in the absence of any other type of practical support.

Religious considerations invade every area of Muslim life, even to the food consumed, especially if this happens to be meat. Flesh from animals killed for sport is taboo. So is the meat of carnivores and animals with claws. The Koran also forbids the ingestion of meat which has not been killed according to *halal*— that is, 'clean meat' resulting from ritual slaughter. According to Muslim belief, only animals which are bled to death retain the correct nutritional value. Pigmeat is not *halal* for Muhammadans, although the reason for this is lost in obscurity. But as with any other of the divine teachings, this dietary rule is always meticulously observed. So also is the annual tradition of abstinence.

In the ninth month of the lunar year—falling in or near the month of September—Muslims celebrate Ramadhan, or Id, when during the hours of daylight they take no food or drink. Pregnant and menstruating women are exempted and those nursing at the breast. Children below the age of eight are also excused Ramadhan; older schoolchildren, weakened by fasting, only attend morning lessons, sleeping through the afternoons until sunset, when they are given a scanty meal of milk and fresh fruit. Anyone who becomes ill during the fast is permitted to eat, but only after a beggar has been called to the house and allowed to eat to repletion!

At Ramadhan mendicants from Hindu settlements inland flock to Borli, eager to cash in on the certainty that no Muhammadan worth his salt will turn any of them away without a donation of rice or money. On a good day in Ramadhan—even in a poor village like Borli—it is said that an agile beggar can make Rs 50!

Another religious obligation is the performance of the *hajj*, or the undertaking of a devotional pilgrimage. At least once in his lifetime every Muslim will try to make the journey to Mecca. If this is beyond attainment, a lesser shrine, such as Ajmer Shariffe, will do. This religious exercise affords pilgrims the opportunity to experience in a holy place the immense brother-hood of Islam.

In the past the isolation of many Muslim communities safe-guarded the continuity of their traditions. They were not exposed to the distracting influences of an increasingly material-istic and hedonistic world. And, in the village, there was always the local branch of the Muslim Society, constantly striving to weld the Muslim community together and make sure no member of it stepped out of line. Noor Pangaka, prominent member of this society, described its responsibilities.

In Borli our council takes care of many practical matters such as maintaining the mosque, arranging marriage cere-monies and funerals and such like. To pay for these services our members contribute $2\frac{1}{2}$ per cent of their annual income. Out of this we pay the *peshmam* who leads prayers in the mosque and those who take turns to call the *muezzin*. We also charge people to borrow the big iron pots which they need for cooking celebration feasts and the coloured canopy which is erected outside the bridegroom's house for the signing of marriage papers.

Other important work of this council is to maintain a school for religious instruction, called *madrusha*. Children come every morning at half past seven to learn to recite the Koran in Arabic and read the original texts.

We always begin our prayers with these words from the Koran: '*Bismillah rachmani rohim* . . .' which means '. . . In the name of God who is beneficent and merciful . . .' In the whole of that particular verse there are ninety-nine letters. When you come to know the Holy Book, you find that this is the recurrent number in all the verses it contains. Always ninety-nine, or multiples of that number, are there. That is why it has never been possible to change a single word of Muhammad's testi-mony and why Muslims everywhere obey them to the last letter. The Koran is perfection. And I'll tell you another thing. When a faithful person recites the holy scriptures, he creates light.

Right here in Borli there lived a simple peasant called Sait Kadre who could neither read nor write. One day he was passing the house of a highly-educated Muslim who was reciting from the Koran. Sait Kadre called out: 'Master, you have made a mistake.' You can imagine how annoyed that erudite person was at such affrontery. So he called back: 'Go away you ignorant fellow. You don't read the Koran so how can you accuse me of mistakes?'

To this the old man replied: 'What you say is true, Master, but I hold the Koran in my heart. When you were reciting just now, I saw the light emerging from your head suddenly go out.' So the educated man checked the holy texts and realised he had indeed mispronounced one of the lines!

The correct moral behaviour of young people also occupies the attention of the village *jammut*, a task somewhat simplified in a place where everyone is well known to everyone else.

We are always strict with those who make trouble. Supposing a boy becomes involved with some girl, it is the council's job to persuade them to break off that liaison. If the boy doesn't obey us, then we will force him to leave our village. This way others learn the lesson and keep it in mind before doing anything wrong. That is our Muslim tradition. When someone doesn't observe the divine laws, he or she will be boycotted. However, if the wrongdoer comes to us and makes a sincere apology, then the council may decide to pardon that person.

What else do we do in this village? Well, the *jammut* keeps track of sons who go to work overseas. If they fail to send support to their parents in the village, we will make contact with the local Muslim Society. It doesn't matter where he is, our members will track down that wrongdoer and make him see the error of his ways.

In 1938 oil was struck in Kuwait and Dubai, and because of our ancient trade connections with Arab countries, it was possible for village Muslims to migrate to new horizons and get better employment than they could find in this poor place. We have many cases where village families sent small boys, no more than seven or eight years old, to work in South African countries. These young boys grew up with little love for their parents, so naturally they don't want to send their hard-earned money to those they have forgotten. This causes hardship to families in Borli who have to depend upon sons for support. If that family consists of devout and obedient people, the *jammut* will try to give financial help once we are certain there's no other way to make the sons provide. But when there are sons to work, we do not give this help. There are always so many poor families hereabouts. We can't give to everybody. That is why in extreme cases we have to advise people to send young sons abroad to become wage-earners. Sometimes they have no choice. It is either a case of starve or sacrifice.

* * *

In 1945 Jainub Undre faced just such a decision as she struggled to feed and clothe her children on Adam's wages and the pittance she made from dressmaking. As the months passed, it became clear that they were rapidly approaching destitution. So when the *jammut* once more told Jainub that there was a man in Borli prepared to take her son Adam to work in South Africa, against her better inclinations, Jainub consented.

> The man say he will teach Adam to work very nice in his shop—to wash floors and clean the shelves. That small boy of mine don't want to be parted from his sisters, but the *jammut* take him aside and tell him: 'Come on, get out Adam. Otherwise your mother and sisters will suffer. It is your duty to earn for them.'
>
> When they came to fetch him, Adam was crying as he put on his broken shoes and one small coat. Then that boy grabs hold of the bed and with all his strength screams he will not go. In the end, they drag him away.

*   *   *

Although Borli Panchatan was on a gently sloping tree-clad mound rising from the flatlands behind Diwaga, scattered in the surrounding valleys lay more abrupt humps of land called *tikera*, a local name for a 'small hill standing by itself'. Against the dramatic escarpments on the skyline, these *tikera* seemed like geodynamic afterthoughts, as though the primeval earth-core subsiding from boiling magnificence to a modest simmer had, with a final exhalation of molten breath, left behind a smattering of petrified bubbles.

Beside the road to Karlia, half a mile from Borli, was just such a *tikera*. A well-worn goat track spiralled up through scrub to the flat summit, where, beneath one old cashew-nut tree and on ground carpeted with wild thyme, was the shell of a two-roomed dwelling. The thatch had long since gone from the rafters; the four window-frames and the door had also disappeared. But one distinctive feature of the house remained. Outside the entrance a long bench made from stones and pebble-dash cement afforded those who sat on it a panoramic view—ox-carts travelling in little clouds of dust along the Karlia road, women trotting home with loads of firewood on their heads, the brilliance of emerald seed patches in the corners of every ricefield, lone eagles over mountain tops, flights of elegant white egret skimming the creek and, in the centre of it all, sienna-coloured rooftops with the bulbous dome of the Borli mosque emerging like a surrealist egg from the dark green foliage of shogun, banyan and mango.

When she discovered the little hill, Jainub had no idea why someone should have bothered to build a home with such an unforgettable view and then abandon it. It was the children who first heard the rumour that it had been occupied by a Hindu leper who was cast out of the village many years before and had chosen to live his life on the hill rather than go to a leper colony for treatment. This unknown man earned Jainub's silent blessing. On days when she felt overwhelmed by her losing battle with loneliness and poverty the derelict house was a much-needed sanctuary. On the *tikera* Jainub felt a spiritual bond with the man who also must have known what it meant to be the victim of circumstances over which he had no control.

Occasionally Jainub received small sums of money from Adam and sometimes from Florina too, although her daughter had also been widowed when her husband had succumbed to tuberculosis. But from Ahmed there was still no word. Then, into a life already hard beyond measure, fate struck yet another blow.

One November day, when Kudbadeen was nearly four years old, the little boy fell off the front veranda on to several large stones which served as front steps to Jainub's house. A festering wound opened up on the base of the child's spine and, when it refused to heal, Jainub consulted Dr Adhikari. His advice was to take Kudbadeen to Bombay for X-rays.

Again Jainub tried to borrow the necessary money from Haji's relations; again they refused her. When, after some months, Kudbadeen's condition became suddenly worse, as a last resort Jainub and the girls walked the two kilometres to Karlia where the herb doctor lived. He gave Jainub a bundle of green leaves with instructions to macerate them and poultice the wound.

As the family retraced their footsteps down the dusty lane to where stepping stones in the river connected it with the Borli road, Jainub's heart felt as heavy as the lethargic child on her hip. When the girls begged for time to play in the river, she consented, and glad of a rest took Kudbadeen to sit in the shade of a mango.

As she sat there, a Hindu man drove a pair of cream-coloured oxen into the shallow water and proceeded to scrub them with handfuls of grass. Holding their skirts bunched up out of the water, the girls paddled upstream to watch. The Hindu asked a few questions and occasionally glanced across to where Jainub sat. When he had finished washing the animals, he led them by their nose-rings up on to the shale margin of the river and taking a small *hunda* from his bundle, squatted against a cow. In a moment a stream of milk was noisily jetting into the brass container.

Jainub watched through half-closed eyes, conscious of little more than Kudbadeen's feverish body held close to her own. So she was startled when the container of milk was suddenly thrust under her nose. The Hindu was smiling, urging her to take it for Kudbadeen. Jainub shook her head, knowing she could not pay for the milk, but the man pushed the *hunda* into her hand. With a friendly wag of the head, he loped back to his waiting animals and thwacking his hand on their wet rumps, herded them out of sight up the lane.

The following day, when the girls returned the empty *hunda* to the Hindu milkman, he refilled it and insisted they take it home again for their sick brother. He would not accept any payment. But even this repeated kindness could not save the child. Shortly before his fourth birthday Kudbadeen died in his sleep.

Jainub's loss was not unique in a village where, in the late 1940s, on average only one out of three children survived to the age of five. If neonatal tetanus did not carry off the newborn infant, there were numerous other endemic health hazards which thrived in a climate of heat and ignorance. Families were large, but so also were their losses—despite the magic talismans hung round their children's necks and the ghoulish concoction of eye-black which parents used to outline their babies' eyes to ward off evil spirits.

As the only qualified physician in the area, Dr Adhikari was hard-pressed to administer a satisfactory medical service. Borli and the nearby villages had a total population of around five thousand. Not only was he hampered by sheer numbers, but also by the people's refusal to have anything much to do with family planning.

> Whenever I talked on this subject, the people gave me a big argument. They told me that to prevent children was a sin against God. I replied: 'So all right, God has given you rain so why do you use umbrellas?' Then they would say: 'If God gives us children then he will also provide food for them.' I used to answer back: 'When you marry you have land. Does God increase the size of that land or the yield of your crops when he gives you fifteen children to feed?'
> But in those days people did not want to listen to modern

ideas. They produced big families and when many of these children died, they said that this also was their God-given destiny.

* * *

The apparently fatalistic attitude Hindus display towards life and death is rooted in their beliefs about reincarnation. The *Bhagavad Gita*, composed about 200 BC, a book as sacred to Hindus as the Koran is to Muslims, says: 'for certain is the death of the born and certain is the birth of the dead; therefore what is unavoidable thou shouldst not regret.'

For Hindus, death is not a final departure from earth, but only one departure in a series of transmigrations of the human soul on its journey towards *atman* (divine awareness). Liberation from this endless cycle of reincarnation is *moksha* (the ultimate level of spiritual development). After death Yama, god of death, reviews his worldly actions, the subsequent score determining the conditions of the next incarnation.

The system of 'caste' in India, which has so often been condemned as cruel by outsiders, can therefore be rationalised in terms of *karma* (destiny). According to Hindu beliefs, a person leading a life of degradation is merely fulfilling his *karmic* inheritance. A privileged person who has led a faulty existence can descend the 'karmic' scale. Equally, the beggar who seeks to overcome adversity could be re-born to more advantageous circumstances. Then again, persistent transgressions at any 'karmic' level could result in the lowest-of-the-low animal incarnations.

Hinduism, regarded as one of the great religions of the world, defies comparison with any other. Hinduism is a complex composite of many ancient forms of worship without a definitive doctrine, with as many facets to it as human nature itself. Unlike the other great world religions, it lacks a divine revelation pinpointed at a precise moment in history. Hindu beliefs are the result of a gradual assimilation of wisdom and wizardry brought to India by a succession of foreign invaders, notably the forceful Aryans who, two and a half thousand years before the birth of Christ, settled down to make India their homeland.

The Aryans originated somewhere in Central Asia. They were tribal people who worshipped the forces of nature; Agni, the god of fire; Dyaus, god of the sky; Prthivi, god of Earth and so on. Aryan invaders first occupied the Indus Valley in northern India and over the next millennium gradually spread east to the Indo-Gangetic plain to found the holy city of Benares, and southwards to the rest of India.

Other ancient civilisations also left their religious imprint on Hindu culture—Greeks, Persians, Egyptians and Chinese to mention some—and all were received with the religious tolerance which is an intrinsic feature of Hindu philosophy.

The first religious literature to emerge was contained in the famous Sanskrit *vedas*, poetic verses composed between about 1500 and 800 BC which spoke at length of the sacred relationship between mankind and his natural surroundings.

Then, between 800 and 600 BC, religious chronicles called the *Upanishads*, exploring the development of mankind's esoteric nature, came into existence. These texts taught that elemental worship described in the early *vedas* was not the only expression of man's spirituality. Man must also strive for karmic liberation of the soul through reincarnation.

> When the body gets to thinness
> Whether through old age or disease
> Just as the mango or the fig or the pepul tree
> Releases seeds from their bond
> So the individual frees himself from these limbs
> And returns again as he came
> To the place from which he started
> Back to life . . .
>
> *Brhad-Aranyaka Upanishad*

Thus began the metaphysical aspect of Hinduism, the belief that it is responsible action in life which speeds the journey of the soul through a series of embodiments, each bringing the 'essential self' nearer to the centre of perfection called *Brahman*.

The lyric poems contained in the *Mahabharata* (seven times longer than the *Iliad* and the *Odyssey* combined!) celebrates the mythical exploits of gods, humans and animals woven into an extravagant pattern of allegorical legends. Extracted from these is the most famous of all Hindu texts, the *Bhagavad Gita* which relates the legend of the greatest of all Hindu heroes, Lord Krishna. The result of an immaculate conception, so the verses relate, Krishna was born a king but sent to live with a humble family. As a boy he was a herdsman, but when he grew up Krishna became a warrior, engaged in furious battles with all forces of evil.

After a saga of memorable adventures, Krishna retired to live alone in the forests. There, in a hunting accident, an arrow penetrated Krishna's heel and he expired. It is the mythical hero Lord Krishna with his androgynous four-armed physical form (and other semi-animal incarnations) who is worshipped in homes and temples all over India.

In the sixth century BC, Buddhism and Jainism came to India, adding yet another religious dimension to Hinduism. Buddhist communities favouring vegetarianism and known as devotees of Jain, to whom the killing or injury of any living creature is anathema, were then founded. (To this day orthodox Jains sweep the path in front of them to avoid accidentally treading on an insect!)

So Hinduism continued to absorb and adapt the beliefs of others into a spiritual celebration which encompassed both the metaphysical and the mundane; which was an appealing expression of faith for illiterates as well as for the literate.

The unique and ancient four-fold caste system of India evolved during the early Aryan conquest, the original meaning of 'caste' probably referring to the differences in complexion between the (superior) light-complexioned Aryans and the (inferior) dark-skinned colouring of the indigenous tribes. The Aryans put the natives to work farming the land, trading goods and making handicrafts. In due course, these dark-skinned workers were classed as *vaisya* and *sudra*, the two lowest castes. Assigned to the highest castes were brahmans, who were priests and teachers, and *kshatriyas*, who comprised the warrior class. So the original four-caste system was an early form of apartheid, segregating the light-skinned Aryan invaders from the dark-skinned labouring indigenes.

Then, sub-castes arose within the four main ones as Greeks, Persians, Jews and other races attempted to preserve their vocational and religious identities in their new homeland. But right at the very bottom of this hierarchal heap came the infamous untouchables or 'outcastes'.

The *Rig-veda* (one of the four *vedas*), said to be the oldest book in the world, reveals how it was that some Hindus never gained the distinction of belonging even to the lowest 'caste'. Many natives, frightened by the Aryan invasion, fled to safety in the hills and jungles where they lived by hunting and fishing only occasionally approaching villages to sell produce and handicrafts. In time some of these refugees were allowed to settle permanently on the outskirts of villages, but the only work they were given consisted of jobs which nobody else wanted—such as scavenging, the removal of dead animals and the disposal of refuse.

Denied affiliation to any particular vocational caste and ostracised by fellow Hindus because they were constantly handling the pollution of others, these people were dubbed 'untouchables'. To exonerate their guilt at such arbitrary treatment, Hindus explained the unfortunate fate of 'outcastes' according to the law of *karma*. Even to this day, workers who handle leather in India are regarded as social pariahs because in the Hindu religion the ox is a sacred animal. As with many pious practices, this probably had practical origins.

In ages past, as settled communities became possible, the ownership of cattle meant survival and self-sufficiency. The family that owned one or two oxen enjoyed perpetual dairy produce. Diluted cow dung weatherproofed house walls, provided hard surfacing for floors and threshing areas and, dried in the sun, served as an excellent fuel. Village farmers cultivated their land with bullocks to pull the plough and, before the advent of pumps, it was oxen-energy that turned the waterwheels which irrigated fields. Understandably the owner lavished extreme care on such a valuable beast and made sure it enjoyed a long and productive life. Doubtless Buddhist and Jain abhorrence of any form of slaughter also contributed to the pampered sanctity of the Indian ox and the taboo concerning the eating of its flesh.

To try and contain and condense the religion which is Hinduism is to try and capture a river of quicksilver. Perhaps the only way to gain some appreciation of it is to suspend all sense of disbelief and open the mind to the possibility of the inexplicable.

Hinduism contains a complex diversity of sects, cults and disciplines, ranging from the esoteric to the erotic, from childlike ritual to profound metaphysical thought; it is rich in poetic beauty and much that, to Western eyes, is downright grotesque. Yet for thousands of years Hindu life and Hindu religion have been inseparable, every move the Indian makes dictated by *puja* and astrological predictions.

So the Hindu *yogi*, calmly disciplining his flesh to withstand the equivalent of a dozen crucifixions, is on the spiritual path. So is the *guru* who turns sand into gold, the bus-driver who lights joss-sticks at a roadside shrine, the family who kneels to worship a statue with features part human, part elephant. For the Hindu, innumerable pathways lead to the liberation of the soul. It is not so much the method used to seek this liberation that matters, but *the act of seeking* in a world which, according to the Buddha, is but a bridge of shadows leading man to the ultimate reality.

☙ CHAPTER FIVE ☙

ON 15 AUGUST 1947 there was a parade of Hindu children in the village of Borli Panchatan. Carrying the new tricolour flag, with garlands of flowers bouncing on their necks, they marched barefoot behind their teachers through the muddy lanes and up the bazaar road. When the procession reached the compound at the top of the hill, the village elders were there to meet it. Assembled in mud-splashed *dhoti* and high-necked tunics, each wearing a white Gandhi cap, they made long speeches about the future of India while the banyan dripped on to their black umbrellas. The children listened in customary silence. Then the head teacher was presented with a large framed print of the prime minister Mr Nehru and the Independence Day celebrations were over—bar the stoning.

That evening—and for several days afterwards—Hindu youths roamed the village throwing stones at Muslim houses. The Muslim community responded by closing its doors and shutters and waiting nervously for this nationalistic fervour to abate. A few veranda railings got broken and empty chicken baskets were used as footballs in the lanes. Otherwise no serious damage was caused to life or property by the citizens of the new India. After all, what satisfaction was there in persecuting one's neighbours?

Generations of Hindus and Muslims had lived and died in Borli. Like shark and remora, like ox and egret, the two communities were undeniably different, but indisputably linked in the same survival pattern. In the cities, poverty and passion exacerbated by appalling living conditions, fuelled the fires of religious intolerance. In the hillside village, living cheek by jowl with natural insecurity dissipated the people's appetites for vindictive behaviour towards one another.

In those days the countryside was still a tangle of bamboo thickets, cactus jungle and, on higher ground, teak forests, all of which supported an abundance of wildlife. Herds of deer and boar, packs of hyena and jackal roamed the forests. The jungles were alive with troupes of chattering grey monkeys and the un-oiled cries of brilliantly coloured parakeets, occasionally interrupted by the muffled roar of *shere* the lion. These, and a multiplicity of other creatures, thrived in the wooded territory separating one village from another, a zoological backdrop as familiar to country people as city traffic to the urban dweller.

The villagers maintained a healthy respect for more dangerous jungle denizens, taking care to leave them strictly alone unless forced to do otherwise. But obviously there were occasions when peaceful coexistence proved impossible, especially in the monsoon period. Then heavy rains turned dry ditches and gullies into raging torrents, washing snakes out of the highlands and stranding them near to human habitation.

Even then people took great care to avoid killing them. According to local superstition, if someone tried to kill a venomous snake but only managed to injure it, that snake would summon seven of its brethren and return to take revenge upon the attacker. So whenever a snake crossed the path of a villager, that person stood still until it had gone on its way. However, snakes washed into the paddyfields proved a more dangerous problem.

Once, so the story goes, a village woman took her baby and older daughter to a ricefield where her husband was working. in order to cook the man's midday meal. The woman's baby had been ill and refusing milk, so while she prepared the food, the mother ordered the daughter to go and sit with the baby in the shade of a nearby tree and see if she could persuade him to drink from a feeding bottle.

Shortly afterwards, she heard her daughter call: 'Ma, he is swallowing. . . .' The woman did not bother to turn round. She thought the girl meant the baby was swallowing the milk. In fact, the terrified girl was trying to convey that the baby was being swallowed by a python which had descended from the tree!

By the time the parents realised what was happening, the snake had consumed the baby and was coiling itself tightly back into the branches in order to crush its meal. Taking a machette, the father climbed the tree and hacked off the python's head. Then he split open its body to retrieve the baby which, very fortunately, was still alive.

It was a much less threatening type of creature which inadvertently sparked off a brief reign of terror in Borli. Under normal circumstances, the villagers had little to fear from the packs of jackals which roamed the countryside, usually on moonlit nights when they ran yelping and howling across the Diwaga ricefields to hunt rodents or merely scavenge for dead meat. During the day, these normally shy animals kept well away from human habitation.

One year, shortly before the rice harvest, a group of Katkari men came into the village to sell firewood, spending the money they earned on bottles of palm toddy. They were last seen stumbling down the Karlia road, uncorked bottle in one hand, short wooden bow and arrows in the other. By the time the Katkari reached their huts, they were extremely drunk, so when they discovered that during their absence an old man who had for days been sick with a raging fever had finally died, the drunks dragged the corpse into the bushes and deposited it in a shallow grave. Sometime during the night, marauding jackals made a midnight meal of the old Katkari. Next day some Hindu women, who had done their usual wood-gathering in the vicinity of the Katkari settlement, saw a scattering of human remains.

Several weeks afterwards, when most of the villagers had forgotten this apparently unimportant event, labourers cutting rice in the fields below the hillside suddenly heard the uncanny scream of jackals. Moments later the animals ran into the fields and launched a ferocious attack on the workers. Fifteen were badly bitten and taken to the doctor, who dressed their wounds and immediately started them on a series of anti-rabies injections. The uncharacteristic behaviour of the jackals prompted questions which soon connected the death of the old Katkari with the attack. It seemed likely that the old man had died of rabies.

Thirteen labourers suffered no more than the discomfort of the preventative treatment. But nearly two weeks after the attack, the other two who were bitten developed hydrophobia. On the lanes where they lived, horrified neighbours were forced to listen to the sound of mad human dogs, snarling and writhing on their *charpoys*, lashed to the frames by wrist and ankle to prevent them savaging and infecting anyone who approached.

In the meantime, the village elders had sent a report of the attack to the district offices at Shriverdhan. This was passed to the health authorities in Bombay, and in due course a lorry arrived in the village carrying armed soldiers with orders to exterminate every jackal in the area.

The soldiers camped under the mango and banyan trees just above the main village well. At night their lorry cruised along the Karlia road, turning a searchlight on the countryside, the intermittent sound of rifle fire echoing in the hills. Next morning another crop of jackal tail trophies was spiked on the cactus hedge at the southern end of the bazaar road. Eventually the soldiers announced that in a few more days they would be leaving the village.

Some believed the danger was over. Others had good reason to disagree. Those who spent their days in the hills reported having seen jackals skulking in the forest above the village. Not that it was at all certain these animals were infected. In any case, the villagers had to trust the soldiers to protect them: by December it would be necessary once again to send the village goats to forage in the hills.

Once grazing in the village was exhausted, after the monsoon, everyone paid two small boys a few paisa a week to drive their goats to pastures a mile or so away. At dawn the boys would wait by the big well until, from the lanes converging at this point, along trotted the goats. Then, swishing their sticks on the rumps of the slowest, the boys set off for the hills. In the late afternoon, the sound of bells and the skitter-skatter of small tapping hooves announced the return of the herd. As the goats reached the well, they automatically dispersed, each one capable of finding its own way home.

One evening early this particular December, the goatherds returned with one of their flock missing. And, as luck would have it, the missing goat belonged to Jainub.

Those two small brothers came crying to my house to say one of my goats is lost. So what can I do except comfort them and say not to worry. It is the will of Allah. But that mother gets so angry with her sons because they has risked the family reputation. She gets a stick and hits them hard, then shouts for them to run quickly and find my poor goat otherwise she will break their legs and give them no food to eat!

It is dangerous for those children to go back to the hills so late in the day, but I can't argue with that woman. So when the boys run off, I go across to the soldiers and tell them what has happened.

Well those boys look everywhere and then they hear those jackals screaming. So they hide in a small hole in the rocks. But they see this is the entrance to a big cave full of bones. It is where those mad animals are living and they are coming to their den by another opening in the rocks! But there, in the middle of the cave, sits my lost goat, fast asleep. So those

Top left Ummie, aged 75, in her garden
Top right Aisa's son Wazir (the 'coconut baby'), now aged 18
Bottom left In Ummie's kitchen (l-r) Halima, Ummie and Aisa
Bottom right Wearing school uniform, Ummie's ten-year-old
granddaughter Reshma poses by the periwinkle bushes

Top The main village well early in the morning
Bottom Moslem couple meet for the first time at their wedding

Top Ox-cart at Diwaga being loaded with coconuts
Bottom Derami and Ummie grind lentils in Ummie's kitchen

Top left Nana Sahib Kulkarni, elder of the village, and his farmer son Ravi
Top right Dr Vasudha Joshi holding a clinic in the Joshi Hospital
Centre Dr Nilkanth Joshi in his new X-ray room
Bottom left Dr Madhusudan Adhikari, the first doctor in Borli
Bottom right The author with young Katkari friends in their
government settlement

brave boys grab his ears and drag him out and run straight back to my house without stopping.

Later, the soldiers went to the cave and exterminated the last of the jackals before returning to Bombay. After that many years passed before sight or sound of a jackal was heard again in the countryside round Borli.

So for the first time but by no means the last, the villagers were the unwitting participants in a pattern of ecological violence which gradually altered the balance of coexistence between them and their natural surroundings.

* * *

Survival for Jainub and the girls during their early years in the village often rested on a knife-edge. Poverty was widespread in the village, but Jainub's neighbours seemed to have a natural resilience to it. Lacking their native cunning, she was forced to learn what village life was all about the hard way.

Throughout her tribulations Jainub was sustained by three factors: a constant hope that somehow circumstances would permit her to return to South Africa, the comfort she obtained from a burgeoning religious faith and her keen and unremitting maternal instincts.

We had so many difficulties during those early years in Borli, I really do not like to speak of them. My health was very poor. I was thin like a stick and many people thought I would surely die. But God kept me safeside. All the same, we have to struggle for our lives. Sometimes there was no other way but to go begging for our food. Everyone in the village was poor, but some used to give to us.

Then we always keep our faith. Every morning I take my five daughters to that small hill outside the village. There we go down on our knees to say our prayers. Then we come home and boil rice for our meal. Sometimes, if we have any, we throw sugar on top. Other times we grind those red chillies on the stone with *lassune* (garlic) and make chutney. We don't eat much but we carry on like that.

Always I keep my children in that free school. And I am strict with them. When they come home from lessons they must go and find wood for the cooking fire and fetch water. And Halima has to help with washing our clothes. I also teach my oldest daughter to use the sewing machine, and soon she is more clever than me at this work. Both of us stitch sari blouses and plain little dresses, so little by little we begin to earn a small income and don't have to beg any more.

I also start to help Hindu people with their deliveries and

95

when they get sick with cholera or typhus. When somebody calls me, I say to God, 'God, I am leaving my house and my children to do some work for these people. Guide me to make them altogether well again.'

In difficult delivery cases when the child is crosswise, I take oil to rub on the woman's stomach, pray hard and then when I put my hand, things come right. When the child is born I cut the navel cord and always use clean string to tie it off. Then I wash the baby and the mother and don't leave until they is altogether tip-top.

When that cholera strike down so many people in the village, I also go to nurse them. Many times those I nurse make a good recovery, but when someone dies, I wash the body and leave it nicely for the family. I nurse lots of people with cholera and typhus when everybody was afraid to go near for fear of catching those illnesses. I was never afraid. I know if I have a strong faith in my heart I will not get sick.

The Hindu people pay what they can for my help, usually a little rice. I grow to love my Hindu neighbours, but of course I am a Muslim woman so my own people tell me it is not my place to go about unveiled doing this kind of dirty work. I don't give them any answer. I just go and speak only to God.

When I was small, I had a good training in English so my Koran, which my late husband bought me, is in English. Often during the day I read and turn to this and after reading I pray to God, kneeling down to hit my head on the ground, so God gives me wiseness. I never lose my faith, even when things look very black for us here in this village.

Early in 1948, after five years of silence, Jainub received a letter from her eldest son Ahmed. By now the young man was twenty-one, working in a small general store in Johannesburg and recently married to the proprietor's youngest daughter. Contact alone would have made Ahmed's letter a memorable one, but it also contained some excellent news. Ahmed had approached the South African immigration authorities to apply for visas for Jainub and the girls to return to their homeland on a government-assisted passage scheme.

Jainub was overjoyed. A terrible weight had been lifted from her shoulders and she eagerly awaited the next letter from Ahmed. In due course it arrived with a sheaf of official documents which Jainub had to complete, giving details of her dependants. Inevitably none of this correspondence and its attendant excitement escaped the attention of the old widows.

When my family members start to know I am trying to go back to South Africa, they all come to me and say, 'We will help you get to Bombay if you agree to take one six-year-old cousin with you.' I ask how I can do that when the visas are only for me and my daughters. Then they tell me that this boy is exactly the same age as the one baby I lost when I first arrived in Borli. They tell me to put this baby's name on the application form and pretend the boy is my son. When I reach South Africa some people there will take the cousin into their home.

At first I did not agree to this dishonesty. Then I think it over again. I must have money and help otherwise how can I get us all to the ship in Bombay? And the relatives promise what I'm doing is not wrong because plenty of people are helping Indian boys to get to South Africa in this way. So I let them put my dead baby's name on the papers. Then I write to Ahmed to make sure he remembers to tell the immigration office that the one boy travelling with us will be his brother Kulsum.

After that I started to get ready for the journey. I sold all my household belongings and packed our clothes into two big baskets. Then, for the first time in such a long time, when I walk out in the bazaar I hold my head up high and look every-one happily in the face. I want to shout out to them, 'Ah, look at me! You thought I was nothing but a poor woman with nobody to care whether I lived or died, but you were wrong. I have a fine son in South Africa who is calling me home to live in the place where I belong.'

Jainub's ecstasy was short-lived. Two days before she was due to leave for Bombay, the runner brought a telegram from Murud and delivered it to the old widows. Together they came along the veranda of their adjoining homes to tap on Jainub's door. Jainub did not have to look twice at their sombre faces to know they brought bad news.

Somehow the immigration authorities at Cape Town had dis-covered Jainub's papers contained false information. The permits had been cancelled.

My husband's relations told me that it would be useless going to South Africa because I would be refused entry and sent back to India. So there I am, with nothing in my house except the baskets of clothes. I have to go round and try to buy back my furniture and cooking pots. I felt so downhearted, but what could I do? It was the will of God that I stay here in Borli for the remainder of my days.

* * *

A few years before the British left India, Mahatma Gandhi described his ideal village as one which was a largely self-supporting community, able to cultivate enough land to feed itself. Gandhi believed that fixture of tenancy would ensure that tenant farmers worked to the best of their ability and that village business conducted on a co-operative basis would be a further incentive to community effort. Any spare land in the village should be utilised for cash crops—other than tobacco and opium, which Gandhi regarded as injurious to health. He also advocated the improvement of farming methods with the proper use of fertilisers, better yielding rice varieties and more robust breeds of livestock. Nor did he express any objection to mechanisation, providing this did not lead to unemployment.

However, work was not the only area which the Mahatma envisaged as needing development. He also advocated the promotion of the social and cultural needs of village people. According to Gandhi, every village should have a recreational area for adults as well as for children, an open-air theatre and a school to provide education up to secondary standard.

It was not until 1952 that the Indian government initiated a nationwide campaign to raise the living standards for rural communities along the lines suggested by Gandhi ten years before. Through democratic processes, country people would be given improved health, educational and other recreational facilities with government grants and a network of administrative bodies.

The first Five Year Plan established the ideology behind this community development programme. Anticipating that ignorance and apathy would be the greatest barriers to progress, government aims were at first directed at raising the social expectations of rural people, showing them how it would be possible to gain for themselves a better all-round standard of living.

The second Five Year Plan, known as the *Panchayat Raj*, established the administrative machinery for putting community development programmes into action. The bureaucratic network was similar to British county councils, district councils and parish councils. The plan contained practical guidance and promises of financial support, but also an idealism which brought with it the ingredient for failure.

Although village *panchayats* were instructed to promote welfare services, improved sanitation and water supplies, they were also instructed not to do so 'without due consideration for existing social patterns and the convenience of the villagers'. Although inspired by the highest motives at national level, this inevitably left the village council working at grass-root level with a weak and watery mandate.

At the inauguration of the plans in 1952, the first chairman of the Borli *panchayat* was Dr Madhusudan Adhikari.

Our job was to work for the good of the village. Whatever we felt was necessary to improve the life of the village, then we would try to do it. But raising our share of the money for these schemes was always difficult. In 1952 there were about 450 houses in Borli and 3,000 people. We used to collect house tax according to how much a house cost to build. For every Rs 100 we took four annas. This way we got about Rs 3,000 a year. Our next source of income was to levy a sales tax on any merchandise sold in the bazaar which was not produced in the village. That used to bring in about Rs 8,000 a year.

When I was chairman, one of our tasks was to try and widen the lanes between the *bungala*, because in places these were too narrow to allow bullock-carts to pass. People had to go on foot through all kinds of unhygienic household rubbish, often with heavy loads on their heads. But villagers were so obstinate. They didn't like to give up land in front of their houses. They claimed it belonged to them and we must pay for it. We said it was their duty to sacrifice a small piece of land for the good of the whole community.

In that part of Borli we call Nangau, the lane used to be so steep there were wide steps between the *bungala*. So I hired labourers to make the road a sloping one instead. But one man owned a big *shoga* tree right in the middle of where we planned to extend the road. He refused to cut this down because that tree is the one which gives plenty of long green pods which people prepare as vegetables. So I went to him and said: 'Your tree is standing in the path of progress. If you don't cut it down, I shall charge you with the hire of all these workmen.' Then he bowed to the will of the *panchayat*.

When the work was finished, people on the Nangau side could get bullock-carts up and down the lanes and were very thankful to the *panchayat* for making their lives much easier. In this way, we widened all the lanes in the village except the main bazaar road. That is always maintained by the state highway department.

But for many years after Gandhi's first idealistic picture of the perfect rural community, Borli was still struggling with fundamental improvements. The government dispensary, opened around 1927 and, staffed by the one qualified physician Dr Adhikari, provided medical services for more than five thousand people in Borli and outlying villages right up until 1962.

On the brow of the hillside, beside the Hindu temple under the obligatory banyan, half an acre of open ground set aside for recreational purposes was seldom used. The ethos of play had little appeal for hard-working peasants and, anyway, where was the money for sporting equipment to come from?

Schooling was another aspect of village development which failed to impress an agricultural community. Farmers' children grew up to develop working skills which they were obliged to put into practice just as soon as they were old enough to make a useful contribution to the hand-to-mouth existence which was the daily reality for eighty per cent of the inhabitants.

The visionary concept of the open-air theatre was also largely wasted on a farming community. Once a year it provided the arena for travelling entertainers who came with jugglers and performing bears. During the 1950s and 1960s it was also a convenient central parking place for the family planning units sent into the countryside by a national government anxious to halt the population explosion.

In Borli, the campaign to curb fertility had little more than entertainment value. Villagers enjoyed the magic lantern slides, but not the message they were intended to convey. Procreation was the poor man's recreation—a pleasurable way to establish a home-grown labour force!

But of all the programmes included in community development legislation, the most ambitious to be undertaken by the Borli *panchayat* was the scheme to bring piped water to the village. In the early 1960s the government set the cost of this at 38 laks and instructed the village to find one tenth of this expenditure. So the project was not completed until 1977, when the novelty of piped water proved something of an anti-climax.

In the village of Borli Panchatan, as in every Indian village, a regular supply of water was a recurrent problem. During the months of March, April and May, the eight rainwater wells in Borli, each with a capacity of 440,000 gallons, were reduced to holding little more than a few feet of brackish water, polluted by sticks, broken buckets, tins and whatever else had fallen in since the previous rains. By May people were often forced to pay Rs 3 or Rs 4 daily to the water-carrier, who took his bullock-cart to Karlia and filled large oil drums with river water to sell in the village.

So the Borli *panchayat* surveyed the countryside and chose a piece of land which, with the construction of a small dam, would form a suitable reservoir. Then, having received government approval, all that remained was for the village to raise its share of the overall cost. Dr Adhikari, and his successors on the *panchayat*, worked tirelessly for the completion of this project.

It took us three years to collect the money to purchase the catchment area in the hills. The man who owned the land wanted to profit by our need and demanded a very high price. When we had collected it, he said the value of his land had increased, so we had to find more.

Altogether it took us nearly twenty years before the reservoir was finished and piping brought to the village. Every main street had cement troughs with four stand-pipes with brass taps. Then, in 1977, we had a grand opening ceremony. The elders toured the village to make speeches, accept garlands of flowers from the people and turn on the taps. As we saw that water pouring out, we felt truly proud of our efforts. Sadly, things soon started to go wrong.

The piped water still had to be boiled, just as water from the wells had to be boiled, to make it suitable for drinking. Nobody had realised that grit and mud would be washed down the pipes and clog those taps. Perhaps the taps were also not very well made, but when they broke, water flowed to waste until we could get them mended. Then people complained because we asked them to bear the cost of these repairs. But the biggest problem was even more unexpected. When the village women fetched water from the well, there was always room for everybody to throw down their buckets at the same time. But when the women went to the taps, they had to wait in line and take turns. This took a long time and the women grumbled and quarrelled. They preferred gathering round together to clean their *hundas* and have a good gossip.

For other reasons the taps were altogether unsatisfactory. Stand-pipes near to houses encouraged some people to use the concrete troughs for washing clothes. Then again there were other dirty people who used them as urinals. I can tell you, it was a deep disappointment to the *panchayat*, who had worked so long and so hard to bring the blessing of running water to our village, only to find that people did not know how to appreciate it.

*   *   *

The fulfilment of Gandhi's hope that the abolition of the feudal system would enable India's peasants to work hard and improve their lifestyles featured high on the agenda for community development. In Borli most of the cultivated land belonged to the Kulkarni family, living in stately isolation at the top of the hill in a rambling old house surrounded by walls and high trees.

The Kulkarni family had moved into the area, from Ratnagiri in southern Maharashtra, in the eighteenth century and purchased virgin land from the nawab of Jungira at concessionary prices. Much of this land was on the Diwaga marches, but when it was gradually reclaimed, it was turned over to the cultivation of *cara*, a variety of rice which thrived in salty water.

In the old days the Kulkarnis leased their land to tenant families, who paid rent either in money or kind, according to the agreement between them. In April 1957 the Land Tenancy Act came into force. Tenants who had previously leased the land were legally entitled to claim ownership of it. In the case of the Kulkarni estates, this meant that about 400 acres were forfeit. Only in hindsight was it possible for Ravi Kulkarni to comment on the practical outcome of such radical changes.

When my family owned most of the land in this area, our livelihood depended upon the rents paid by our tenants. Those large barns across the yard, which now house the Borli High School, were formerly our granaries. Before our land was given away, even those buildings were not sufficient to hold all our grain. But when the land passed to the peasants, it was up to me to find ways to support our family on a much smaller acreage.

We were left with about ten acres, spread out in different places. Some was on the hills outside Borli and had never been cultivated. So what I did was to develop those un-cultivated pieces and then exchange them for land closer to our home. In this way we managed quite well, but certainly our life has changed. Neither my father nor my grandfather worked. Servants and tenants did all the cultivation. Now I must attend daily to the land we own to make sure the labourers we employ carry out my instructions. Because every year we have tried to improve cultivation by using intensive farming methods to get better yields—not just rice, but also bananas, mangoes and coconuts as well. The old ways had to go.

In 1960 I went to Japan to study rice cultivation methods. Like India, Japan was a feudal country before the Second World War, unable to grow enough rice to satisfy her own needs and having to import from Burma and Malaya. But when Japan came under American occupation, the Japanese Tenancy Act was introduced and, after 1960, Japanese peasant landowners were not only growing enough rice for themselves, but also exporting to other countries. The Americans taught them new cultivation methods and they were quick to learn. Sadly, in India this transformation did not happen.

We thought the Tenancy Act would mean that new land-owners would work hard to improve yields and then spend the money to get better housing conditions, better clothes and send their children to be educated. These hopes did not bear fruit. Although rice cultivated round here is sufficient for local needs, nearly thirty years after the Tenancy Act we cannot grow enough to export any.

What has gone wrong? It is only the human factor. As a defeated nation, the Japanese were forced to adopt new ways and work for the recovery of their country. Here in India the Hindu peasant landowners never got that feeling of national urgency. There is an English saying which applies: 'You can take a horse to water, but you cannot make it drink.' We did what we were told to do by our government and that was to give tenants their chance. It was up to them whether or not they took it.

* * *

In many ways, once she had accustomed herself to the realisation that Borli Panchatan was henceforth to be her permanent home, Jainub found life easier. At least, she no longer yearned for the impossible. Instead she took stock of her situation and reached a practical conclusion. For the sake of her daughters and their future she must assume the traditional trappings of Muslim respectability.

Although she never wore the *bourka*, Jainub made sure that her five daughters remained in strict *purdah*. Already of marriageable age, she knew that their humble circumstances would be a distinct handicap on the local marriage market, where parents were expected to provide daughters with substantial dowries of gold and household goods. Jainub resigned herself to having to accept whatever offers came along.

In 1948, aged just seventeen, Halima was the first to marry. Dawood Khan, whose family home was on the other side of the bazaar road not five minutes walk from Jainub's house, was already married with four small children when he instructed his parents to approach Jainub and arrange a second match with Halima.

The boy's family came to my house and said they wanted Halima for their son. I replied that I would think it over. Halima was very upset. She cried so hard and begged me not to send her to live in someone else's house. But after eight days the family came back for my answer and I give my consent to the marriage. I know my daughter may never get another offer.

These good people help in every way. They say: 'We know you are a poor widow so don't worry. We don't expect any dowry and we are giving seven *tollas* (of gold) for the wedding ornaments. But I felt obliged to hold up my end of the bargain and promised to arrange a small wedding reception for the guests.

I write to Adam and that good son sends me a little money. Then I booked the *Kadi* (civilian official who performs Muslim wedding ceremonies) and we set a table and chairs on my front *stoep* for the signing of the documents. When the day come, we women is all inside dressing Halima in a wedding sari and the gold wedding necklace her husband did give. Outside on the veranda the men sign the papers. Then we give simple refreshments, cups of tea and rice-cakes. At evening time there comes to my door an ox-cart decorated with a canopy of flowers and a cushion on the back. So away goes my Halima with her husband to live with his other wife and children in his family house.

Next year my daughter Aisha was given to a man in the village who is a builder. A year later, Amina got married to a man in Diwaga who has a fine coconut plantation. Then, in 1952, Howabi also got a husband. He was a butcher in Bombay, a friend of Halima's husband. This Hussein already had one wife and six children, but I understand that he is earning good money and can give Howabi a nice home. And as this daughter received no offers in the village, I have to give my consent to this match. Only later do I come to realise it is a mistake. But I only did what was best for my children to give them the chance of a better life. I was also thankful that each of my daughters marry with modern Muslim husbands who do not force them to cover up when they go out.

So I have two daughters living near to me in Borli and two in Bombay. Then there is my last daughter, Kadija. Kadija, the clever one, did well at lessons. She study to get her matric exam and at sixteen start to be a teacher here in the kindergarten school. She don't marry until she is eighteen to a fine man from Bombayside. He works on the docks, but is also a *maulana* (Muslim lay-preacher).

So then I am alone in my house, earning a little money to keep myself going, amusing myself with planting flowers in the small garden beside it. Life for me at last becomes quite calm.

* * *

One year after Kadija's marriage, Jainub's first grandchild was born to her daughter Amina in Diwaga. So began a new phase in Jainub's life as she attended each of her daughters' subsequent confinements and took on the role of grandmother to her many descendants. She became known as 'Ummie', the old mother, an affectionate sobriquet used at first by family and friends but eventually by all her village neighbours. At last the hillside village had come to love the South African stranger and accept her as one of them. And, with the advent of a telegraph office, better roads, electricity and transistor sets, medieval Borli Panchatan—Place of the Five Holy Graves—was reluctantly drawn into a modern future, as the first generation of new Indians set off to catch up with the rest of the civilised world.

❧ PART TWO ❧

How it is today . . .

❧ CHAPTER SIX ❧

BENEATH A CANOPY of diamond chips scattered into reeling space, the village sleeps. Only the sonic squeak of cicadas disturbs the warm velvet night.

Shortly before four o'clock, the khaki-uniformed night-watchman leaves the police block near the main well and starts on his final rounds. Up the bazaar road he goes, weaving back and forth into darkened lanes, his footsteps illuminated by the beam of his 'battery', the rattle of his staff along veranda railings, on walls and stone steps, marking his progress.

Slumped on the ground like leather sacks, oxen gently regurgitate. Dogs growl in sleepy recognition of the watchman's familiar tread, and here and there the baleful eyes of large rats momentarily gleam yellow in the torchlight. With the comforting tap of the nightwatchman's stick penetrating their dreams, the people breathe more easily. All is well with Borli.

The watchman walks the length of the bazaar road to the northern perimeter of the village, pausing on the bridge to light a cigarette and observe the light from the neon strip above the tomb of Kwaja Shabbudin reflected on the river. Then he turns back up the hill until he reaches the bus-shelter. Thwacking his stick on the concrete steps, he hears the muffled whine of the old beggars lying on the floor behind the parapet, tightly rolled up in cotton sacking. The bus-shelter is a regular dormitory for wandering mendicants. The resident village beggar sleeps opposite in a small mango orchard behind the broken stone wall, which separates it from the main road.

The watchman flashes the beam of his torch on the tent-like structure of scrap wood and rusty tin sheeting which houses the legless man and his family. Then he moves on up the bazaar road and turns left into the untouchable quarter.

Scrupulously swept, the lanes occasionally broaden into open compounds, where in neatly bricked earth containers little *tulsi* trees flourish, evidence of good luck for the neo-Buddhists or untouchables who live there. Most of these dwellings are respectably pipe-tiled and shuttered. However, clustered at the lower end of the district are the raggle-taggle palm-thatch huts occupied by the poorest of the poor, up against the high bamboo fence of the new *nartuk* (outdoor theatre) built to make sure only paying customers see the show.

As he leaves the poor quarter, the nightwatchman rattles his stick for fun along the iron gate which fronts the smart new brick shrine housing a large plaster likeness of the Buddha. Inside, one small flickering lamp illuminates the gold-painted plaster halo behind the plump lipped face. Opposite, a steep narrow lane twists up between terraced *bungala*, each ramshackle structure of timber and wattle apparently relying on the next for precarious support.

Shining his 'battery' on the open drain which gleams wet and odoriferous at his feet, the watchman carefully navigates through the crowded dwellings of the leather-workers, not caring to linger in the acrid atmosphere created by raw hides tanned to pliability with rock salt and urine.

At the top, as if emerging from a tunnel, the watchman reaches the main village compound dominated by the oldest local banyan, festooned by thick roots dangling from its topmost branches which have been severed above ground level to prevent the old tree re-roofing and duplicating itself many times over. Close by, a raised concrete dais with a pagoda roof shelters a large concrete statue of the god Shiva.

At the highest point on the hillside, the far side of the compound is occupied by the shabby but imposing grandeur of the Kulkarni residence, a double-storey house encompassed by mossy walls draped in flowering creepers. After tapping the front veranda, the watchman sets off to inspect the network of lanes leading down between the homes of the goldsmiths. On past the cracked well, into the long shadowy street where the Hindu fieldworkers live, he carefully side-steps to avoid tethered goats, crouching oxen and heavy-wheeled carts.

At the mosque gates he turns left, tapping his way back to the bazaar road, where here and there lights are already beginning to appear in some of the ramshackle shops. The man who owns the café is squatting in the doorway vigorously rubbing a black powder on his teeth with his forefinger and spitting. He flaps an acknowledging hand at the nightwatchman as he trudges on his way up the sloping lane to Nangau, past the homes of the pot-makers, until at last he reaches the compound at the top.

Then he retraces his steps, taking another route which loops back down the hill, past the second and smaller village mosque, on past the towering monolith of the government 'go-down' (grain store), the rice-mill and so back to the Karlia end of the main road. There a quick turn to the right brings him back to the lighted doorway of the police station.

Yawning, the watchman squats on the step and checks his wristwatch. It is ten to five. As though switched off by an unseen hand, with one accord the cicadas cease their nocturnal twitterings and a deep stillness descends over the village. In the faintly luminous skies above the Diwaga ricefields clouds of fruit-bats flap home to roost in the old banyans and, from a distance, the first cockerel crows. In quick response, the donkey tethered behind the rice-mill raises its head, curls its top lip and shatters the silence with a raucous braying which disturbs flocks of equally noisy crows.

Then, as a lemony evanescence edges the eastern hills, the rich throaty cry of the dawn *muezzin* soars into the archway of fading stars.

Another day has broken in the hillside village.

* * *

The village wakes up quickly. Lights appear in barred windows, the soft glow of oil *buttees* where there is no electricity, the wicked glare of fluorescent tubes on the verandas of the more affluent. In Hindu homes, framed pictures of severe-faced paternal ancestors and exotic household gods are illuminated. On Muslim verandas the neon strips light up framed blessings, Arabic lettering cut from polystyrene sprayed with glitter and pasted on to a religious background such as the Kaballa or some other holy place.

For the majority of villagers electricity is limited to lighting. Without benefit of gas rings, the women's first job of the day is to make breakfast on traditional clay ovens.

By pushing several long sticks in at the front opening, adding a splash of paraffin, a lighted match and then blowing down a metal tube, a good hot fire is soon kindled. The first meal of the day is invariably simple. Both Hindus and Muslims take tea made by boiling leaves in one pot, buffalo milk and sugar in another and combining the two in a cup or bowl. Muslims dip in small round rusks; Hindus, needing something more substantial to generate energy for the day's heavy labours, also eat chappattis and fermented rice porridge called *ambhil* made from soaking rice flour overnight in a covered container until it becomes sour.

Once the first meal of the day is finished, activity in the village gains momentum. First to appear on the lanes are groups of Hindu women. Carrying one, two or three metal water-pots balanced on their heads, and in their hands empty tins or plastic gerry-cans for baling, they converge upon the grey stone parapet of the main well.

The twice-daily task of fetching water provides village women with the opportunity to exchange gossip as they scour the copper *hundas* with handfuls of wet earth, only satisfied when they shine with the lustre of burnished gold. Only then do they haul the water to fill them.

In October, soon after the last of the rains, the well is brimming, so the women only need short lengths of rope to reach it with the gerry-cans. Then, with much spillage and merriment, they help one another lift the *hundas* on to the rings of protective padding each wears on top of her head. Small of stature and slight of frame, none of the water-carriers weigh more than 36 kilos. Yet with straight backs and gracefully swaying hips, they effortlessly carry loads amounting to more than half their own body weights.

Next on the lanes come the ox-carts. Trundling fast between the *bungala*, the yolked beasts are urged on by Hindu drivers wearing ragged cotton vests and *lunghi* and wielding sticks. Some carts come down the lane below the primary school or along the one just above it. Others choose the steeper lane behind Ummie's house, scattering chickens pecking in the refuse-filled ditches, only slowing the mad dash when they arrive at the place where the three lanes converge on the bazaar road.

Here a large reinforced concrete pipe has been used to bridge a shallow rainwater ditch and has developed a sizeable hole. With care, there is just sufficient room for a cart to pass without dropping a wheel into it. Once over the hump, the animals are whipped back into a brisk trot again, the velvet folds of skin under their necks wagging from side to side, bunches of harness bells supplying a frenzied accompaniment to the muffled tap of unshod hooves as the carts disappear down the road to the Karlia brickworks or out across the mist-streaked ricefields to Diwaga.

Promptly at a quarter past seven Muslim children straggle down the hill to attend an hour's religious instruction in the building by the Karlia bus-stop. The wood-gathering women also appear, striding along in colourful saris looped up between their legs and secured at the waist. Most wear gold nose-rings, fresh flowers in their hair, and balanced on the padded head-rings are machettes and sandals for wearing when they get into thorny territory. With a five-mile hike in front of them, they are wasting no time as they set off up the Karlia road, soon over-taking the more leisurely progression of goat-herds and buffalo bound for ploughing.

By eight o'clock plenty of mechanised activity appears on the main road through the village: lorries bringing supplies to local shops, others *en route* for Bombay with loads of coconut, pausing for *char* and a wad of *paan* before continuing. Parked on the bazaar road the gaily-painted vehicles dwarf the squat open-fronted shops and snarl up the movement of other, less imposing, traffic. But nobody complains. The splendid decorations provide pedestrians with a spectacle.

Care of a high order has been lavished upon them by their owners. Bonnets and mudguards are hand-painted with multi-coloured floral designs and scrollwork, large bunches of plastic flowers decorate the inside and outside of every cab, mirrors and bumpers are adorned with plastic tassels and link-chain fringes—these trucks are indeed the worthy successors to the ornately caparisoned elephants of another age. And latter-day *mahouts* do not hesitate to acknowledge the patronage of contemporary overlords by lettering the legend, 'Thanks to the Bank of Maharashtra for the Purchase of this Truck' along the sides of their mechanical mammoths.

Shortly before nine o'clock, Koli women arrive in Borli with fresh fish. Some travel by bus from Barotkol, the next fishing village down the coast from Diwaga. Others, come from the nearby seashore, elect to travel in style, bringing their dripping baskets to market in rickshaw taxis.

A brand new form of transport, these frenetic little vehicles first appeared in Borli in 1980. Basically three-wheeled scooters encased in hard covers and open at both sides for easy access, they were designed to carry two passengers but invariably carry more. Four in one rickshaw is usual, six not unusual when one sits beside the driver. As for juvenile passengers, the rickshaw affords limitless possibilities.

During term-time the newly-rich Muslim families, living in their fine new houses on the Diwaga road, frequently taxi their youngest offspring to the English-speaking kindergarten near the bazaar. As many as ten infants clinging together on the back seat is a familiar sight as the elasticated rickshaw bounces through the lanes like a demented perambulator!

By the 1980s a few saloon cars have made their appearance in Borli and at least one local farmer owns the Indian equivalent of a Land-rover. Before, ownership of a car in rural areas was more of a liability than a convenience, due to lack of proper repair and spare-part facilities. But when an enterprising Hindu had opened a motor repair garage on the Karlia side of the village, a fair number of cars, rickshaws and, especially, motor-cycles became a permanent feature of the local scene.

Once reliable lines of communication had extended village business interests with inland India, a new breed of white collar workers sprung up in Borli. Bank clerks, school teachers and shop-keepers found motorcycles ideally suited to local road conditions. And, being Indians, nobody allowed a little matter of personal safety to prevent these becoming family conveyances.

A wife wishing to accompany her husband rides side-saddle on the pillion, sari flowing in the slipstream. If there are children, the smallest sits on her knee, another rides sandwiched between the parents and a third perches on the fuel-tank, the only concession to safety being crash-bars fitted to the frames.

Most of the village tradesmen still use pushbikes, the sturdy upright Indian models. The baker uses his bike to carry four large battered tins containing freshly-made bread and biscuits. The milkman, cycling daily from Diwaga, brings two churns of buffalo milk clanking against the wheels, and the bottled-gas vendor, with heavy metal cylinders suspended from the handlebars of his pushbike, always announces his arrival long before he pedals into sight.

So, first thing each morning as the bazaar prepares for business, trucks, cars, rickshaws, motorcycles, pushbikes, ox-carts, donkey-carts, hand-carts and pedestrians with loads on their heads create a mini rush-hour on the crossroads which form the hub of the village. Adding to this congestion come the buses, the main street of Borli being on every scheduled route.

Run by the Maharashtra State Transport (known locally as STs), these rugged single-decker vehicles—which originated in the factories of British Leyland—by 1980 were running regular services along the peninsula from Dighi in the north, through Borli and on to Mahsla and Shriverdhan in the south, where the newly-surfaced road snakes over the mountains to connect with highways further inland.

In the past villagers travelling to Bombay used the Dighi ferry to link up with the steamship at Murud. In the 1960s, after the initial construction of the mountain road, the sea-route was discontinued and going by bus became the regular mode of travel both within the peninsular villages and to more distant places. An ST bus ride often resembles a sea-voyage as passengers are pitched and tossed on winding country roads in varying stages of disrepair.

Several STs stop in Borli throughout the day, their combined function as country buses and long-distance coaches resulting in an extraordinary assortment of travellers. A paddy-field worker in loincloth with a long harvest knife suspended from his waist might rub shoulders with a surgeon travelling complete with the tools of his trade (*not* stuck in his belt!) bound for some remote rural clinic; schoolboys carrying bundles of books, brilliantly adorned wedding guests, occasionally an invalid stretched out on one whole seat *en route* for a Bombay hospital. STs are an extremely democratic form of transport; in fact, caste distinctions are not allowed. Where Western buses might carry advertisements for soap powder or insurance companies, Indian buses carry the message 'Untouchability is a Crime Against God and Man'.

There are two bus-stops in Borli, one at the concrete bus shelter, the second on the other side of the bazaar at the junction of the Karlia and Diwaga roads. Those waiting to embark never queue. The arrival of the bus involves a chaotic free-for-all at the door as young men in slim-line shirts and tight-fitting trousers push in front of women. Hindu women, their sharp elbows working in the scrum, are never far behind. Then come their Muslim sisters, hampered by flowing *bourkas* and the need to try and maintain their composure in the undignified struggle to get up the steps.

The *maulana* from the next village, going home from a funeral and still dressed in immaculate white clothes, is pushing and shoving alongside the local Hindu *saddu*, with matted hair and less than pristine robes; and all this before passengers wanting to get off have succeeded in fighting their way off the bus!

When one more person will prevent the door from closing, the bus is declared full. Then the ticket collector (always a thin man) pulls the looped string which connects with a bell in the driving cab, and lurching forward, the ST bucks over the purpose-built concrete 'speed-stopper' on the village boundary and gathering speed (and dust) heads for the open countryside.

Designed to carry fifty-four passengers on an arrangement of high-backed seats and benches, the more usual complement is around eighty, including those standing in the central gangway. And seasoned travellers, left without a seat, are known to employ an artful stratagem for getting a seat on the long bench across the back of the bus. Tightly packed with passengers, the ST, when it careers round the first corner, causes a human landslide which opens up a space at one end of the bench. Before those seated can regain their equilibrium, two more people have sat down in it!

Vibrations inside the ST make conversation difficult and the deplorable state of the roads keeps flesh and bone in constant torment, yet this does not prevent long-distance passengers from nodding off, lolling against their neighbours in an effort to find a comfortable position. The remainder are left cramped in limbo, peering through windows open on the lower half to admit the dust and whitewashed over the top half to reduce sun-glare. Not that the inland landscape offers much in the way of spectacular scenery.

Since Jainub Undre first came to live in Borli, the countryside has changed out of all recognition. Tracts of jungle, which formerly hugged the boundaries of the hillside village, have been cleared to make way for ricefields to feed a population which has increased from 3,000 to 5,000. Indiscriminate wood-felling has gradually denuded the surrounding hills until, stripped of trees, they emerge as sharply-contoured mounds covered by a scattering of black boulders and thorn scrub toasted to a uniform shade of pale saffron.

When the Indian government took steps to curtail timber-cutting and encourage tree-planting programmes in the 1970s, most of the central part of the peninsula had already lost its forests. But how else could country people manage? Local timber was essential for the construction of their houses, for making household furniture and farm implements, as well as for fuel to make cooking fires. In addition, Hindus needed wood for traditional funeral pyres.

Access to wood was as much an imperative for survival as access to water—at least, until such time as cheap alternatives were available. The arrival of electricity in the village in 1963 might have been one such answer. However, the cost of having a meter installed in the home denied the facility to poorer villagers. Those who could afford a connection used electricity mostly for lighting and small appliances, such as portable fans and radios. Those who experimented with electric rings for cooking declared categorically that this method spoiled the taste of food and went back to their clay ovens. Electricity did not replace wood for cooking purposes in spite of the increasing scarcity of cordwood which gradually forced up the asking price. By the 1980s Hindu wood-gatherers were getting around Rs 8 for a 25-kilo bundle, which, on average, lasts a family for three or four days. Cooking fuel is, therefore, an expensive item on a weekly wage of Rs 80.

Children still go out on the lanes collecting ox-turds, which, when dried in the sun, make excellent fuel for the little ovens. But the new generation of hygiene-conscious doctors in the village strongly discourage the practice as a dangerous source of family infection in homes where the mother hand-stoking the cooking fire is probably also hand-feeding her youngest children.

In the late 1970s bottled gas (LPG) had become another possible alternative to firewood. It was certainly cheaper, costing only Rs 25 for a month's supply, but there was a snag. The people who were in most need of cheap cooking fuel were those who cooked in low-raftered and poorly ventilated kitchens. The authorities would not allow them to use it.

Not that getting a supply of LPG in the first place was easy. Manufactured by a nationalised industry, the demand for bottled gas far exceeded supplies. Householders had to wait at least a year before getting their first delivery. So, bottled gas was not a practical substitute for wood.

Easily the most practical alternative fuel for home cooking is 'gober-gas'. Installed in the back yard, these units produce natural methane gas from fresh manure, a raw material both free and readily available. Unfortunately the cost of constructing the necessary concrete pits and purchasing a metal storage tank and pipes amounts to about Rs 3,000, which puts this system beyond the reach of all but a few village homes.

So wood-gatherers leave the village each morning to scavenge the countryside for cordwood, trekking across areas where once had flourished acres of fine teak, sesum and shiva pine forests.

Up until 1970 these timbers were still being cut in forests along the coastline, lashed together in rafts and floated by sea to Diwaga for building purposes. At that time Noor Pangaka was a fourteen-year-old Muslim boy working in his father's timber business in Borli Panchatan.

When the logs came ashore at high tide, we secured them with ropes. At low water we loaded them on to ox-carts to haul to our yard. Teak was the best wood for building because it had qualities superior to other woods. Teak is not a hardwood as most people think. It is made hard by soaking in salt water and then left to season for one year. In this way it is also protected from mice and other destructive wood pests. This wood is very suitable for building in our monsoon climate.

In my father's day teak logs were cut by hand. The log was hoisted on to a *kaychee*, which is a high wooden stand. Then two men with a five-foot hand-saw cut the planks. One sat on top of the log, the other pulled from below. They needed no guide-lines to cut a perfectly straight piece of timber, but it took altogether two hours to saw one cubic foot. Now my modern machinery does this same work in about two minutes.

In olden days, everything in our workshops was done by hand; for example, planing and carving furniture with tradi-tional designs such as you see in the big two-poster beds called *palangs*, which our people like.

Formerly there were no architects in this village. When some-body wanted a house, the builders built it from experience. The framework was of unhewn logs and rough timber sup-ports with walls made from mud and wattle; the roofs were either thatched or pipetiled with local tiles. But even these simple houses were of good construction. Many are still standing today although they were put up more than one hundred and fifty years ago.

My father had no education, but he designed and made our family house. Everything wooden in it is made from teak: rafters, ceilings, windows, shutters and doors. Even our furni-ture is made from polished teak. But in my father's day it was cheap, only about one rupee for a cubic foot. Today the same measure costs Rs 300. That is because the mountains in this area are now barren. The trees have all gone, and nobody is permitted to cut any hardwood. We must transport it by road from Gujarat, Udder Pradesh and other parts of Maharashtra, and this is very costly.

But luckily for us these days there is plenty of money in this village due to overseas workers. People used to be content to occupy the same house as all their relatives, but today the fashion for separate houses is spreading. People come back from Saudi Arabia with ideas about Arab-style houses and insist on having the finest materials to make them. Nowadays this timber business relies on money coming from our Muslims working in the Gulf. Otherwise, I don't think we should be doing so well.

It was about 1970 that, after generations of poverty-line existence, the first Muslim men from Borli elected to leave their families for years at a time to earn overseas the kind of wages that would raise their standards of living. Five centuries after Arabs first landed on the Konkana coast and settled on the hillside above Diwaga, their village descendants made the reverse journey to help turn desert wastelands into industrial conurbations.

* * *

The renaissance of Saudi Arabia began in 1932, when Abdul Aziz Ibu Saud proclaimed himself king in order to unite nomadic tribes into one cohesive nation. To strengthen the royal autonomy, Abdul took three hundred wives. In two generations his descendants numbered five thousand princes and princesses, thus founding a dynasty able to dominate the economic future of the country.

World oil prices steadily rose over this period, and by 1970 the kingdom of Saudi Arabia found its treasuries overflowing with unspent 'petro-dollars'. So an ambitious vision took shape as the emirs began the momentous task of transforming eight million backward people into a modern superpower.

Churning bulldozers carved the foundations for airports and highways, schools and universities, hospitals, hotels, sports centres and luxury housing out of windswept sand dunes. In less than a decade the mirage became reality as out of thin desert air grew sophisticated cities where the inhabitants enjoyed a standard of living second to none in the world.

Free education to university level, excellent free medical facilities, subsidised food and housing and full employment in a thriving industrial economy created a near-Utopian society. But for all its wealth and progressiveness, Saudi Arabia could not have achieved this development miracle without the muscle and artisan expertise of migrant workers, and it made sense to recruit these from amongst Indian Muslims with the same religious upbringing as the Arab people, able to tolerate the climate and the restrictions imposed on personal freedoms.

As the birthplace of the Prophet and protector of Islam's two most sacred cities (Mecca and Medina), Saudi Arabia was the fountain-head of Islam and expected her subjects to honour the teachings of the Koran in every last respect. Gambling, pornographic literature and films were banned. So also was the consumption of alcohol; drunkenness was punished by public flogging. Saudi law also imposed merciless penalties for criminal acts. A convicted thief would have one or both hands amputated. Murder and adultery were punished by decapitation. Nevertheless, such Draconian rule had a salutary effect on public morality. Shopkeepers never hesitated to leave their premises unattended when answering calls to prayer and nobody went about in fear of life, limb or property. Indian

Muslims, weaned on the same religious ethics, easily identified with the Saudi way of life.

Between 1970 and 1984, more than two hundred Muslim men left Borli to work in the Arab Emirates, despite the cunning imposition of a large premium demanded by Bombay agents determined to capitalise on the desperation of migrant applicants. Before an agent would enter the name of a prospective worker on the application list, a premium of Rs 5,000 had to change hands, the equivalent of around eight years' wages for the average Indian artisan.

Impoverished village Muslims had no option but to raise this money as best they could. Some used their wives' gold wedding ornaments as collateral to moneylenders, sold or mortgaged ricefields and borrowed from family and friends, confident that the illegal payment would ultimately prove to be a worthwhile investment. They were usually right.

By village standards the salaries paid in Saudi Arabia are colossal. A carpenter, one of the best paid village craftsmen, earns a weekly wage of Rs 175. Helping to build Jiddah airport, he could earn Rs 7,200 a week. There never was much work for unskilled Muslims in Borli and once they left school, most went to work in the city for a meagre weekly wage of Rs 100.

In Gulf countries, a man who operates a mechanical street-sweeper is paid a tax-free salary of Rs 1,150 a week, plus free board and lodging in hostel accommodation. Apart from a few personal expenses, his entire wages can therefore be sent home to the village, first to repay his debts and thereafter to improve the living standard of his family.

Those who go to Saudi Arabia are not particular about what they do. Some work as airport cleaners, others as lorry drivers, electricians or building labourers. Whatever the work, it is highly paid for as long as the indenture lasts, generally for five years with options renewed each year after that until the employer has no further use for the foreign worker. When a man is finally sent home for good, if he has been prudent, he can afford to finance a small business of his own as well as to build a fine new house.

Amongst the rustic shabbiness of traditional *bungala* built of natural materials, new village houses stick out like white sugar lumps in a bowl of demerara. Usually where an old dwelling has been demolished the replacement is erected on the same site; so in a row where each house snuggles against its neighbour, the incongruity is even more remarkable.

Up on the Nangau compound stood some of the oldest houses

in the village, those which had escaped the great fire of 1899. One in particular, set behind a cactus hedge, had thick adobe walls, small bamboo-barred windows and a low doorway to three dark rooms with hardened dung floors. Unhewn timbers propped up the ponderous overhang of the roof made from pipe-tiles so large and coarse that they resembled chunky knitting. Then one day it was yanked like a rotten tooth out of a row of similar *bungala* and, within weeks, a grand new house of cement and plastered bricks and painted a brilliant duck-egg blue, had grown in its place.

Now at night the faulty neon tube on the veranda flickers like bottled lightning, while from neighbouring houses the gentle glow of lamplight casts pools of yellow on the dusty lanes.

The new house is the property of Ousman Pardeshi, the youngest son of a large family. When he went to work in Kuwait, he left behind in the old *bungala* his wife, baby daughter and ancient mother. When, after two years away, Ousman learned that the old lady had died, on his first leave home he ordered builders to pull down the old house and construct a new one. When he returned to the Gulf on a second spell of duty, he left his wife and daughter living in solitary splendour.

Ousman's wife yearns for her absent husband. She also yearns for more children. Instead, as the years pass, she has to take consolation in showing off her latest disco saris, so-called because of their exotic gold-weave geometric designs on dark silk, and her solid gold wristwatch, man-sized because that was the only way her husband could get it through customs without paying duty.

On the shelf above the glass china cupboard in the front living-room, a large stereophonic radio floods her fine house (and the Nangau compound) with Indian pop music taped from the sound-tracks of the latest Bombay cinema epic. When letters arrive from Ousman, his wife must wait until her ten-year-old daughter returns from school so that the child can read them to her.

Like the rest of her Muslim neighbours with sons or husbands working overseas, once a month Ousman's wife puts on her best *bourka* and walks down to the bazaar to bank her husband's monthly pay cheque at the local branch of the Maharashtra bank. Then she goes shopping, with plenty of spending money tied up in the waistband of her sari alongside a big bunch of dangling house keys. Pandering to the extravagant fancies of well-to-do Muslim housewives, the general stores stock the latest luxuries: nail varnish and 'Romantic Moonlight' talc, cheap plastic toys, bubble-gum and—in Borli, where mangoes, papayas and jackfruit grow in abundance—the most popular luxury of all, tinned peaches.

The Borli bazaar is a mixture of shops fronted by dirty glass counters and others which are scarcely more than clapboard cubby-holes squeezed between them. At a glance, the entire area resembles an untidy attic that has somehow spilled an accumulation of shabby bric-à-brac out on to the street, where a continual baptism of dust stirred up by passing traffic covers everything with the patina of age.

The cleanest and brightest goods on sale are treasure troves of fruit and vegetables heaped on mats and shallow baskets on the ground or piled on hand-carts. There are mauve-skinned onions, pink carrots, peas and many other kinds of bean-pods; purple brinjal and tiny limes, bunches of fresh coriander, shaggy-leaved cabbages—some sold by the piece after much haggling, some deftly weighed on hand-held pan scales.

In season, there are papayas and sweet-scented mangoes, mounds of tart-flavoured *ber* (like small brown plums) and sacks of scented guavas mixed up with twigs and leaves as though they have been picked in a hurry. There are hand-carts bearing weirdly-shaped 'beefsteak' tomatoes and small earth-crusted potatoes, baskets of green and red chillies shining as though painted with enamel. There are papery-skinned garlics and a profusion of small bananas as pink and plump as a sumo wrestler's fingers.

Each morning a fresh supply of coconuts appears in the bazaar, green ones full of pearly milk and mature nuts for grating—indispensable constituents for home-made curries as well as bearded symbols of fertility at every Hindu festival.

The permanent shops in the bazaar, raised above street level to protect them from flooding in the monsoon months, are reached by way of flat stones which serve as steps. The shop selling rice and dried goods is beside the hardware shop; the baker's shop, displaying large jars of chunky biscuits, is opposite a narrow shed where a gaunt-faced man with tragic eyes presses trousers with an old-fashioned cinder-iron.

Next door the barber's scissors snip busily and the heady smell of patchouli wafts into the street. A few doors down the optician stands in a cubicle lined with sunglasses; next to him the tailor, greasy tapemeasure around his neck, supervises his workers sitting cross-legged in front of old Singer sewing-machines. Opposite, in the hub of the bazaar, is a small general store so overstocked with a mad medley of goods it looks like a giant rag-bag which has burst its seams.

Beyond the main crossroads, on the Diwaga side—past the old Muslim who sells dabs of scent from an unpromising array of dirty bottles, past the man crouched on the counter of his *paan* stall outside the corrugated iron fish-market, is the most modern shop in Borli—the chemist.

Facing the street, two high glass counters contain a sun-warmed assortment of medicaments from suppositories and muscle liniment to antibiotics. With charming incongruity, the old Hindu *saddu* sometimes purchases 'military' cough lozenges there.

Next to the chemist is the metalsmith, a family business conducted on the front veranda, the excruciating sound of hammers beating red-hot metal into kitchen pots vibrating on the mid-morning air. Just below the metalsmiths, a flight of stone stairs leads to the balcony of the bank, where inside ceiling fans cool the impatience of customers waiting inter-minably to transact their business. Back on the street, below the bank is the Joshi clinic, infusing the air with the sharp smell of antiseptics. Thereafter the street tapers and merges with the tree-shaded lanes on the Diwaga side of the hill.

But the village bazaar is much more than a market-place for material needs. In the absence of local newspapers, it provides a fountainhead for gossip. Mostly this is chatter of a domestic nature: the rising price of marriage dowries, illnesses and deaths, the quality of the rice harvest or the late arrival of the itinerant basket-makers, who always camp under the trees outside the municipal building and make all the baskets the villagers need to store rice and root vegetables. Just occasionally, stories of a more sensational nature make verbal headlines in Borli to be remembered and mulled over for months afterwards.

Although crime is never a prominent feature of village life, the occasional case of suicide or petty theft does occur. One incident involving both was memorable. An old woman was robbed of her wedding ornaments by two Hindus she employed to plant her ricefield. Since neither man was capable of sustain-ing a convincing alibi, the local police locked them in the single cell at the village police station. The confession of one of the culprits quickly revealed the hiding place of the missing valuables in the branches of a mango tree. Then the two men settled down to await trial at Shriverdhan.

According to custom, the prisoners' wives were expected to

take them food twice a day. But in a small community the shame inflicted upon these women was greater than the crime itself. Netteha's wife refused to have anything more to do with her husband. Goowin's wife dutifully carried food to the jail until the men were sent to trial to Shriverdhan where they were sentenced to two years' imprisonment. Only then did the dutiful wife seek the ultimate escape from her humiliation. One morning, when the water-carriers went to the main well, they found the body of Goowin's wife floating in it. On that particular morning people were more than willing to go and fill their *hundas* at the stand-pipes.

But the story which kept tongues wagging the longest as it circulated and re-circulated in increasingly lurid versions, concerned two young Muslims from Dighi who went overseas to work as kitchen porters in a hotel in Dubai.

Both came from extremely deprived backgrounds; once they began earning good money they looked for ways to amuse themselves, soon finding precious little to do, particularly in a country where there were strict laws governing segregation of the sexes. So they formed a relationship with a young Egyptian boy who also worked in the hotel. It was a friendship which ended with the death of all three of them.

One evening the two Dighi men took their Egyptian friend to their living quarters and persuaded him to play the game known as 'homosexual roulette'. This involved seeing who could introduce the most air into the anus by means of a foot pump. In the event, the Egyptian boy won this gruesome contest but that same night was taken to hospital dying, his intestines literally burst asunder.

Eventually the two Dighi boys were extradited for trial at the Delhi High Court, convicted of murder and executed in the electric chair.

But more often the most exciting disruptions to Borli life consist of domestic squabbles exacerbated by too much palm toddy, and the most onerous duties the local constabulary are called upon to perform are the nightwatch patrols. Even these are not really such impositions when they enable the policemen to extract two rupees a month from every householder as a form of 'protection money'. (Quite what they are protecting the community from is debatable: the fashion for barred windows and heavily padlocked doors turns all but the most simple homes into miniature fortresses.)

* * *

When the midday *muezzin* sounds, Muslims have already gone home to perform their ablutions in readiness for prayer and as most businesses are run by Muslim merchants, this effectively puts an end to the morning's transactions.

Where there was bustling activity, now a heavy stillness settles over the bazaar. At its zenith, the sun banishes every last shadow from the streets, which for the next two hours are left to leather-skinned pye dogs with lolling tongues and bantams with rich metallic bronze and green tailfeathers diligently scratching through vegetable debris. It was siesta time and the villagers dozed. All, that is, except Jainub Undre.

In her house on the lane below the kindergarten school, Ummie was at pains to calm her hysterical granddaughter. A short while before the noon *muezzin*, the girl had rushed home from visiting a schoolfriend in Nangau and had flung herself on Ummie's *palang* in floods of tears. Waiting for coherence to return, the old lady sat patting Reshma's back, heavy thumping pats such as those given to comfort small babies. Not since the death of Dawood Khan had she seen the child so distraught.

I can get no sense out of that small child and have to wait until my daughter Halima also gets back from Nangau. Then I hear what has happened. One stupid woman has told Reshma she's not a real daughter, but was fetched from a Bombay hospital when she was a baby. This is a big difficulty for us. We know that in this village no family can keep a secret, but for ten years Reshma live a happy life with us and we don't worry her young head with such troublesome thoughts. Then that busy-body on the high side of the village must show her spite because Reshma is a clever student and her own daughter is a dunce.

We do all we can to soothe that child, telling her the silly woman got the story wrong. We explain that when she was a baby she got very sick and her father and mother have to take her to a Bombay hospital so she can get better.

At first she don't listen. Then by and by Reshma gets calm again. Mind you, what we tell isn't the proper truth. But nor is it altogether lies. One day she will know how she came to be Halima's daughter, but only when she is old enough to understand.

Amongst her five married daughters, only Ummie's eldest remained childless. Halima's shared husband was absent for long periods working on an oiltanker and as the years passed, whenever he came home on leave, Halima hoped for a pregnancy. But although the other wife conceived, she remained barren.

By the time Halima had reached the age of forty, her husband's first wife's daughters were married and had gone to live elsewhere; his only son, who had very little education, went away to work in Bombay as a shop cleaner.

Since the first wife could take care of Dawood Khan's old parents, Halima asked permission to return to live with Ummie. She also raised the possibility of adopting a baby from the Asha Sadan orphanage in Bombay.

Dawood was not an unreasonable man. He sympathised with his wife's maternal needs and agreed to the adoption, providing Halima chose a girl baby to ensure that there would be no question of dividing his son's inheritance. As for the request to return to live with her mother, Dawood opposed it. He had plans to take Halima to live in Bombay, a prospect she found appalling.

Halima knew from her sister Howabi what city life could be like. Howabi lived with her husband and seven children in two small rooms on the third floor of an insanitary concrete tenement. Each landing had one cold-water tap and two toilets to service the occupants of ten similar family 'apartments'. Even at its very worst, Borli was a paradise compared to Bombay, and dreading the thought of going to live there, Halima confided as much to her mother. So Ummie devised a way to persuade Dawood Khan to leave Halima in Borli Panchatan.

My son-in-law was a fine person, but had no patience with strong-minded women like me. So from the beginning I do not argue with him. I have to find another way to make him change his mind. Now, out of all my daughters, Halima was always most close to me. I cannot bear to see her unhappy. During hard times when I thought we would surely die of starvation, it was always Halima who gave me strong courage. So I think to myself, how can I get Halima close to me again without upsetting her husband.

Well, the garden of my home which Haji did build was large enough for another house. So I say to Dawood, 'Look here, son-in-law. I will give you the land for nothing and you can build a fine house for you and Halima and the new baby.'

After that he come very nice, because in 1972 land values in Borli were already rising fast. Luckily I don't get any quarrel from the old wives about this decision because by then they are both in the graveyard.

126

When Halima's house was finished, there remained a fair-sized yard between Ummie's old house and the new one. Halima's house also possessed a walled triangle of land on the lower side, where Dawood had a concrete privvy built in one corner with a proper soakaway. Near the back door, a concrete slab was laid for washing purposes.

The house itself, made of dark brown bricks baked at the brickworks down by the Karlia river, was on two floors, and the spacious verandas on the front faced out across the ricefields to the Diwaga coconut plantations. From the ground floor veranda, large wooden double-doors led into the high-ceilinged living room. On the left side of the house another set of double doors gave access to Ummie's yard. From the back of the living-room, one door led to a small bedroom and the other to the kitchen, where a flight of wooden steps connected with the storage rooms above. The pipe-tiled roof, with a generous overhang to give adequate protection from both heat and rain, was supported on square columns of brick.

The amenities in Halima's house featured innovations which, at the time, were unusual in village homes. Each room had one electric light bulb, and in the downstairs bedroom a low cement parapet in one corner, with a drainhole to the outside, provided the privacy of an indoor bathroom. In the kitchen another departure from convention was the elevated position of Halima's two clay ovens. She had them placed on a brick platform so she could cook standing up instead of squatting on the floor to do her cooking. And she had a concrete sink alongside for washing pots, the drain flowing out into the public lane.

Wrought iron panels in the front windows were different from the usual wood or iron bars, and so were the coloured-glass sections in the shutters fitted to every window.

Furnishings were simple, with one exception. The marriage bed in the downstairs bedroom was a fine *palang* constructed from carved teak, the head and foot of the bed inlaid with little heart-shaped pieces of glass hand-painted with flowers. Overhead, a square frame supported on two central posts was draped with an embroidered canopy and, instead of webbing, the solid wood base of the bed had a thin mattress stuffed with raw cotton. There was also a heavy wooden wardrobe with ornamental mirrors on the doors in which Halima stored towels, cotton bed covers, saris and other personal items, a sewing machine which folded down into a table and a collapsible chair. In keeping with the rest of the house, the bedroom floor was surfaced with cow dung, spread on a hardcore of coarse sand and left to harden.

The living-room was sparsely furnished with three string beds, a small table, four metal folding chairs and the two glass wall-cupboards, one displaying an assortment of photographs, china and plastic nick-nacks, the other used to store provisions.

In the kitchen, there were shelves for pots and pans and in the space beneath the staircase, Halima kept a stack of dry firewood and metal *hundas* for water, brought daily by 'Mama' Jadhar, an old neo-Buddhist Hindu who undertook household chores to finance his nightly visits to the liquor store in the bazaar.

Built in 1972 it was one of the first new houses to appear in Borli and cost Rs 40,000 (£2,700) to build. By 1982 similar houses were costing one lak (£7,000) or more as migrant earnings encouraged local landowners and builders to ask inflated prices.

In the winter of 1972, when Dawood Khan went back to sea, he left his wife happily ensconced in the new house. Although mother and daughter were not under the same roof, it was still an ideal arrangement for both. Next year Halima and her husband made a preliminary visit to the Asha Sadan orphanage in Bombay and were promised that their application to adopt would be favourably considered.

The orphanage was a converted corner of a penitentiary, built during the early days of the British rāj, in Bombay's Umarkhadi district. In the heart of a labyrinth of squalid back streets, the institution was surrounded by high walls spiked with broken glass. A flight of crumbling stone steps led to a huge iron-studded door with a smaller one set in it. Beyond was a doorkeeper's lodge guarding an archway of vines to a cobbled courtyard. All around rose the bleak walls of the 'Rescue Home', its small barred windows at monotonously regular intervals in the sombre greystone exterior resounding with the continuous babble of children's voices.

On her first visit, the sound of children reciting in class, of children chanting prayers, of children shouting in play and, above all, of the miserable rasping cries of countless babies was music to Halima's ears.

The superintendent asked us many questions to make sure we were in a good position to care for a baby. Then she asked what age of orphan we wanted because the home kept children of all ages living there until they were old enough to go and work in the city.

We told her we wanted a new-born girl. Then we were taken up many stone staircases until we got to the nurseries. There we saw rows and rows of iron cots all close together. Sometimes there was one baby in a cot, sometimes two. The superintendent said: 'My older girls try to care for these babies, but many die. If you decide to take one, you must be prepared to lose it. All these small babies are neglected when they reach us. Most have been abandoned.

Before we left that day, my husband and I chose a tiny Muslim girl. She was sickly, but I fell in love with her as soon as I saw her. The superintendent said we must go away and wait. If the baby lived, she would write and then I could come and fetch her back to Borli to stay for a few months and see if I could manage.

When the orphanage finally wrote to Halima, it was to inform her that the baby she had chosen had been taken to the hospital in Bombay suffering from smallpox. Halima caught the next bus to the city and for three weeks lived in the hospital compound, along with many other country people who wanted to be near their sick relatives. Each day she spent helping to nurse the baby, and gradually it began to recover. Then, just when the infant was ready to leave hospital, the child developed measles. Halima suffered another wearisome and worrisome week at the cotside, willing the child she now considered her own to stay alive. Miraculously Reshma did, although it was an exceedingly fragile baby that Halima eventually took with her on the long bus-ride back to Borli.

In her daughter's absence, and with consummate optimism, Ummie had borrowed an iron crib, the kind which a village mother would suspend from a rafter by long chains. In this, the infant was safe from the rats and mice, which infested houses at night, as well as crawling insects, and in particular the ubiquitous ants. Anything edible inadvertently left exposed would in minutes be swarming with black ants marching in dark columns from cracks in walls or ceilings, homing in on the target with uncanny precision. It was a foolish housewife who did not keep her staple goods in air-tight containers, and the baby with sweet milk on its mouth out of reach of these miniscule armies of destruction.

Inundated with love and care, and fortified by clean country air and nourishing goat's milk, the orphan soon started to thrive. In her hanging crib, with *kajal* outlining her large and lustrous eyes, Reshma resembled an exotic little cage bird.

Ummie's pleasure in her latest grandchild was enhanced by Halima's delight at middle-aged motherhood. The baby roused memories of Ummie's own childhood in Cape Town, so each evening, with the orphan baby nestling on her shoulder, the old lady serenaded her in English, shuffling her feet in time to the lullaby: 'Go to sleep my little piccaninny, mummy's going to smack you if you don't . . .'

When Reshma was a year old, Halima took her to the new lady doctor in the village, who pierced both the child's ear-lobes and one nostril so she could wear the gold ornaments her father had bought. She also gave a donation to the mosque so that the *peshmam* would write a Sanskrit blessing on a small piece of paper. This Halima carefully sewed into a tiny skin packet to hang round Reshma's neck. Most village babies wore this kind of amulet as protection during the hours of darkness, when superstition had it that children were most vulnerable to possession by mischievous spirits.

When Reshma was three, her father retired from his job at sea and came home to the village for good. Realising his company pension would scarcely provide more than the basic necessities for his two wives and small daughter, Dawood Khan had carefully saved for his retirement. However, he had not been home long before he was faced by a serious family crisis.

His only son Sultan, with a low-paid menial job in Bombay, declared that he intended marrying a girl not of his parents' choosing. Having already promised his son to a girl in the village, Dawood Khan refused his consent. In fact, he felt so strongly about the proposed misalliance that he devised a stratagem that would, he hoped, effectively kill two birds with one stone.

Dawood Khan offered to give Sultan the necessary money to get work in Saudi Arabia. Once his son was overseas, Dawood felt sure he would forget his infatuation. Moreover, the wages Sultan was duty bound to send home to his parents would also help to augment Dawood's meagre company pension.

The young man accepted his father's offer. So Dawood Khan withdrew Rs 15,000 from his life's savings of Rs 17,000 (about £1,000) to pay the agent's handling premium, to secure both a visa and a passport for his son and to buy the air ticket. He also purchased new clothes and luggage for the young man and gave him spending money.

On the eve of Sultan's departure for Kuwait, Dawood Khan, Halima and Sultan's mother went to his Bombay lodgings to bid the young man farewell. As they sat waiting until it was time to catch the airport bus, Sultan suddenly flung his passport and ticket on the floor at his father's feet and issued an ultimatum. 'Either you agree to my marriage with the girl I love or I won't go,' he declared.

In a society where marriage unions were strictly pre-arranged, this was heresy. However, having spent so much on his son's future, Dawood Khan found himself in an invidious position. He badly needed the money his son would be sending home, and there was no way he could retrieve what he had already spent. So there was no option but to lose face and agree to his son's demand. A message was dispatched to Sultan's girl who, already prepared for the summons, arrived by taxi with her parents. As the ceremonial saucer of sugar was passed round to seal the engagement, Dawood Khan refused his share, quietly seething at the way he had been tricked.

*　　*　　*

When she was seven, Reshma started lessons at the kinder-garten school not fifty yards up the lane from where she lived. Dressed in a uniform of white Punjabi trousers, Prussian-blue frock, a white muslin *dupatta* draped over her carefully plaited hair, she sat cross-legged on the floor of a crowded classroom to make her first attempts at numeracy and literacy on a slate. (Only senior students did schoolwork on paper.)

Kindergarten children are taught parrot-fashion. Teachers shout out the lesson and, in a loud chorus, the children repeat it . . . and repeat it again and again until it is mastered. As the dividing walls between the classrooms have no ceilings and children from the ages of seven to twelve are taught in the same building, each class teacher is obliged to keep raising his voice in order to command the attention of his pupils. Consequently, as the school day progresses the resulting noise can be heard half way to Diwaga!

School does not begin until eleven each morning, to give those coming from outlying villages time to walk over the hills. But Muslim children will have already spent an hour and a half taking religious instruction, leaving home soon after seven and returning at nine o'clock for a breakfast of tea and hard bread rolls or perhaps a chappatti left over from the previous day.

At two o'clock classes are dismissed for the midday siesta and begun again at three, continuing until five-thirty. The school is closed on Wednesday afternoons, but opens again each Saturday morning. The curriculum is a surprisingly heavy one for village children, most of whom come from homes where the parents are illiterate. Not only were the children taught the basic aptitudes of reading, writing, arithmetic and geo-metry, but also how to speak and write in English, Urdu and Marathi. In addition, they have enough homework each evening to keep them busy for at least an hour.

At the age of ten, Reshma is able to read and write with some fluency in Urdu and Marathi and make a tolerable attempt at English. Because of her Muslim religious instruction, she can also chant in Arabic from the Koran.

After reaching the top class, the most able children can go on to the Borli High School, founded in 1963 in premises converted from the Kulkarni family's grainstore. So, for the first time, village children were given the chance to prepare for the possibility of entrance to a college or university. Amongst Muslims, it was initially only the boys who continued their schooling after the fifth standard; once they reached puberty, usually in their last year at the kindergarten, the girls would retire into *purdah* to learn from their mothers the domestic skills and womanly virtues which in a few more years would enhance their value on the local marriage market.

After little more than a year at school, Reshma was proving herself an apt and diligent pupil. When she was eight, her father gave her permission to take part in her first Rammadhan and bought Reshma a gold necklace in honour of the event. Proudly the little girl looked forward to joining Ummie and her parents as they embarked upon a month of self-denial, taking neither food nor drink during daylight hours. Then, only three days into the fast, for the second time in her short life, Reshma became fatherless.

Dawood Khan had been suffering for some time from chest pains, periodically going to a Bombay clinic for treatment. Then, one night early in August he awoke gasping for breath. Grabbing her husband's big black umbrella, Halima went out in the pouring rain to seek help from her sister-in-law Kerima, who lived just up the lane. Kerima's son Ysouf was promptly sent running through the rainsoaked village first to fetch Dawood Khan's other wife, then Dr Vasudha Joshi.

An hour or so later, when medicaments failed to relieve Dawood Khan's distress, another village doctor was summoned. After examining the patient he expressed the opinion that the best thing would be for Dawood to go to Bombay to be seen by his hospital consultants. Providing he was prepared to meet the expense, the doctor offered to take him to Bombay in his own car. Dawood Khan agreed to a price of Rs 800 for the journey, although at the height of the monsoon it was obvious that the first stretch of the drive was going to prove arduous. But the prospect of hospital treatment seemed to revive Dawood and, while the doctor went to fill his petrol tank, the sick man got up, shaved and dressed himself in clean clothes.

When Reshma saw her parents preparing to leave, she flung herself into her father's arms and begged to be taken with them. At first Ummie tried to dissuade her but when the girl clung to her father and refused to be parted from him, Halima agreed she could go.

A little after midnight, the car set off. Dawood Khan sat in the back between his wives, with Reshma on his lap and Kerima sat in front next to the doctor. Slowly the car climbed the brow of the bazaar road, coasted down the incline and, crossing the bridge by the tomb of Kwaja Shabbudin, took the winding road across the flatlands to Mahsla and the mountains.

Pounded by deluges of rain which rendered the windscreen-wipers practically useless and normal conversation impossible, the long drive through the night seemed interminable. Every so often Halima glanced at her husband trying to gauge his condition, but all she could see was the dim outline of his profile as his head rested on the back of the seat. Despite the lurching, sliding progress of the car, Reshma slept, sometimes flung against her father, sometimes against her mother.

On the other side of the mountains, equidistant between the village and Bombay, lay the unremarkable market town of Pen. From there the journey could be made on a hard-top highway and having wrestled with the gears up and down the rain-sodden mountain roads, the doctor welcomed the chance to accomplish the remainder of the journey at a reasonable pace. But as the car reached the outskirts of Pen, Dawood Khan begged for a drink of water. The pain in his chest had returned with a vengeance and he was once again gasping for air.

Pulling into the forecourt of a ramshackle roadside hotel, the doctor went to find the proprietor. The women helped the sick man out of the car and retired to a discreet distance as, leaning heavily on the open door, he relieved himself. Hearing him groan, they came running back to find Dawood slumped half in and half out of the car.

It was just getting light when the doctor's car once more drew up outside Halima's house and honked its horn to alert Ummie.

When I unbolt the front door, what a sad sight to see! There on the back seat lies my son-in-law and, crouching on the floor, three women and Reshma weeping loud enough to wake the village.

The *jammut* took Dawood Khan for burial that same afternoon. He was put in the graveyard behind the kindergarten. Right after the funeral, Kerima comes with other women of the family, to break all Halima's glass bangles and take off her wedding ornaments.

Then my daughter says, 'Ummie, now you must come to sleep here in my house because Reshma and me cannot bear to be alone.' So that is what I do. Every night I cross the yard to Halima's house and we bolt the doors and lock the shutters. Then we push two *charpoys* close together and lie like that.

For many weeks Reshma don't sleep so good. The poor child is crying out many times in the night, 'Why did Allah take my father, why, why, why . . .?'

So there we are, us two widows and Reshma, managing on the small pension Halima gets from her husband's old company and whatever my Florina in Cape Town sends. But Allah is great. I still have my one ricefield and that Muslim doctor was good to us. Instead of taking full payment for Dawood Khan's last car ride, he charge us only half.

After the funeral, according to custom, Halima had to go into mourning for forty days. During this time she wore a white sari and remained mostly sitting on her bed. When visitors came to commiserate, the new widow was expected to pour out her grief in a frenzy of loud wailing, thus fulfilling the Arabic definition of the word 'widow' which, literally translated, means 'empty woman'.

At the end of forty days Halima could once more dress in coloured saris, but never again could she wear jewellery or her wedding gold. Her status within her dead husband's family, with that of the other bereaved wife, dropped to the bottom of the pecking order. If anything, Halima's position was even more ignominious since she was the second wife and without a natural son. As Ummie sadly explained, her daughter's name had proved prophetic.

'Halima comes from the Koran. When the prophet Muhammad was born, his mother died. The baby was given to a neighbour called Halima who fed him at her own breast. Then the time came for this woman to give up the baby she had come to love. So the name Halima has come to mean someone who will be unable to possess wealth or happiness in this life but can expect great rewards in the next.'

In all her misfortunes Halima's consolation was her adopted daughter. After the death of her husband Halima's main purpose in life was to find a good match for Reshma. And with the winter wedding season fast approaching, she started to sew dresses which would show the little girl to best advantage.

✺ CHAPTER SEVEN ✺

WHEN THE LAST field of rice has been threshed, winnowed and safely stored, when days become pleasantly hot and nights refreshingly cool, the inhabitants of the hillside village turn their attention to more festive matters.

Traditionally the winter season is reserved for village weddings. First come Muslim nuptials, held during November and December, occasions heavily laced with religious ritual. Next, in the months of January and February, Hindus marry strictly in accordance with astrological predictions. But if Muslims and Hindus have widely divergent views on ceremonial protocol, one element of marriage finds them in agreement. Both believe that every marriage partnership should be negotiated with as much romance as a business transaction.

But for country people this is logical. Is the soil not painstakingly prepared in order to establish the best possible foundations for a healthy crop? So also meticulous husbandry is needed to prepare the ground for the seeding of human growth. Only weeds and mongrels seed themselves.

Hindu betrothals between families of the same caste are arranged far in advance of the wedding, sometimes between children of eleven or twelve. A fishing family will not seek marriage with the child of a farm-worker or sandalmaker. Nor will Hindus marry Muslims, at least not in the village. But Muslims, on the whole a classless society, arrange their marriages between young people of more mature years. Sixteen is usually the age for the girl; the bridegroom might be considerably older. In both cultures, marriage is popular between cousins and in an isolated rural community like Borli, this means that families become linked and cross-linked by an incredibly tangled web of relationships.

For instance, because she has married early, a woman can be a grandmother in her early thirties and yet still be producing her own children. This means that if her sister's son marries her daughter, she is both aunt and mother-in-law to her daughter's husband. Supposing that her married daughter produces a son at the age of sixteen and five years later she herself produces another daughter and, in due course, these second-cousins marry, then the grandmother will become her grandson's mother-in-law, and her grandson's mother (the grandmother's daughter) will become his half-sister, while his paternal grandmother (who is also his great-aunt) will become his aunt . . .! Should polygamy complicate this alliance, the genetic cat's-cradle becomes even more impenetrable. Small wonder that the often-heard phrases 'cousin brother' and 'cousin sister' are coined to identify such devious family connections.

In the village, the typical arranged marriage involves the asking of a dowry by the girl's family; the more beautiful the girl, the larger the asking price. This practice was made illegal in 1961, largely due to the social reforms instigated by Mahatma Gandhi. In Borli, however, the dowry system continues to flourish, despite the fact that its payment invariably inflicts considerable hardship, especially on low-caste Hindu families with meagre incomes. But two factors insure the perpetuation of bride barter. One is the social imperative for every man and woman to be married. (In a population of 5,000, unmarried men and women can be counted on the fingers of one hand.) The second is simply that in a close-knit community no family is prepared to invite the ridicule of neighbours by being the first to dishonour an age-old tradition.

One old farmworker, recalling his marriage in 1930, explained the typical lengths to which a man would go in order to fulfil the marriage contract made on his behalf by his father.

When I was a boy I helped my father in the fields and collected cow dung on the lanes for my mother's cooking fires. That is all. I got no schooling. When I was about nineteen, I got a better-paid job as houseboy to a well-to-do family. I earned Rs 10 a week. So my father decided it was time to marry the girl I was betrothed to when I was ten.

When the arrangement was made between our two families,

my father had to say how much we would spend on gold ornaments and how much on the wedding feast. Rice for the feast cost Rs 30. Chickens and vegetables cost another Rs 125. On top of this there was the wedding gold. I had to borrow Rs 350 from a lady in the village to pay for my wedding. Then my brother and me worked nine years without wages to repay the loan. (In the 1930s rice cost Rs 2 for 25 kg; enough to feed a family of ten for two weeks.)

It will be the same for my sons, but nowadays money goes into thousands of rupees, not hundreds, because girls' families ask for more ornaments and more clothes. Now farmworkers can earn Rs 10 a day, but have to spend more than a thousand rupees for the wedding of a son.

It's like this. If one man offers five *tollas* (500 gm) of gold ornaments for a girl, then I must promise my future daughter-in-law seven or ten *tollas*. It is a matter of family pride and necessity. No dowry, no marriage. Sons must have wives or how else can they get the children to support them in their old age?

Some years ago my caste association, the *agri* (farmworkers), held meetings to try and agree to set a fixed amount of expenses for marriages so that everybody paid the same. People from sixteen villages came to discuss the matter of simple weddings without pomp or show. Everybody agreed this was a good idea, but when we got home to our villages, we could see it would never work. If we don't pay a good price, how can we get wives for our sons? And nowadays everybody is spending more on marriages. I think it will always be like that. It is our custom.

The principles of the marriage contract are settled long before the young couple is ready for marriage. Eventually the parents will consult the village soothsayer, who determines the most propitious astrological moment for the wedding ceremony to take place. The date settled, the prospective bridegroom then pays an official visit to the girl's home to seal the betrothal over a cup of *char*. On his way there, dressed in his best clothes and carrying a bunch of marigolds, the young Hindu is escorted through the lanes by a pipe-and-drum ensemble and a following of barefoot urchins kicking up the dust.

At the girl's house, the boy may be meeting his future wife for the first time. He squats down on the rush mat and the girl offers him a cup of tea. If he drinks it, this signifies that he is quite happy with the liaison. Final details of the promised dowry are then reviewed to make certain everybody fully understands the financial side of the arrangement. The betrothal ceremony ends with the boy giving a needle to the girl and requesting her to thread it. This little ritual has nothing to do with the girl's ability to sew. It had much more serious implications in days when a wife had to raise a family and perform all her domestic duties in a dark hut lit by oil lamps. However beautiful the girl, the prospective bridegroom had to make sure he was not being tricked into supporting a partially-sighted partner, at a time when cataracts and even congenital blindness were all too prevalent in the village.

Today, most village homes have electric lighting, but every few months an optician comes from Pune to treat eye patients. But as with so many superstitions and ritual practices, the observance continues long after its practical relevance.

The Hindu marriage ceremony follows hard on the heels of the betrothal—sometimes in the middle of the night if the soothsayer's predictions indicate this to be the most auspicious moment. Then the lonely song of the cicadas is rudely interrupted by the piercing nasal resonance of wooden pipes and the nervous thump of skin drums as the newly-weds parade through the village. Riding on a bullock-cart decorated with hoops of fresh flowers, they are followed by the bride's brothers, cousins and other men in slim-fit shirts and even tighter trousers, dancing along with the contents of the bride's bottom drawer on their heads. Amongst the chattels she takes to her husband's home are such items as copper *hundas*, cooking pots and plastic cases bulging with enough saris and sandals to last her for ten years. Then there will probably be some really heavy pieces of furniture proving a formidable burden for the slim Hindu lads, whose prancing becomes slightly heavy-footed when hindered by steel cupboards and tables with plastic-laminated tops coloured like oil-slicks on water. Easy access to Bombay has opened up markets for manufactured furniture and, amongst the young people of the village, squatting on the floor to eat meals is rapidly going out of fashion.

Weddings between high-class Brahmans in the village are much more sedate events, a mixture of picturesque symbolism and innovations introduced by the younger generation. The young Brahman couple will very likely already have met and mixed socially in college. So behind their formal betrothal is a strong element of free choice. However, if it takes place in the village, the wedding ceremony will tend, for the sake of the older generation, to conform to tradition.

The day before the marriage ceremony, the bride and bridegroom, together with close family members, hold a prayer meeting. Next day, early in the morning the family gather again for *puja*, this time accompanied by a ritual grinding of rice using mortar and pestle. Presents of saris and rings are made to the bridal pair, each gift given together with a coconut and a handful of rice to symbolise fertility. Afterwards, the girl's parents kneel to wash the feet of their future son-in-law, acknowledging their acceptance of him as an honoured member of the family whose welfare will in future be of more concern to them than their own.

At eleven the bridal pair enter the room which contains the family shrine, usually featuring Gunapatti, the elephant god of learning. A tray of coloured rice is passed to the guests, while the young couple take up their positions on either side of an embroidered cloth held high enough to hide them from one another.

As the room becomes heavily scented with incense, the priests and elders dressed in white *lunghi*, black high-necked coats and Gandhi caps, keep a watchful eye on the time. At the exact moment decreed by the soothsayer, they start to chant seven Vedic mantras, pausing between each to allow guests to shower the couple with rice and for the bride and groom, each on their respective side of the screen, to step on one of the seven small mounds of rice at their feet to represent the seven vows of marital responsibility.

The ceremony concludes when the screen is lowered so that bride and groom can exchange garlands of flowers. Then, while the newly-weds remain to sign the marriage documents and listen to advice about the more intimate side of married life provided by the priest, women guests retire to an adjoining room, where a small girl distributes fresh flowers. Then cups of tea are passed round together with plates of bananas, *burfi* (fudge made from buffalo cream) and a hotly-spiced mixture of rice, coconut, peanuts and chillies.

Meanwhile the bridal pair take their places on two high-backed chairs out on the forecourt of the house which has been canopied over with a network of cottons threaded with mango leaves, marigolds and *crêpe* paper.

First to pay homage to the newly-weds are the bride's parents, who place spots of turmeric on the husband's sacred thread. (The sacred thread ceremony is performed when a high-class Brahman boy reaches the age of eight. It is a string worn like a sash as a protection against evil spirits.) Then yellow marks are made on the foreheads and hands of both bride and groom who make sure not to remove them until the following day. Last, the mother hangs the *mongra sutra* round her daughter's neck, the traditional marriage necklace of ebony and gold beads with two small fluted discs suspended from it.

Guests then form a line for presentation to the couple, each offering obeisance in the correct Hindu manner before inspecting a display of symbolic wedding gifts made by the female members of the bride's family; coconuts covered with embroidered jackets, paper footprints each inscribed with a prayer, rice and other cereals arranged into *mandala* (the diagram of the Buddhist cosmos) patterns, perhaps tiny felt embroidered baby shoes, a replica of the wedding invitation made out of icing sugar and even a model of the Taj Mahal ingeniously constructed from small glass bottles which had once contained doses for injections!

Later that same day, the Brahman couple may leave for Kashmir, a location which for grand Indian families is what Acapulco, Niagara Falls or Paris is to Western honeymooners. Once there, the custom is to dress in Kashmir costumes and pose against the spectacular back-drop of the Himalayas for colour photographs, portraits which are a far cry from those of their parents who stood stern-faced and stiffly to attention for black-and-white exposures.

* * *

The Muslim *shardi* is a more extravagant occasion and in recent years has usually been financed by the earnings of fiancés working in Gulf countries, and generates lavish displays of matrimonial one-upmanship in the village. If, at the start of the wedding season, four goats are slaughtered for the marriage stewpots, the next family will kill four goats and a dozen chickens. Not to be outdone, the third wedding feast will have a whole ox on the menu. And, in 1984, the largest wedding Borli had ever seen was held at one of the new Muslim houses on the Diwaga road.

On the day before the ceremony, a chartered bus brought a group of classical musicians from Bombay. Boys toured the lanes inviting everyone to come for evening tea and refreshments and to stay to listen to the concert. Needless to say, it was an occasion which few could resist although, for religious reasons, Hindus would not partake of food prepared by Muslim hands.

Loudspeakers were fastened to the outside of the house, and from eleven that night until dawn the rippling sound of *zitars* and the staccato percussion of *tabors* interspersed with the clear soaring voice of the soprano gave Borli a treat it long remembered.

Next day, in the bazaar, it was rumoured that the cost of the wedding extravaganza had topped Rs 7,000 although, of course, this was only one item in a long list of expenses, the bride's gold ornaments accounting for the largest.

There are three goldsmith families in the village, one Muslim and two Hindu, all making a good living. The Muslim goldsmith (who was also a silversmith) works from his small clapboard house on the Nangau side of the bazaar. Lit by one dangling electric light bulb, this room is open to the street. In front is a small glass cabinet, its dusty shelf displaying silver anklets and toe-rings—charming complements to well-shaped legs and feet of Hindu peasants. Samples of goldware are kept under the counter, which is also the goldsmith's workbench with brass balance, a variety of blackened implements and an oil burner. When a customer comes into the shop to discuss gold, samples are flung on to the counter with the careless flourish of a duelist casting a gauntlet before an adversary. But in this case, the duel is verbal, a session of polite but protracted haggling between customer and craftsman.

In contrast to the traditional Hindu wedding necklace, Muslims favour intricate filigree collars made from several *tollas* of gold, the weight of a *tolla* being roughly equivalent to 100 gms, and costing Rs 1,800. As well as the obligatory necklace, a bride also demands rings and bangles, nose-pieces and ear-rings and, if she can get it, the exquisitely beautiful gold forehead ornament called a *bindia*.

The average outlay on wedding gold often costs the bridegroom between £2,000 and £3,000, even though some migrant workers might try to economise by bringing cheaper gold from Saudi Arabia, furtively hiding it inside shoulder pads, bars of soap or the plaster cast on a conveniently 'broken' ankle. But recently customs officials have started to use metal detectors, forcing the adoption of other tactics to avoid paying duty. Nowadays heavy gold rings and neck chains with outsize links are worn through customs as 'personal jewellery'. Once safely in the village, these items quickly find their way into the goldsmith's melting pot.

This obsession with gold has both aesthetic and practical reasons. Black shining hair and smooth brown skin provide the perfect setting for gold ornaments and, in the absence of any kind of social security, gold is an insurance against unforeseen hardship. In Borli there are always one or two traders prepared to accept gold as collateral against a loan.

Once the bridal dowry has been satisfactorily settled, plans for the winter wedding get under way, stagemanaged by the *jammut* who takes care to see that each ceremony is well spaced. The enormous cauldrons needed to boil huge quantities of tea, rice and curries for anything up to two hundred guests belong to the *jammut*. So do other indispensable items of wedding equipment. It is the *jammut* who erects the high coloured canopy outside the bride's family home and sets up rows of metal folding chairs for male guests to witness the signatures on the marriage papers. The Muslim elders also own the loud-speaker system, which in recent years has become an indispensable feature of every Muslim wedding, to relay both devotional passages of the ceremony and the latest Bombay cinema music.

There is only one *kadi*, a diminutive old man with a straggling goatee beard, who arrives on the bus from the Shriverdhan District Offices, bringing in his battered plastic briefcase the wedding documents. The *kadi* officiates at every Muslim wedding, his quavering incantations amplified by the loud-speaker system, his left eye grotesquely magnified by the extra thick lens on one side of his horn-rimmed *chessma*.

The Muslim *shardi* is a prolonged series of rituals which take place both before and after the actual marriage ceremony. First of these is the betrothal party. Five days before the wedding, the *jammut* assemble on the veranda of the bride's family house, although neither the bride nor bridegroom are present. Loudspeakers fixed to the trees outside the house relay a lengthy recitation from the Koran, officially announcing the engagement of the young couple. At this point, the bride's mother begins to weep and wail with inconsolable fervour. The fact that she has been preparing for this from the moment of her daughter's birth makes no difference. Nor is her grief in any way diminished by the knowledge that, once married, the girl will only be living down the road from her family home. The betrothal marks a highly emotional moment in the life of every Muslim mother.

Out on the veranda the elders conclude their part in the ceremony by sprinkling one another with 'Attah of Roses' out of long-necked silver containers, so the sweet smell permeates the *bungala*. The men then give refreshments, trays of sweet vermicelli sprinkled with cardomum and raisins and flat rice cakes wrapped in paper for the men to dunk in their tea.

Plates heaped with the ingredients for making *paan* and twig-like brown-papered cigarettes called *bidis*, which some of the less orthodox Muslims choose to smoke, are passed around.

After the men have eaten, the living room is prepared for the women. A rattan mat is unrolled and in the centre another large tray piled high with the popular vermicelli mixture. Tea is brought in a big aluminium kettle and served in small china cups, which each guest in turn pours into the saucer and drinks with loud slurping sounds. Some three hours after the ceremony has begun, the tea party ends with the distribution of small pink scented plastic button-holes.

Three days before the wedding the ritual of *chiksa* is held when the womenfolk anoint both bride and groom (but on separate occasions so they shall not meet) with a mixture of coconut oil and ghee. The origins of this ritual have been lost in antiquity, although it may once have been an expedient for obliging both partners to reveal in public that they were not harbouring any hidden deformity or disease, since the ceremony demanded that all but the scantiest of pubic coverings be removed. While one group of women sang the traditional songs extolling the joys of connubial bliss, another group massaged the *nosha* (groom) or *nouri* (bride) from head to toe. Today *chiksa* is modified to a token rubbing of arms and feet, although the folk songs are preserved in a repertoire which lasts a full two hours.

The day before the wedding both the *nosha* and the *nouri* held tea parties in their respective homes; he for his men friends, she for her female relations and acquaintances.

In the bride's home, guests bring gifts which are put into open suitcases on the floor or stacked at the back of the living-room. While the older women drink tea and gossip, the bride and her friends prepare a henna dye made from boiling leaves of a privet-like shrub which grows in village hedgerows. This red juice is used to stain the palms and soles. The more talented of the girls use small pointed sticks to work a lacy pattern with the dye. Others content themselves with simpler application as an attractive adornment, but also as a medicament which cools the blood and induces a peaceful state of mind for the bride during the following day's ordeal.

In Borli, pre-wedding occasions are presided over by Kerima, the arbiter of custom at each ritual gathering. An able mistress of ceremonies, Kerima organises the distribution of refreshments in rooms so crowded everything has to be passed from hand to hand out of the dark kitchen. Amazingly enough, scalding tea is never spilled on the children and babies crawling about the floor. Then, at the appropriate moment, Kerima calls for silence and kneeling by the suitcases proceeds to hold up each present for inspection, identifying the name of the donor as she does so—no mean feat of memory for someone who cannot read.

Finally the bride brings her gold jewellery to show her friends who each press a sum of money into her hand. The tea party ends when the *nouri* bids a formal farewell to her mother— a touching ceremony inevitably accompanied by a further outburst of wailing which quickly spreads to the rest of the female guests, who dab away tears with the ends of their *dupattas*.

In twenty-four hours the daughter, guarded so carefully in *purdah* for perhaps four or five years, will leave her parents for ever. Every woman present can remember with emotion the moment in her own life when she too had to fulfil her Muslim destiny.

* * *

On the day her aunt Najimunissa Undre and Rashid were married, Reshma and most of her young friends missed school. At eight in the morning, her new red and white long dress with puffed sleeves was taken out of the wardrobe. Dragging the plastic case from under her bed, Ummie's granddaughter rummaged about until she found a little pair of high-heeled sandals. The previous day Halima had spent over an hour combing her daughter's hair for nits, before taking her out in the back yard to wash it. After a decade without cutting, Reshma's luxuriant cascade of jet black tresses had grown well below her buttocks.

Still too young either to arrange her own hair or put it up in the coiled bun most village women favoured, Reshma stood quietly grimacing while her mother brushed out the tangles, occasionally stopping to sprinkle on quantities of coconut oil until it shone like patent leather. Then Halima made a single braid laced with coloured ribbons and fixed a spray of red blossoms to the end.

Mother and daughter sat on the edge of a *charpoy* to sort through a tin box of baubles to decide which ones Reshma should wear. Gold ear- and nose-rings were obligatory. So were the glass bangles worn on both of her satin-smooth arms. Then, after much deliberation and tryings-on, a necklace of crystal beads was chosen to complete the little girl's finery.

She was, in effect, a novice bride, practising for her own marriage day.

Shortly after eight o'clock, carrying her sandals so she could hurry on bare feet up the dusty lanes, Reshma left to join the other women already congregating for *nikka* at Najimunissa's family home on the other side of the bazaar road.

The signing was to take place at eleven o'clock. In front of the house rows of empty chairs flanked a table covered by a thin plastic cloth set with microphone, a vase of artificial flowers and a saucer of greyish granulated sugar. Fluttering sea breezes occasionally billowed the high canopy, but otherwise the hot dusty lane was strangely still and deserted.

By contrast, the back yard of the house buzzed with activity as gangs of women squatted at their appointed tasks. Some peeled miniature mountains of purple onions and pink carrots, others shelled peas or worked with small stone rollers on worn grind-stones to pound garlics, gingers, chillies and other spices for the curry. Rhythmic accompaniment to their subdued chatter was the patting sound made by hands moving with unhurried expertise, shaping chappatti dough into pancakes, each one exactly fitting the circumference of the skillets set on rows of earthenware ovens. Smoke spiralled up through the branches of the mango tree, flocks of noisy crows waited their chance to swoop down and scavenge for scraps. Under the thatched byre in one corner of the yard, the butcher stirred the stewpots with a long stick. The only man in the yard, he was of enormous height and girth, a bearded giant dressed in white shirt and trousers stained by blood and sweat.

On the previous evening it was the butcher who had slaughtered six goats and two calves for the feast, holding them head down over a shallow pit scooped from the sandy soil in the yard to catch the blood. As his knife severed their jugulars he intoned the ritual prayers for *halal*, while a cluster of small boys stood round to witness the death throes of the beasts and boast about who would eat the most at the next day's feast.

Inside the house, women relatives robed the bride, the last Undre daughter to marry and now attended by her married sisters. Dressed in a wedding sari of white and blue silk threaded with gold lurex, Najimunissa sat with eyes closed as her eldest sister attached the gossamer thin chain dangling from one side of the *bindia* to the drooping nose ornament. Another sister knelt to fasten on dainty silver anklets, while a third unfolded the white muslin veil with lurex borders and draped this over the *nouri*'s head and shoulders so that she was hidden from sight. And still it was only nine in the morning.

Once the robing was completed the eldest sister took up her position behind the bride, clasping the girl's temples in her hands to help support her head for the long vigil ahead. From time to time women brought drinks of water and young girls, including Reshma, waved *punkas* (fans) to circulate the air, which, as more and more women and children crowded into the room, became stifling.

Outside on the lane, twenty minutes before the signing, male guests arrived to sit under the canopy, some fidgeting self-consciously in tight new cotton suits, others more comfortably attired in loose white *pyjama* and *kurta*, every man wearing a white lace skull-cap.

Promptly at eleven, a commotion up the lane caused every head to turn. A procession of young men approached, led by the *nosha* dressed in gleaming white *salwar* (trousers), high-necked *kurta* edged with gold braiding and on his head a splendid pink silk turban. Walking beside him and vigorously flapping a plastic *punka* came the bridegroom's brother, a portly and hirsute young man, stomach bulging out of his too-slim-fit shirt and perspiring freely from his efforts to keep the *nosha* cool.

With stately step, the *nosha* took his place at the table where the *kadi*, his father, his father-in-law and members of the *jammut* were already seated. As he intoned the conditions set out in the documents, the frequent clearing of the *kadi*'s throat was faithfully amplified in every glutinous detail by the microphone. Forty minutes later, after the bridegroom had muttered his marriage vows, the papers were signed with a flourish of signatures full of hooks and loops going from left to right on the paper. Everyone was given a pinch of sugar and then all that remained was for the *nosha*'s friends to collect the envelopes of money each guest had ready in his hand. The ceremony was over. Although they had yet to meet, Rashid the mechanical streetsweeper from Kuwait had become the husband of Najimunissa, virgin of Borli Panchatan.

Inside the house, the bride's long wait was nearly over. While the men dispersed to the mosque to answer the midday *muezzin*, she was helped to her feet and, with eyes still closed, took a few steps to ease the stiffness in her limbs. When runners came to say the *nosha* was on his way back, a wicker basket containing two magnificent cloaks of flowers was produced. Made to order in Bombay at a cost of Rs 7,000 and brought to

Borli on the overnight bus, one was for the bride and the other for her husband. The cloaks were fashioned from a network of cottons threaded through hundreds of sweet-scented *mongra* blossoms interspersed with variegated astors, traditional adornments to symbolise the 'flowering' before the 'de-flowering'.

As soon as the bridegroom was dressed in his cloak, the young couple were at last brought together to stand side by side with little fingers linked as the bride's mother parted the flowers over her daughter's face to expose it for the husband's gaze. This signalled the entrance of the bridegroom's friends, who, with ostentatious posturing to obtain the best angles, flashed off the bulbs in their Japanese cameras. It was also the moment for Reshma and her young friends to try and get themselves into the photographs so, when later these were inspected by the families, their faces would be there for all to remark upon.

The couple were then ushered into an adjoining side-room and seated on the edge of the bed. The bridegroom's mother gave her son a cup of milk to drink. Then she held a looking-glass in front of the couple. At long last the girl was permitted to open her eyes and perceive her husband's face reflected in the mirror. For both it must have been a moment of truth. If so, neither gave any hint of their feelings. There were no coy glances, no embraces, merely impassive acceptance—perhaps because they were, after all, the puppets in a marriage game where only their elders and betters pulled the strings.

At one o'clock, trestle tables under the canopy were loaded with platters of rice and curry, chappattis and popadums. For the next two hours, while loudspeakers blared Indian pop music, dozens of hungry hands dipped into the communal feast. As each platter was emptied it was replenished by women hovering nearby. No guest was permitted to leave without eating his fill. Only when the final guest had rinsed his eating hand, politely belched and departed was it the turn of the women.

The back yard was swept clean of debris and rush mats were laid on the ground to enable the womenfolk to squat round the food. Widows like Halima made sure everyone had enough, their turn to eat coming last of all. Thus was the pecking order properly observed.

After the four o'clock *muezzin*, the bridal pair left for Naji-munissa's family home. The wedding gifts were loaded on to a lorry (Muslims never carry anything on their heads except their prayer caps) and still dressed in wedding attire, the young couple were driven at reckless speed through the lanes in a topless jeep.

On the morning after the first honeymoon night, it is customary for the bride's mother to rise before daybreak and pluck and clean a cockerel that has been ritually beheaded by the butcher. Once made into chicken broth, she takes it to the bridal chamber, knocking loudly on the door. The new wife opens the door, and spoon-feeds the soup to her husband, a form of ritual nourishment thought to stimulate the young husband's virility and enhance the bride's chances of early insemination. Each morning for five days this dawn aphrodisiac is brought to the newly-weds. On the fifth day, five young men from the groom's family come with a basket of food for his mother-in-law and escort the bridal couple back to the husband's abode. After another five days, a group of the bride's friends come to take them back again—comings-and-goings which are repeated for twenty days, when the wedding formalities are officially at an end.

After this, the young bride settles down to live a life of unquestioning obedience with her husband's family—a subjugation which causes considerable unhappiness if the mother-in-law happens to be too strict, and the young husband is working overseas. Without her husband's protection, the young bride finds herself trapped in an invidious position. If she is illiterate, she may not even be able to contact her husband with letters of complaint.

In Borli there are a number of cases of young husbands, returning home after an absence of several years and expecting to be welcomed with open arms, walking straight into fierce family quarrels. These are only resolved when the men agree to build separate homes for their wives and children. Thus, the structure of Muslim family life is changing as young wives with affluent husbands are able to demand domestic independence.

But for Reshma, it was only the glamour and excitement of the Muslim *shardi* which captured her imagination. Long after Rashid and Najimunissa had departed for Rashid's home, the little girl cheerfully helped Halima and the other women clear away the rubbish, listening intently to talk which had already turned its attention to plans for the next wedding.

The moon had not yet risen as Halima and her daughter walked home along the lanes, Reshma's animated chatter about the day's events punctuated by yawning. Holding her 'battery' in one hand to light their path, Halima carefully carried in the crook of her other arm a pot of left-over rice and goat-meat curry for Ummie, kindly sent by the bride's mother.

As she grows older, Ummie seldom accepts invitations to village nuptials, insisting that one wedding is too much like another. But although she avoids going to these celebrations, she makes a point of sending presents. The latest fashion in domestic accessories is imported nickel-plated jugs, tumblers and air-tight storage tins which are sold in the bazaar. Engraved with the donor's name and wrapped in pink tissue wound with cotton thread, these items regularly appear at every bridal tea party and are regarded as much more acceptable than locally handcrafted copper and stone utensils.

Behind a display of prodigality Ummie can scarcely afford is the motive that her generosity will be remembered and reciprocated at the betrothal of her own grandchild.

It seems that every village marriage is bound by materialistic considerations, even those which, due to force of circumstances, have to be conducted with simplicity. Not that there are many such events, but when they do occur it is invariably between families who in the eyes of the local community are seriously disadvantaged. Such was the marriage arranged between Fatima and Aziz.

Aziz lived with his widowed mother in the next village to Borli. Not only was he exceedingly poor, but also exceedingly ugly—a fatal combination when it came to his mother's efforts to find him a wife. Her attempts were not entirely altruistic: she also hankered after a daughter-in-law who would be obliged to work for her. Eventually she approached the *jammut* to ask if they could find a girl who, for reasons of her own, was in no position to be particular.

It so happened that in Borli there lived a spinster called Amila. Although Amila was quite a good-looking girl, she had two distinct drawbacks when it came to finding a marriage partner. She was already in her mid-twenties and in childhood she had had the misfortune to lose one eye.

When the offer of marriage was made to Amila's widowed mother, it was refused. She did not want to lose the services of her last unmarried child who was a hard worker. But seeing her last chance of marriage slipping away, Amila nagged her mother into accepting the match with Aziz.

So one day, shortly after the four o'clock *muezzin*, the *jammut* called the couple together in a back room of the mosque, where marriage papers were duly signed and witnessed by the congregation. A bowl of fresh dates were served as refreshments and the couple then returned to the boy's home village, where kindly neighbours had made a small collection of money and gifts.

All might have gone well had it not been for Amila's aspirations for her ugly husband. Day and night she wheedled and coaxed Aziz to make an effort to better himself. Even if he was ugly, could he not work as well as the next man? He must borrow the money which would enable him to apply for employment in Saudi Arabia. Eventually Aziz gave in to his wife, found someone who would loan him enough to pay the labour agent's premium and duly departed for the Gulf. Soon he was earning good wages and, according to custom, sent most of them home to his wife and mother. But Amila's new-found prosperity was short-lived. Before long the ugly husband realised that as a substantial wage-earner his lack of physical attributes was no longer a matrimonial hindrance. He therefore found himself a wife who was more presentable than the one he had left at home.

To Hindus, divorce is anathema. However, if a Muslim union fails to produce children, the husband can either take a second wife and support both women, or he can divorce the childless one and revoke all responsibilities to her. Having failed to conceive, Amila was easily rejected. As a disabled, deserted and childless woman, she had thus descended to the very foot of the social ladder; all she could do was return to her mother.

But if female subjugation is an accepted part of village life, there are signs that, in the city at least, a more independent breed of Muslim girls are prepared to challenge the arranged marriage.

One of Ummie's granddaughters found the courage to rebel against this form of parental manipulation. When Ummie heard that Kowserie, eldest child of her daughter Howabi, was to be married, she and Halima padlocked their doors and taking Reshma with them, caught the overnight bus to Bombay.

> This granddaughter of mine was fifteen and fail to get her ninth standard examinations. So my son-in-law Hussein got angry, saying he wouldn't feed her any more and she must get married. Now Hussein got a friend who owned a small hotel somewhere in the city and this man wanted a wife for his son. So Hussein fix up a match for Kowserie. Halima and me arrive eight days before the wedding to help Howabi with the

preparations. Howabi only have a two-room apartment in a big block of flats, so this means her seven children must sleep nose-to-nose on the floor, with only three beds for us grown-ups. But anyway, we make the best of it.

Then six days before the marriage, Kowserie comes to me and says: 'Ummie, please speak to my father and help me. How can I marry with a man I never meet? If my parents force me to this boy I will chuck myself under a train.' So that evening when my son-in-law get back from his shop, I take big courage and ask him if he has seen the man he has promised to Kowserie. Then he got so hot-blooded and shout back to me: 'Old woman, keep your nose out of this affair. Why must I see the boy when I have the word of a man who is my friend and also very rich and respectable?'

But I can see how unhappy my granddaughter is so I call Howabi and Halima and say that we must stand together and force Hussein to show us the boy he wants for Kowserie. We is all trembling like a leaf because we dare to speak in such an open way to the man of the house, but luckily Hussein gets quite calm and agree to send for the rich old man and his family.

Three days go by, and then one morning a taxi pulls up in the street and small children run upstairs to tell us visitors is arriving. Kowserie got so nervous she crawl under one bed. Then the old man and his big fat wife come in with two daughters and that one son. My Howabi give refreshments and then she ask if the boy is the one promised to Kowserie. The fat mother nod her head and give her son a pat on the back. Then we all get such a shock! That boy's eyes roll back in his head and he starts to laugh and laugh and flap his arms like a rooster in the yard. I can't stand to see such a sight and pull my *dupatta* tight over my head and start to pray. Then my Howabi asks the fat mother why her son is laughing so much. The woman replied it is because he is so happy to be getting married to Kowserie. Then she asks where is Kowserie? At that my granddaughter rush out of hiding and shout: 'Go away from here with your son. I never get married to such a foolish person!' and start to cry as loud as she can—more loud than that boy is laughing. Such a commotion you never did hear! That rich old man call his fat wife and children and they walk out without a *salaam*, so everybody knows the marriage is now broke off.

Once the storm had blown over, Ummie, full of concern for her granddaughter's future, encouraged the girl to go back to school and study for her matriculation. A year later, Kowserie left school with this qualification and started to nurse at the Goopal-Dass Free Government Hospital in Bombay. Before long she met and fell in love with a laboratory technician. The young couple insisted on another departure from tradition, opting for a modern Bombay ceremony known as an 'ice-cream wedding', a complete contrast to the expensive and protracted traditional marriage.

The event took place in a hired hotel reception room, and the male and female guests intermingled freely. The marriage documents were signed and witnessed in the usual way, the newly-weds condescended to wear cloaks of flowers, but thereafter conventions were thrown to the wind.

Instead of a wedding feast, guests were treated to unlimited quantities of ice-cream. Thirsts were quenched with a choice of tea or 'Thums Up' (the Indian equivalent to Coca Cola), after which a team of professional dancers entertained the assembly. Then, while the older guests sat and watched, the youngsters spent some happy hours dancing to the music of rock 'n' roll.

Muslim parents who have little if any schooling, and lack the broader outlook on life which education and travel give to their children, hope the old religious conditioning will prevail. In the village there are many signs that this is not going to be the case. The opportunity to come and go between the peninsula and the city inevitably nurtures in the younger generation expectations which cannot be satisfied in the country. Exposed to a tide of Western influences which colour every aspect of urban living, young people—like young people everywhere—are only too eager to sample fresh experiences and adopt new ideas and attitudes.

India is already placed ninth in the world's industrial league and is striving to improve this position. The social and economic changes which have altered city lifestyles are rapidly affecting the course of village life, which for centuries has maintained a steady orbit around its own internal culture rooted to an agricultural ecology. Like a satellite starting to burn up as it re-enters earth's atmosphere, the hillside village has begun to shed the protective outer covering which for so long has been its source of strength and survival.

Yet, in the face of outside influences which are tempting other young people to drift away from their country origins and to embrace a synthetic environment, in Borli one young woman called Fhamida deliberately turned her back on an industrial civilisation to enter married *purdah*.

My parents came from the town of Shriverdhan near here. They went to East Africa and us five children were born there.

My dad had a good job as a printer in Kenya, but when the government was trying to get rid of Asians, my family moved to Blackburn in England. That was in 1973 and my dad couldn't find work there, so we went to live in Birmingham.

In Africa I spoke Urdu and Swahili. So my parents sent me to special classes to learn English. School was hard for me at first, but we lived in a neighbourhood where everyone spoke English, so I soon managed to catch up. I studied to O-level standard and led a perfectly normal English life. I got used to being in a mixed school, wearing English clothes, going to cinemas, discos and coffee bars—everything like that.

When I left school at seventeen I wanted to work in a bank, but my mother told me she'd fixed for me to marry her sister's son Mustaq, who lived in the Indian village of Borli Pan-chatan. Well at first, I got really upset. I didn't want to go to a foreign place to be given to a strange man for the rest of my life. So my parents said I should go for a visit and meet my cousin. Then I could decide what I wanted. So that is what I did.

Usually girls cannot meet their future husbands, but my aunt was a very forward-looking person. While I stayed in Borli I lived with other relations, but most days I went to visit Mustaq and his family. This was allowed because he was my blood relation. If he had been a boy outside my family, even a college graduate or somebody very respectable, I could not have seen him. And even with my cousin, we couldn't go out-side the house together. That would have looked very bad. Anyway, I really liked my cousin. He was six months older than me, but we had the same likings and thinkings. So I agreed to the match. We got married a year later in the village and, of course, now I live with Mustaq's parents.

Before I met my husband, he had trained as an electrician and worked in Bombay, although his parents are quite well off. They own ricefields and dairy cattle in Borli, with Hindu people to do all the work. After our marriage, Mustaq gave up his job in Bombay because his father told him to try for work in Saudi Arabia, where he could earn better money. So my husband paid Rs 5,000 to an agent in Bombay to get employ-ment as an electrician in Kuwait. He was lucky he didn't pay more. We know some people who had to pay those agents as much as Rs 6,000. Nobody questions giving this money. It goes into the agent's pockets as we all know, but what can anybody do? Down here in the country there are no good chances of work. But sometimes when people pay those big amounts, they don't get the job they signed for. We knew a man who took out a contract to work in an office and when he got to Dubai he was forced to dig roads.

I got pregnant soon after I married. Although my husband had signed to go to Kuwait, he didn't go until our son was seventeen days old. He wanted to see his son before he left. Now he won't be back for two years and I miss him very much. But I'm lucky with my mother-in-law, perhaps because she's also my aunt. Some mothers-in-law can be very strict. The girl must do all the housework and hardly go out at all. If the mother-in-law is in the room, the girl must not sit and things like that. But my mother-in-law is only thirty-five. She laughs and jokes with me and lets me go to sewing classes in the village, so that one day, if I've got the time, I can earn a little pocket money with dress-making. As for having to wear a veil, she does force me to put it on when I go about the village, but when we go to Bombay she lets me go without. Now quite a few of my Muslim friends wear a short style of *bourka* which is more like a coat. I think this custom of the veil is dying out with younger women.

I don't feel like I'm in *purdah* here. Nor do I miss the kind of life I had in Birmingham. You can get used to country ways when you have to, and anyway my in-laws have a lot of modern things in the house such as a stereo radio and a gas stove and electric fans in the ceiling. When Mustaq gets home, he will probably bring a television and a video. He will have to pay duty, but it will still be cheaper than buying in India.

I'm also pleased about schooling for my son. Right across the lane there's the English-speaking school for Muslim children. When he's four, he can start. I can help him with his lessons, even though I know I've got a Birmingham accent. If my son speaks English, he'll get a good job abroad when he grows up.

I've been in Borli two years now and don't regret giving up my freedom. In fact, I think I am more free here because I know exactly who I am and what I'm supposed to do. This way I don't have anything to worry about. After all, my family roots are here. This is where I really belong.

❧ CHAPTER EIGHT ❧

FOUR MILES WEST of Borli Panchatan, deep in a range of hilly pasture-lands, lives a caste of Hindu dairy farmers called the Wakulgar. Much of the milk sold in Borli comes from their herds; it is especially valued because of the richness of the curds which can be made from it. But the Wakulgar region is celebrated for much more than the excellence of its milk; it is in these hills that once every three years the miracle of the 'Gunga' takes place.

The Gunga always arrives in the middle of winter; the exact time is unpredictable. One morning towards the end of December or the beginning of January, a Wakulgar herdsman will take his cows to graze near a certain rocky hollow and there it will be—a deep pool of water that was not there the day before, water that is ice-cold and crystal-clear. And that is the Gunga, sent by the gods to bless and heal all those who bathe in it. Sometimes the Gunga remains for a full fifteen days, in other years only for a mere nine. But the level of the pool always remains constant. Then just as suddenly as it appeared, the Gunga departs, without even a damp patch in the hillside declivity to indicate it has been there at all.

Once the news of its arrival has spread, Hindus flock in their hundreds to take advantage of the pool's healing properties. Every bus that stops in Borli brings a fresh influx of pilgrims stoically setting off along the steep and dusty track behind Nangau which leads directly to the pool.

The Gunga was expected the year a Harijan ('untouchable') boy called Bakha fell off his bicycle. For weeks after the accident he remained inside the hovel at the back of the neo-Buddhist quarter of Borli, nursing his painfully swollen genitalia, too weak and ashamed at the indignity of his affliction to move off his *charpoy*. Old Padma, his mother, almost blinded by double cataracts, squatted at his bedside interminably offering *puja* for her son's recovery, a muttering which so got on her daughter's nerves that Derami frequently felt like slapping the old woman into silence. Instead, and not for the first time, she tried bullying Bakha into taking the village doctor's advice to go to Bombay for treatment at the free hospital. As always, Bakha's response was to turn his face to the wall.

Derami realised he had made up his mind to die—unless a miracle could save him. As soon as news came that the Gunga had arrived, the girl planned to be first at the pool to bring back *hundas* of the precious fluid so that Bakha could bathe himself in the privacy of the hut.

Adversity had toughened the girl both inside and out. Aged about twenty-five, a scant one and a half metres tall, Derami possessed physical strength, a graceful figure and a temperament which brought swiftly changing moods. In a flash her face could turn from beautiful to ugly and back again. Her unpredictable temper made Derami's neighbours more than a little wary of the girl and she had few, if any, friends. Not that she cared. On top of a volatile nature, she was also fiercely independent, qualities which might have frightened off any offers of marriage. Paradoxically, there was something about Derami which, far from repulsing prospective suitors (from among her own caste), encouraged numerous offers of marriage. Some even included support of Bakha and Padma, which, in the face of this family's poverty, would have solved their difficulties. But Derami scornfully rejected all proposals, silencing her mother's entreaties with outbursts of rage which made the leaves of every *tulsi* tree tremble.

Before his accident, Bakha had managed to earn a small income doing odd jobs around the village, loading and unloading lorries in the bazaar or fetching water for households where there were no lingering prejudices about his 'unclean' origins. Although Gandhi's long struggle for the emancipation of six million Harijans had become a national movement, in country areas especially social acceptance of the 'children of God' was often difficult to achieve.

The elders of Borli, learning that a nearby community was adopting a recalcitrant attitude towards the integration of Harijans, paid a visit to the village. They called the people together and lectured them about 'untouchability' being a crime against God. Fired with missionary zeal, they then took the Harijans to the main well and instructed them to throw down their buckets. This was to demonstrate to the rest of the villagers that pollution would not result if 'untouchables' were permitted to use the well.

Some weeks later, returning to find out if successful integration had indeed taken place, in this particular village, the elders found to their consternation that it was the Harijans who were refusing to exercise their rights. They preferred to use their own water well and to settle for peaceful, if inferior, co-existence rather than risk causing overt hostility.

In Borli, the same segregation prevailed. Although the community as a whole no longer displayed open prejudice against their Harijan neighbours, the neo-Buddhists chose to retain their identity and pursue an entirely independent way of life, rather than be absorbed into a society which for centuries had treated them as pariahs. Padma and her generation remembered only too well what it meant to be forced to announce their presence in public places with loud warning cries of 'unclean,

unclean' so that others might avoid physical contact with them. In those days, if another Hindu happened to brush against an 'untouchable', after giving the outcaste a good beating, he was obliged to go home, take a bath and change his clothes. Unless, that is, he could quickly find a Muslim to touch, in which case the taint was neutralised.

* * *

It was just getting light when Derami left home, treading silently on bare feet through lanes kept cleaner than anywhere else in the village. Soon the houses of Nangau were behind her and she was striding into open country, where humpy hills were silhouetted against the sky. She walked in the centre of the track and covered the miles at a pace that never altered, despite steeper gradients which forced her to shorten her stride.

After three miles, Derami made a detour into the scrub where she had spotted a papaya tree, finding at its base, as she had hoped, a fallen fruit still good enough to eat. Using her teeth to rip off the skin, the girl sucked the soft flesh, leaving behind on the path a trail of shiny black seeds. On the final stretch of her journey, Derami quickened her step, feeling her heart pound not from exertion but with excited anticipation as, rounding the final curve in the track, she saw the outcrop of flat granite rocks which marked the end of her pilgrimage.

She had visited the Gunga before, but on this occasion she gazed with renewed amazement at what could so easily have been mistaken for a pool of liquid light. Setting the *hunda* close by the edge, Derami squatted down beside it and, mesmerised by her own reflection, soon lost all sense of time.

As if from below the surface, a hand moved the water, dissolving the girl's image in a ripple of concentric circles. When the water became still again, she glimpsed below her the distorted features of a leper floating in a tangle of black weed. The apparition then dissolved to be replaced by five faces with closed eyes suspended in the translucent depths. Derami experienced a deep sensation of peace before another flurry of ripples caused these faces to vanish, leaving only her own reflection and that of her *hunda* and a passing dragonfly.

* * *

When she got back, Derami longed to relate her experience beside the Gunga, but she lacked a sympathetic ear. Her brother Bakha, who reluctantly agreed to wash with the magic water,

157

was too preoccupied with his own discomfort to display any interest in his sister's daydreams. As for Padma, the old lady was incapable of absorbing anything other than reference to food or money. But Derami was bursting to tell someone and, as luck would have it, within a day or so she found the ideal person.

Although Ummie and Halima were reduced to the category of poor villagers, occasionally even they employed the poorest of the poor to help with certain domestic chores.

They paid Rs 4 to an old soldier called Mama (who was also a neo-Buddhist) to fetch a day's supply of water, wash clothes, and sweep up and burn the leaves and rubbish which drifted off the back lane into Ummie's yard. A spider-thin Hindu woman also came to polish the floors, using her hand to spread a slurry of cow-dung and water over the badly cracked surfaces to hold them together for another four or five weeks.

The other household task needing keen eyesight and deft fingers was the hand-sorting of large quantities of rice. Now and again relatives returning from overseas, instead of the usual gifts of saris and lengths of dress material, bought Halima a sack of rice which they purchased locally. Then she called Derami to do the necessary cleaning. Emptying the sack on to a clean sheet spread out on the living-room floor, Derami scooped small quantities of rice into a shallow rattan tray, flicking the good grains into a basket and discarding the grit and other debris. The cleaned rice was carried up to Halima's loft and was poured into a cylindrical basket, one of those made by the itinerant basket-makers who each winter lived and worked under the trees just above the village well. To protect it against vermin, the rice basket was plastered with a thin layer of cow-dung, which once hardened became quite odourless.

Derami also came to grind rice into flour for Ummie. The day after her visit to Gunga, she was called to perform this task, and as the Harijan girl sat on the kitchen floor rhythmically turning the handle of the big stone grinder, she told the old Muslim lady all about the strange poolside mirage. Ummie listened quietly, but in the end was unable to offer any explanation. However, her obvious solicitude encouraged the girl to confide the rest of her family troubles. Thereafter, even when there was no work for her to do, Derami became a frequent visitor, recognising in her new friend an independent and fearless soul to match her own.

Ummie, for her part, recognised in the tempestuous Harijan girl the frustrations of an illiterate young person with no prospect of ever finding a satisfactory outlet for her natural energies and intelligence. Although Derami had been born at a time when legislation made it possible for every child to attend school, like most children of destitute families, once she was old enough she worked in the fields. At that time Derami, like other Harijan children, would have been forced to sit apart from the other pupils and treated as inferiors. It was only very recently in Borli that a new generation of teachers had emerged who were at last free from the ingrained prejudices of their predecessors. In 1983, the headmistress of the Janata Shikshan Saristha High School in Borli, was able to point to the fact that the first boy from a family of illiterates had been awarded a scholarship to go on to higher education. But in a village where the livelihoods of 5,000 inhabitants revolved around the annual rice harvest, this was indeed a unique occurrence. 'Rice before reading' was the unwritten motto of *agri* peasants. Their reluctant decision to compromise with the demands of state education authorities meant that they sent half their children to school; the rest—as always—were sent to work in the fields.

Bitter experience had taught the paddyfield workers that the margins between enough and not enough were slim. The family who did not work together might very well starve.

In Borli, the widespread famine of 1952 in India was complicated by another catastrophe, as one farmworker, who was for many years employed by the Kulkarnis, recalled.

> The dam which crossed the creek behind Diwaga was washed out by a big storm. All our paddy was covered by salt water. The good land was swallowed up. All my neighbours suffered. We had to work to mend that dam. The government paid us small wages, but not enough to feed our families.
>
> I took my ox and plough to cultivate a patch of ground in the hills by the seashore and planted millet. This way my family ate once a day. The government ration shop in Borli allowed every family four kilos of grain for one week, but I only had money for some of this. And they sold us spoiled grains. For three years we make our bread with mouldy rice until that salty land was ready to plant again.
>
> That is why I always say, What do *agri* people want with school? Can our children eat chalk and books?

Introducing new ways to replace the old was always a gradual process; people found it difficult to grasp the concept of long-term advantages. The village attitude towards agricultural innovations was typical.

The village economy was based on rice cultivation. Although ownership of the land had passed to the peasants, they continued to live from one crop to the next, perpetuating a form of husbandry that had not changed since ancient times. The cultivation of rice needs standing water, which is why the crop is particularly suitable for monsoon areas. Grown on inland terraces carefully positioned so that contours of the land ensured that they would catch the water running off the hillsides, the grain was called sweetland rice. The variety of rice grown on land by the sea was called *kharapat* and renowned for its particularly fine flavour.

Getting the paddyfield ready for the new crop began in the winter months. The farm labourer went into the hills to collect large quantities of brushwood which he carried back on his head, thus presenting the extraordinary sight of what appeared to be an enormous walking bush moving down the road on a pair of thin, naked legs! Ox-dung and brushwood were spread on the fields and set alight, the resulting potash then ploughed in with the traditional ox-and-stick plough. Next, the low mud parapets surrounding and separating each field were repaired and strengthened, and, during the hot and humid months of March and April, seed saved from the previous harvest was planted. When this germinated in May, all across the valleys red-earth paddyfields were patched with squares of brilliant emerald-green.

If the monsoon arrived on time, preliminary showers in late May consolidated these seedlings for planting out the following month. This was undertaken by Hindu women, working knee-deep in water, with rattan capes on their backs to protect them from the pounding of the rain.

Throughout the wet months from June to the end of August, rice crops grew to maturity, and in late September and early October they were harvested into bundles and dried out in stacks built on wooden platforms in the fields or lodged in the forks of trees. Finally, to complete the annual rice cycle, in October these stacks were dismantled for threshing, again by hand.

It was a precarious existence, but, nevertheless, the only one the people knew. Which was why attempts to introduce improvements invariably met with opposition. Since 1964, agricultural research stations had been developing new and stronger varieties of rice to withstand storm damage and produce better yielding crops. But in Borli Ravi Kulkarni, a progressive farmer with extensive knowledge of the land and the people, found it difficult to convince his neighbours of the benefits.

On my land I planted a short-stemmed rice variety which was especially suitable for our local seashore conditions. This rice has strong stems, can withstand heavy winds and rain and produce more food grains. But the secret of success is artificial fertiliser. Now there's a good road inland, it is easily obtainable. But when I tried to persuade my neighbours to grow this rice variety, they were full of objections. They pointed out that the short-stemmed rice did not give enough straw for cattle fodder. So I showed them how to compensate for this by planting seedlings closer together. That way they got more rice, and at the same time, sufficient straw. But I also explained that this intensive form of cultivation could not be done without using chemical fertilisers.

At this they threw up their hands in horror. Artificial fertilisers, they said, would surely damage the sweetness of the soil. So I explained that if they combined chemical fertilisers with compost and dung, this would not be the case. Then they argued that once a person started using chemicals on the ground he would have to use them every year because the rain would wash them away. I replied that the scientists already had an answer for this. Farmers could buy bags of ready-mixed soil and urea, with slow-release granular compounds which wouldn't easily wash away.

But we still can't afford them, they said. So I carefully outlined the whole scheme again. If you grow this improved rice variety, I said, you will get more rice than you need for yourselves. Then you can sell the surplus, purchase fertilisers and still have cash in hand. After that, they said they would go away and consider my words.

Well, at our next meeting my neighbours said to me: 'Sahib, what you said must be true because you are an educated person, but we see it like this. All we need is enough rice to feed our families and enough straw to keep our cattle going strong. Why must we work harder to plant more crops and get more rice in order to buy these scientific products, when our cattle dung is free? Is it to put money into the pockets of these city gentlemen? And we also say this, Sahib. What happens if we spend on chemical fertilisers and it is a drought year? Then all that hard work and money is lost and we shall fall into debt. Unless, Sahib, those important scientists can also sell us artificial rain . . .!

Clinging to a comparatively simple hand-to-mouth existence in the face of scientific innovation was no longer a viable alternative if the farmers on the little peninsula hoped to continue to live off the land. In the past self-sufficiency may very well have constituted a legitimate claim to security, but, as the population increased, self-sufficiency had within it the seeds of self-destruction.

The natural resources which the people relied upon were not enough to sustain so many, so relentlessly, for so long. And as educated farmers like Ravi Kulkarni well knew, the villagers were already on the brink of an ecological crisis.

This whole area has a sub-stratum of latrite rocks covered by a poor red top-soil to a depth of about twelve inches. This is the result of erosion which over the decades has been getting steadily worse. Now it threatens the future of rice cultivation in this area. When the hills were thickly covered by forests, we never had this problem because, when monsoon rains fell, the big trees absorbed large quantities of water. The rest flowed gently down to the lowlands, bringing with it leafmould and other valuable humus. This provided a natural distribution of organic matter to supplement cow-dung. Then the paddy-fields were extremely fertile.

Now the trees have been cut down for building and firewood. During the monsoon season, we get about 120 inches of rain. Without trees to absorb it, this water forms torrents which cut deep gullies in the hillsides, washing rocks, pebbles and sandy soil into the fields. That is why for many years now, rice yields have been getting less and less. And I will tell you something else. Without trees, the erosion on the hills is serious. If we don't make a big social effort to plant new trees, there will be no top-soil up there even to support grass for grazing cattle. Then I really hate to think how the farmers will manage.

It was ironical that the family in Borli best able to administer the land had been forced by the 1961 Tenancy Act to hand it over to those least able to do so. After twenty years of ownership, the peasantry had neither improved their living standards nor the proportion of literacy amongst their caste. Moreover, when advised by their ex-landlord to introduce modern methods of cultivation in order to safeguard the fertility of their lands, they could not grasp the advantages of doing so.

Apart from farming Ravi Kulkarni's other interest is education. Serving on the administrative board of the local high school he feels sure that education will help where democratic evolution has failed, to produce a new breed of farmer able to grasp the concept of ecological conservation and the need to remove some of the emphasis from rice growing.

Rice is labour-intensive and nowadays costs a lot to produce. Even in Borli, labour costs have gone too high. I must pay one man Rs 15 a day and a woman Rs 7. I get about Rs 1,500 per ton of grain and out of this Rs 1,200 must be spent on cultivation. So rice is not a profitable crop unless I can find ways to reduce labour costs. The planting out of the seedlings is where much of the expense goes. In Japan there are rice-transplanting machines, but even if this type of mechanical device was introduced to India, I would not use it. No humanitarian person would, when there are so many needing work.

But I do think that power-tillers have a place in rice farming. Three years ago I tried one and found it much better than ploughing with oxen. The machine broke up the soil nice and fine all over, so it was in excellent condition for planting. This type of small cultivator is suitable for use in small paddyfields, where trying to steer something like a tractor would damage the mud-banks. I had to get rid of my tiller. When it went wrong, I couldn't get spare parts. All the same, I personally feel that when there is an efficient after-sales service in India, this automatic tiller will become widely used by rice farmers, especially as using it will not deprive others of a job. But as I see it, in the future our main concern must be reafforestation programmes. Perhaps this is the opportunity we need to get away from emphasis on rice cultivation and plant trees which will produce valuable cash crops—not only such trees as teak and pine for building purposes, but others such as mango, jackfruit and cashew, which will give our farmers other sources of income. Once such trees were not profitable because we couldn't market the fruits before they deteriorated. Nowadays, we actually send mangoes by air freight to Saudi Arabia. With fast road transport, six hours after the fruit is picked off the trees in Borli, it reaches Bombay.

Mango trees grow everywhere along this coast and must surely be nature's most luxurious fruiting tree. There are several kinds, but queen of them all is the dessert mango called *Kulmi*, which fetches a high price in the city. Then there are *Appus* and *Pairi*, which we call 'jungly' mangoes because they grow wild in the hills and have a slightly salty flavour. Mostly these go to the factories in Bombay to be made into chutney.

Here in Borli, I cultivate the *Alfonso* mango, which originally came from Goa. It is almost as good as the *Kulmi* with a deep-yellow flesh and rich flavour. What I do is grow the *Kulmi* stone in a pot for two years. Then we prune back the 'jungly' mango and graft on the *Kulmi* shoot. Then outdoor cultivation is simple. The tree needs plenty of water in the dry season and manure after it has fruited, which is about six or seven years after grafting.

As the crop matures, we have to pay Katkari families to go

and live under the mango trees and guard them from thieves. Then from the middle of April to the middle of May, the fruit is harvested. This is very specialised work because the trees are tall and plucking must be done with great care. Any fruit that falls is spoiled. So only the Katkari men can do the plucking because nobody climbs with such care as they do. They take a basket on a rope and pluck the mangoes with a net fixed to the end of a long pole. Then the full baskets are lowered to the ground, where the fruit is packed into larger baskets padded with straw. The trouble is, the Katkari know they are the best people to perform this task. They demand a very high price for picking. Last year (1983) we had to pay them Rs 30 a day.

But there are disadvantages to the *Alfonso* mango because the trees only bear on alternate years and the parent tree, when fully grown, compares in size with your English oak. What we need is a dwarf variety which also fruits every year. I'm pleased to tell you that our horticultural researchers are now perfecting just such a kind. This new mango tree is a cross between *Alfonso* and a mango which only grows in the Madras area. When it becomes available, I for one will certainly plant this dwarf variety. I intend to establish proper orchards where the trees can be easily harvested from the ground to reduce the cost of picking and sprayed with pesticides to prevent mango fly.

There's an amusing story about the little pest called the *Rumali* fly. People hereabouts believe it is one of nature's great mysteries because sometimes, when they cut into a *Rumali* mango which shows not the slightest blemish, out comes this small butterfly which is always impossible to catch. I myself once believed this to be a magical insect until I went to college and learned the truth. When the *Rumali* mango is still small and hard, the female mango fly uses her oviparus duct (which is like a hypodermic needle) to deposit an egg just under the skin, leaving no trace of penetration. When the larva hatches, it feeds on the pulp, which at this stage is very acidic. But the creature thrives on it and soon eats its way to the centre of the fruit, where it pupates. Just before the fruit ripens, this pupa turns into a pretty little butterfly. Someone takes a mango, cuts it open and hey presto – out it flies!

* * *

In the winter month of January, if the temperature drops to a chilly 50°F or 60°F, the feathery honey-coloured mango blossom 'sets' well, and by early February marble-sized fruits have formed to renew the villagers' love affair with the mango. Even at this stage, the immature fruits are much relished for the sour flavour they add to fish stews and, rather as Western schoolchildren hunt for conkers under chestnut trees, Borli children rake about under the mango trees searching for windfalls.

Towards the end of March, every tree is hung with green and yellow fruits and beneath each, guarding nature's treasure trove in the branches above, lives at least one Katkari family. These diminutive dark-skinned people, once nomads on the peninsula, have recently accepted government protection. On a few acres of ground on the Karlia road—just beyond the *tikera* with the ruined house on top—a settlement of rudimentary hovels has been built, together with one small schoolroom staffed by a resident teacher. Lacking all refinements, these huts serve as the first step towards civilising the Katkari, who have for so long preferred the impermanence of a wandering existence. It is therefore no hardship for them to return for a few months each year to their customary alfresco lifestyle to become guardians of the mango trees.

Nor are potential poachers deceived by the unimposing stature of those arboreal sentinels. The average Katkari is an infallible marksman with a sling-shot, and at close quarters able to wield a stick with shin-cracking accuracy. Only small and naked Katkari children get away with free mangoes, gorging themselves on juicy windfalls, the envy of their better-clothed contemporaries just up the road.

Mangoes too ripe to travel are sold in the bazaar for one or two rupees, depending on size and condition and at this time of the year the exotic *punnus* (jackfruit) are also ripening. This strange marrow-like fruit grows directly out of the trunk of a tall solid-limbed tree. Under the dark green skin lie a mass of seeds imbedded in rose-coloured pulp with a deliciously fragrant taste which lingers on the tongue long after it has been swallowed. Then there are the big pink-skinned citrus fruits called *pomelos*, yet another pre-monsoon fruit which helps to quench the thirsts of people who, in May, are suffering from an acute shortage of water.

Hard on the heels of the mango harvest comes the monsoon. Skies, which for months have remained an unchanging pellucid blue, become the backdrop for iron-grey cumuli boiling over the northern horizon. At first the village is bombarded with a few preliminary showers, a flurry of large raindrops hitting the rooftops like a fusillade of buckshot, in moments transforming dusty lanes into little rivers of red water. Then, as if turned off by a celestial stopcock, the rain ceases and, in sunshine which seems hotter than ever, the entire countryside starts to steam. These first showers transform the scorched land. Long spikes of green sprout from apparently dead cactus hedges, and everywhere seeds that have remained dormant for months spring to life, spreading a green haze across the landscape.

But the showers which bring relief soon give way to the tedium of an almost continuous inundation which lasts a full twelve weeks or more. Unglazed windows are either shuttered or protected against driving rain by roughly-woven lean-to panels of palmleaf. Nobody ventures far without taking a large black umbrella and everywhere the sound of hawking and spitting announces the arrival of the first bout of seasonal chills. Even the *muezzin*'s call to prayer is interspersed by amplified coughing!

Hindu women, bent double in waterlogged ricefields, sing as they work. Muslim women kindle their *shagris* and in the semi-gloom of shuttered houses sit diligently stitching patchwork quilts, as day after day the heavens return the blessing they have so long withheld.

* * *

Although rice is the staple crop in Borli, not far behind in importance comes the cultivation of coconut palms in the sun-dappled 'gardens' of Diwaga. But compared to rice, the lifecycle of the coconut is indeed bizarre. With self-perpetuating fecundity these extraordinary trees produce an unending succession of nuts which only age or natural calamity can interrupt. Sixty or seventy feet tall with unruly heads of feathery foliage on long and supple necks, these beautiful hermaphrodites flirt with sea breezes, the only outside influence necessary to pollinate the male and female flowers, which every four weeks produce a new crop of bulbous progeny. At any time several clumps of nuts in varying stages of development can be found on a single tree.

As with mangoes, picking the ripe nuts is a job for experts, in this case—not Katkari but—Hindu boys renowned for physical fitness and a head for heights. Knotting a loop of rope round the trunk, the climber pushes the rope upwards on the rough bark and then, using it as a handhold, walks his bare feet up to the same level, a repeated caterpillar movement which in minutes enables the boy to reach the swaying summit. With a combination of agility and expertise he is able to identify and cut out only those nuts which have reached the required degree of ripeness. This he does by tapping the nut, the sound it makes telling him the exact state of the kernel embedded in a fibrous covering several inches thick within the nutshell.

There are several different types of coconut. 'Green' ones contain only milky juice, providing a naturally refrigerated drink, because, although the fruit grows in direct sunlight at temperatures often exceeding 100° F, the sterile contents remain insulated by the husk.

A slightly more mature nut, called a 'temptation' coconut, contains sweet milk in a womb of pliant kernel, providing both a drink and a succulent snack. Finally, there are coconuts that have gone to 'full term'. Inside these the milk has turned to hard flesh, and is used for grating into curries and other foods. These coconuts also go to oil mills, where the oil is extracted for cooking, soap and other cosmetics.

At Diwaga the three-mile stretch of palms along the coast is divided into plantations, each extending from about three to five acres. They are called 'gardens' because, in effect, this is just what they are—the back gardens of plantation owners who live and work in the shade of these graceful trees. Planted in rows some twenty feet apart, the palms are irrigated by a network of shallow ditches mostly fed by electrically pumped water from deep brick-lined springwater wells. But here and there in the 'gardens', the old method of raising water by ox-powered waterwheels is still in use.

The plantations at Diwaga are kept in immaculate condition. Nothing that might interfere with the nourishment of the palms is allowed to grow in the sandy soil; every last scrap of debris is carefully collected and put to good use. Fallen palm leaves are used for thatching cattle sheds or bought by Hindu women, who strip off the fronds and bundle the flexible leaf 'spines' into brooms to sell in the villages.

The fibrous outer casing of the nuts is set aside for cooking fuel, although once it would have been a more valuable commodity. In the old days this *coir* was soaked in the creek for two or three months, after which ropemakers twisted it into ropes and strings for making fishnets. Once cheap nylon ropes reached the village, this practice was discontinued.

Unless felled by hurricanes, which from time to time sweep up the coast from the south-west, the androgynous coconut palms live long and fruitful lives. When, after sixty or seventy years they are finally cut down to make way for saplings, the tough timber provides excellent building material. Since the coconut palms provide a cornucopia of food and drink, fuel and shelter, ropes and nets, they have come to be regarded by those who live beneath them as sacred trees. And, furthermore, the juice from their flowers is the raw material for palm toddy.

Usually one tree in each plantation is set aside for this purpose; deep wedges are cut out of the trunk to facilitate the toddy tapper's twice-daily trip to the summit in order to collect the sap. It is obtained by punching a hole in the thick flower stems so that the juice drips into containers. When fermented, this liquid produces a mildly intoxicating drink comparable to beer. After distillation, coconut 'moonshine' becomes a potent and fiery liquor much enjoyed by Hindu men and women returning from a hard day's toil in the paddyfields.

Yet there are indications that the lofty nature of the all-providing coconut palms is about to change. Just as he has been a keen promoter of improved varieties of rice, so Ravi Kulkarni's interests have already spread to a new breed of coconut tree.

> Until recently not much research had been done into coconut cultivation. The trees which grow up the west coast of India are *Narial*, *Karderucta* and *Kalpadruma*, all varieties of 'West Coast Tall'. Young coconut palms start to fruit when they are seven years old and about fifteen feet high. At this height, cropping is easy, but when that same tree grows to eighty feet, then it is very difficult. If you look up, you can see there are many distinct bunches in the same tree. Every twenty-eight days a new leaf grows and along with every new leaf a fresh flower bunch comes out. So every month each tree produces one ripe bunch consisting of about twenty coconuts. That is why picking goes on all the time.

> Nowadays skilled climbers are difficult to get. Sometimes I must reserve the services of a boy a week ahead because he is kept so busy. And the charge for climbing has gone up too – almost as high as the coconut tree! The profit from these tall trees is not so much: from one palm I can earn about Rs 300 a year.

> So now I am interested in the 'Singapore Dwarf', a coconut palm which is a cross between our 'West Coast Tall' and one grown in the Laccadive Islands off the Malabar coast. They say the quality of nut and oil is inferior, but the dwarf bears early and is, of course, easier to crop. There may be just one problem. We shall have to put the 'Singapore Dwarfs' in the centre of the coconut *waddis*, away from boundary fences, to prevent pillaging.

> The coconuts we grow here in Diwaga are sold locally. Each nut fetches Rs 3.50, or Rs 2 if it is a 'green' one. Nowadays these nuts are only used for cooking but, when I was young

I can remember seeing oil-makers in Borli preparing oil from coconut meat. Their place was where Dr Joshi's dispensary is now. The oil press was worked by bullock-power and those who did this work were Jewish people. Now they have all gone back to Israel.

In my childhood (1950s) everything we needed was right here in the village. There were spinners and weavers who made cotton for saris and other clothes, ropemakers, oil-pressers, everything. Then in the mid-1950s they put the road through and by 1960 all that had changed. Once we were like the coconut tree – able to stand proudly in one place and look after ourselves. Now we must rely on outside help. Personally I feel that to be forward-looking is not such a bad thing; if we keep what is good from the past and take only what is best from today, like the palm trees, perhaps we also can learn to bend with the winds, whichever way they blow.

*   *   *

Viewed from the seashore, there is little to indicate that the Diwaga palms shelter a thriving community of nearly one thousand people in surroundings which, to an outsider at least, seem idyllic. At the southern end, near the estuary of the Karlia, live the Koli, the shaded lanes between their simple thatched dwellings strewn with fishing nets and lobster pots. Brightly feathered poultry scratch in the sand, hairless pye bitches with distended dugs trailing in the dirt bark listlessly and children chase vivid red-and-black swallow-tail butterflies, their shrill cries lost in the cathedral-like vault of the tall trees.

Sweet air, fragrant with woodsmoke and damp earth, is also tinged with salt breezes coming off the seashore beyond the dunes which back the fishing village. There a three-mile stretch of sands is usually quite deserted, except for the fisher-men wading chest high in the waves to trawl for pomfret and surmay. At sunset, when the sea changes to a vista of beaten brass, white-breasted sea-eagles circle the estuary and flocks of egret angle their way across an orange sky to roost on the other side of the bay.

The coastal road from the south, after switchbacking over a long range of humpy hills, drops to sea-level and enters Diwaga by way of the new concrete bridge across the Karlia. Almost immediately the semblance of 'hard top' merges with a sandy track tunnelling the length of the 'gardens' to emerge at the opposite end, where there is another smaller fishing village at the edge of the creek. Then, on a series of small concrete bridges, the gravelled route traverses the marshes to connect with the inland road. But half way through the coconut 'gardens', at the junction of this road and the one which crosses the ricefields to Borli, is the 'commercial centre' of Diwaga, consisting of post-office, small store, metal forge and barber shop.

Diwaga has both a junior school at the Karlia end and, a mile further up the road, the high school, built on land donated by the Hindu owner of the Borli ricemill, who lives opposite in one of the fine old houses typical of those occupied by plantation families. With a shabbiness which has about it a certain grandeur, these spacious dwellings with their huge tiled roofs sweeping down and out over broad verandas are screened from the road by mellow brick walls hung with flowering creepers. In front of the houses well-swept forecourts edged with flowerbeds and shrubs lead to a flight of wooden or stone steps on to the front veranda. This is often used as the plantation owner's office. Here each week his 'servants' line up for their pay and his neighbours congregate to discuss farming matters over glasses of coconut juice.

Inside, the rooms are dark and cool with high ceilings and stone-tiled floors. By Western standards, they are sparsely furnished, especially where the older members of the family still prefer to squat on the floor rather than to sit on chairs. But usually there is a large wooden swing seat suspended by chains from the rafters and covered with patchwork cushions. And every Hindu living-room contains a family shrine—a corner alcove where the household god is illuminated by small brass oil lamps and decorated with fresh flowers.

The side rooms are also furnished with ascetic simplicity, no more than simple wood-frame beds covered with coloured cotton covers, a cupboard and in one corner a concrete sump with a low wooden stool for the bather and a stainless steel water urn.

The kitchen at the back often contains the only signs of local wealth; refrigerators, sinks with taps and gas rings for cooking fuelled either by bottled gas or home-made methane from 'gober gas' installations in the yard. As a concession to modernity, there may also be a formica-topped table and chairs on which the younger generation take their meals, even though the food is still usually served on shining clean banana leaves and eaten, in the customary way, with the fingers of the right hand.

At the back of the typical plantation home is a second large veranda, perhaps with one or two enclosed toilets with keyhole-shapes set into tiled floors. They are 'flushed' by containers of water which also serves as 'toilet paper'; personal cleansing is done only with the left hand.

But perhaps the most delightful feature is the effect created by the custom of extending the hardened dung-slurry floor of the back veranda out into the area behind the house, and of supporting the veranda roof and those of the outbuildings with unhewn timbers and growing trees. In this way the inside and the outside flow together, the fabric of the house merging first with the flowerbeds surrounding the obligatory *tulsi* tree and then with the shaded avenues of the coconut 'gardens' beyond.

Although coconut is the predominant crop, Diwaga residents also grow a number of other plants, mostly for domestic use. In the sandy soil between the palms are pineapples, black-pepper vines and nutmeg trees. Also *punnus*, *pomelo* and small brown fruits called *chicos*, a substitute for apples which only grow further north.

Banana palms also flourish throughout the Diwaga 'gardens'. They are planted not as a cash crop, but to give protection against winds for immature coconut saplings. Nevertheless, bananas form an integral part of the local diet. Banana palms reach a height of about twenty feet. Once they are ready for harvesting they are cut down and a new shoot then grows on the same root for the next crop.

There are three varieties of banana, the most popular being the thumb-sized *welchis* with paper-thin skins. Next comes a larger type with pink skins and deep yellow flesh called *rasbeli* and finally there are plantains, the granddaddies of bananas, with thick skins and hard greenish flesh ideal for curries.

But the crop which a new generation of Diwaga farmers is finding increasingly profitable is betel nut, the quality of those grown in the salt air at Diwaga having gained a reputation for excellence amongst the *paan* connoisseurs of Bombay. Betel palms thrive in the shade of coconut trees and once every year produce massive dangling bunches of nuts covered by tan-coloured fibre. When harvested in January, this fibre is roughly sliced off, leaving the nuts still imbedded in a thin layer of pith. The crop is then spread out on flat-roofed outbuildings to dry in the sun before being bagged and sent to Bombay.

In the city, 'Borli Betel', as it has come to be known, fetches as much as Rs 80 for one kilo. One mature tree yields close on 100 kilos, and most planters grow up to 200 trees on an acre. So long as the habit for chewing *paan* is never superseded by cigarette smoking, there is an excellent living to be made from this crop.

About the size of a large conker, the rock-hard betel nut has a white-mottled grain. Cracked into fragments it is added to the little leaf-wrapped parcels which also contain *chuna* (lime), shreds of *tombaku* (tobacco) and *kath* (scraps of bark from the *catachou* tree which gave *paan* its characteristic red colour). It is the alkaloid content of betel nuts which produces the slightly euphoric effect enjoyed by millions of *paan* addicts.

* * *

Ummie's daughter Amina lives at the northern end of Diwaga, where her husband Jamil is fast turning from coconuts to the more profitable betel nut palms. Kadija, Ummie's youngest middle-aged daughter, also owns property on the opposite side of the lane, although most of the time she and her large family occupy a flat in a suburb of Bombay and only come to Diwaga for the children's school holidays.

Kadija and her husband Zeoudi also own ricefields and a mango orchard at Elas, a small village two miles north of Borli. Despite their underprivileged upbringing, two of Ummie's daughters have become women of substance. Yet the good fortune enjoyed by her daughters makes little difference to Ummie's, Halima's and Reshma's somewhat impoverished existence, for the simple reason that according to the dictates of Islam, sons, not sons-in-law, are obliged to support parents.

Entirely reconciled to this traditional pattern of family responsibility, Ummie neither expects nor receives assistance from her better-off daughters. However, when she goes to stay with either Aisha, Howabi or Kadija in Bombay, they go to great lengths to make a fuss of her.

> They feed me with the best fruits and nice dinners, so all the time butter shines on my lips. But in those small city flats I feel like a bird in a cage and only long to get back to my old nest in the jungle!
>
> I could leave my home here in Borli and live always with my other daughters so I have no more worries, but then what would Halima do? Better we two widows stay close together, then we do not bow down to anybody for our bread.

Neither of Ummie's two sons in South Africa has fulfilled his filial obligations, although considering the harsh circumstances under which they left Borli, perhaps this is understandable. Having been forcibly parted from their mother and sisters, they could scarcely be expected to retain an affectionate recollection of the woman they are supposed to support for the rest of her life.

In 1979 Ummie's eldest son Ahmed was killed in a Cape Town traffic accident. Although Adam continues to evade his financial duties, he once wrote to suggest that Ummie return to South Africa and live with him and his family. But the old lady refused.

Adam sends me photos of his nice house and car and promises to send money for my air ticket if I say I will come. But how can I give up all that I know and love for that new life? Once I get there, perhaps his wife don't like me, then what would I do? So I write back and say: 'Son, I am old now and too much afraid to fly in that big machine. Supposing it drops in the sea, then where would I be? Much better I stay here on the ground where Allah put me.'

❧ CHAPTER NINE ❧

ONE DAY ASHUMA, a Muslim widow of Borli, and her daughter Amila went to console a family member in Mahsla who had just lost her husband. Much to their consternation, they were not invited to remain overnight. As there was no bus back to the village until the early hours of the next morning, the two women decided to walk. The distance between Mahsla and Borli was twelve kilometres, but the road was good and there was a full moon. So off they set, the old woman always a few steps ahead of her daughter and occasionally muttering encouragement when the girl showed signs of lagging too far behind.

When they reached a place where the road was hemmed in by trees which cast weird shadows in their path, Ashuma's pace quickened. She was well aware of the local legend that this particular wood was haunted by evil spirits waiting to take possession of unsuspecting travellers. So, clutching her *bourka* more closely around her, Ashuma hurried on, looking neither to right nor left. By the time the two women had reached home, they were both exhausted and, after quickly washing their feet, they rolled themselves up in their blankets and fell instantly asleep.

In the morning, Amila awoke to the sound of her mother's wailing. The old woman was standing in front of the mirror and wringing her hands at the sight of her reflection. During the night Ashuma's normally long hair had twisted itself into a hard matted tangle on top of her head, which no amount of combing could dislodge.

Without waiting to eat or drink, Ashuma donned her *bourka* and hurried off down the road to Karlia to consult the *fakir*. After probing the hairy mass with his fingers and reciting a litany of incantations, the seer confirmed Ashuma's worst fears. A Hindu wood sprite had settled in her hair and on no account must she try to cut away the tangle and evict it. If Ashuma did so, the *djin* would penetrate further into the old woman's head and drive her to madness. Only by remaining patient and by avoiding uncharitable thoughts about her unwelcome lodger could she ensure that one day it would vanish as mysteriously as it had appeared.

Two years later, Ashuma was still playing host to the Hindu wood sprite; her head crowned by a grotesque and rock-hard protuberance. Had she been persuaded to consult one of the five medical doctors in Borli, Ashuma's affliction would soon have been diagnosed. It was a sebaceous cyst which, unfortunately for the superstitious widow, just happened to burst on the night she walked home through the wood. In the following years, without a simple operation for its removal, this painless wen continued to exude matter which hardened into a hairy top-knot.

* * *

When Dr Adhikari first came to Borli in the early 1930s this kind of ignorance and superstition was no more than he expected in an isolated rural community. Almost without exception, villagers believed that evil spirits, magic and witchcraft had the power to affect their health. So, in order to gain people's confidence the doctor had to embark on a long and patient campaign to convince them that it was not the super-natural which caused sickness amongst them, but unboiled water and poor standards of hygiene. Although he had no patience with the *fakirs*, Dr Adhikari had a great respect for nature-cure medicine as practised by Nana Kulkarni's father, a traditional physician who had learned the ancient art of Ayurveda from his father before him.

Amongst the earliest forms of health care in the world, Ayurveda bridged science and religion, reason and faith, medication and meditation to create a form of medicine which was part human creation and part divine revelation. And in many respects, it was the metaphysical component of Ayurveda which appealed to Hindu people with their devout respect for elemental gods.

According to Hindu belief, everything in the world is ultimately composed of the five *bhutas* (elements); earth, water, fire, air and ether. The art of Ayurvedic medicine was always based on the principle that these elements in various combinations conferred upon food its six basic characteristics; sweet, sour, salty, pungent, bitter and astringent. Thus food containing a predominance of water would taste sweet; water and fire combined to produce salinity; air and fire made food taste hot and pungent and a predominance of air and ether produced bitterness. Lastly, food mostly composed of air and earth would be astringent.

Ayurvedic practitioners believed that the elemental nature of food accounted for the internal disharmony which produced physical symptoms. So their diagnosis and treatment was also based on the premise that elemental imbalance in the sick person caused by eating an incorrect diet could also be reversed by prescribing herbal remedies and foods known to contain the elemental properties needed to restore the equilibrium.

In the fifth century BC, Hippocrates, so-called 'father of medicine', taught that food and medicine were indistinguishable; he believed that medicine was an extension of man's search for food and congenial surroundings, combined with his ability to adapt to his environment. Ayurveda extended these concepts by insisting that nature cure and prayer belonged together, since both were potent forces for healing the sick.

The remedies supplied by the *vaidya* (practitioners of Ayurveda) are never directed at the patient's symptoms, but at fortifying his entire system so that he could emerge after recovery with a greater power of resistance to any future disturbance. In this context, every remedy has to be tailor-made for the individual according to temperament and physiological characteristics.

An 'earth' person can be recognised as being cold and dry; a 'water' person as cold and moist; a 'fire' person as hot and dry and those akin to air and ether, hot and moist. By treating diseases according to whether they were hot, cold or moist with remedies from plants with similar qualities, the Ayurvedic doctor sought to reharmonise the patient's internal *prahna* (life-force).

The taste of the plant remedy is also matched to the idiosyncratic disposition of the patient—whether he is a 'sweet' person, or one better described as 'sour', or 'salty', or 'acid'. And when all these considerations have been taken into account, sometimes the actual appearance of the plant will be selected because it imitates the visible nature of the patient's symptoms. Trembling diseases are often treated with the leaves of the *pepul* tree, which also trembles in the wind; the spotted leaves of the plant *phadukanar* are used to salve the bite of a certain spotted snake, and following the principle that 'hot should be treated with hot', black pepper is a common treatment for venereal diseases.

With an extensive knowledge of local botany, the Ayurvedic physician is able to concoct the antidotes for a whole range of complaints ranging from a simple sore throat to a potentially fatal poisonous bite. Centipede or scorpion bites are treated with crushed *adambuvalli*, a creeper-like plant which produces a sticky juice. Rubbed on the bite, this instantly relieves the pain. The much-dreaded bite from a rabid dog or cat is treated with a poultice of *ankolam* leaves applied to the wound, a medicament which is also supposed to prevent the infection spreading to the patient's bloodstream with fatal results.

The rudiments of Ayurvedic medicine are also in common usage amongst the villagers to treat themselves or their children for minor complaints. Leaves from the *neem* tree, mixed with turmeric, remove the kind of skin blemishes left by chicken-pox or smallpox. The diverse medicinal value of the delicious papaya is legendary. Papaya juice cures warts and staunches the bleeding from external wounds; a paste made from crushed papaya seeds is an excellent home-remedy for ringworm and intestinal worms, and latex from papaya bark heals carbuncles and burns. Garlic is another potent home remedy. A clove of garlic, warmed in water and plugged into an aching ear, brings immediate relief. Persistent coughs are treated by rubbing the patient's feet with oil and then applying a poultice of crushed garlics.

In rural areas where contaminated water and lack of sanitation invariably cause certain chronic conditions, wise Ayurvedic practitioners gain the co-operation of the community by means of mass medication disguised as religious ritual. At appropriate intervals, holy days are accompanied by ceremonies which involve the swallowing of 'sacred' leaves, which can, in fact, eradicate intestinal parasites or, due to their high vitamin C content, alleviate coughs and catarrh brought on by the monsoon climate.

So Ayurvedic pundits skilfully administer a combination of prayer, prophylactics and practical remedies to fortify the resistance of the community to health hazards directly related to the personal circumstances of their daily lives and the local environment.

Before the arrival of the first 'scientific' doctor in Borli, Dr Adhikari, the villagers went up the hill to the Kulkarni house whenever they needed treatment.

My father learned his Ayurvedic skills from his father and from many books containing the medicinal properties of herbs and plants growing in this area and the formulae for their preparation. He used to send servants out into the countryside to collect what he required, and then he'd mix the remedies himself in front of the patients. Everything had to be freshly made. The villagers had a high respect for Dada Sahib Kulkarni, and faith that what he administered would bring them relief. My father always said that faith was the last and most important ingredient that the patient himself added to the mixture.

By the time my father was an old man, allopathic medicine had come to India from the West, so he did not pass his training on to me. Dada Sahib used only his hands and his eyes and his knowledge of the patient to make a diagnosis. When he saw how Dr Adhikari had a stethoscope and thermometer and modern analysis methods, my father reached the conclusion that traditional treatments would be no longer needed.

Towards the end of their imperial rule, the British had encouraged scientific medicine in India and young doctors were using penicillin and other antibiotics to treat endemic problems such as dysentery, worms and eye infections. Those who received this form of treatment found that, when the problem recurred, they had to return for more of the same—provided that the doctor who originally gave the antibiotics was still around, since in India mobile clinics were more usual in rural areas than dispensaries. When the patient could not get further allopathic treatment and turned back to traditional remedies, often it was to find that these no longer worked with the same efficacy on a system 'polluted' by synthetic medicines.

In the 1940s, health ministers were saying that traditional health care did not befit the progressive outlook India needed to cultivate if she wished to follow in the footsteps of developing nations. (The first health minister of independent India actually predicted the disappearance of traditional forms of medicine within the decade.)

Fortunately, colleagues of Mahatma Gandhi, who during his lifetime was a staunch advocate of nature-cure methods, strenuously campaigned to protect the future of Ayurvedic centres with, as it transpired, commendable acuity. By the 1980s not only had the allopathic approach failed to supersede traditional health care, but the number of officially-recognised Ayurvedic physicians registered with the Central Council of Indian Medicine had actually risen to 225,000. There were 97 teaching centres attached to Indian universities, where graduates received the same rigorous training as was demanded by the ancient Ayurvedic manuscripts.

There was a time when, as the legend goes, a group of eminent sages met on the slopes of the Himalayas to discuss how they might get rid of the diseases which were blighting mankind. They decided to consult Indra, lord of immortals, who was in possession of the ancient secrets of longevity. Bharadvaja, the oldest sage, was chosen to approach Indra and this he did, saying: 'Diseases have arisen, O Lord, which are the terror of all human beings. Pray tell me the means of curing them'. Thus it was that Indra gave Bharadvaja the ancient knowledge of Ayurveda, and in turn the old man taught his disciples.

By the fifth century AD, Ayurveda had become the medicine of the people. Students wishing to learn the art came from all parts of India and from abroad, such was the reputation created by a form of health care which comprised all the necessary ingredients for the natural treatment of body, mind and spirit. During the seven-year training period every student was expected to complete, equal emphasis was placed upon theoretical and practical aspects of Ayurveda. The pupil who displayed an aptitude for one but not the other was regarded as 'a bird with only one wing' and considered unworthy of further instruction.

Dissection of the human body was also part of this training— long before other early medical institutions taught anatomy. Again the *vaidas*' knowledge of botany enabled them to devise an ingenious method to prepare the cadaver for anatomical study. Carefully wrapped in a certain type of grass, it was then concealed on the river bank. In four or five days the skin had fallen away and exposed for the students' inspection all the veins, arteries and muscles still perfectly intact.

Ayurvedic physicians were also taught certain surgical procedures. The *Sushruta Samhita* was one of the earliest manuscripts to describe surgical operations (using narcotics as anaesthesia). It included instructions, for example, for the rebuilding of the human nose by incorporating a flap of skin from the patient's forehead, a procedure used today by modern plastic surgeons.

At the end of his training the Ayurvedic student was given a qualifying examination. The following anecdote illustrates exactly the quality of graduate the examiner was seeking. After passing his written tests without difficulty, an Ayurvedic student called Jivaka was taken by his tutor out into the country and given a spade. Using a small hill as the centrepoint of a one-mile area, he was told to bring to his teacher all the plants he could find which had *no* medicinal value. For close on a week Jivaka diligently searched the prescribed area. Then, with reluctance, he returned to his examiner and admitted that he could not find a single plant which did not have some medicinal value for one disease or another. Satisfied that his pupil had learned his final lesson, the examiner declared Jivaka qualified.

* * *

The people of Borli Panchatan are fortunate when it comes to health care. Before Dr Adhikari came in 1935, they had a resident Ayurvedic practitioner in the person of Dada Sahib Kulkarni. When he died, they had already become used to Dr Adhikari's more modern forms of treatment. But for three more decades no other doctors came to the village.

In the early years of independence, although a new generation of doctors trained in Western methods graduated from medical schools up and down the country, few chose to grapple with the multiple disadvantages of rural practice. Their training had proved costly and, once qualified, these ambitious young doctors wanted lucrative city appointments. They also wanted to practise medicine where they had the backing of modern medical facilities such as hospitals and laboratories. And the final deterrent was the education of their children; the inferior quality of village schools was not good enough for them.

So although eighty per cent of the Indian population lived in villages, most continued to lack a source of primary health care and had to rely on occasional visits from mobile medical units.

But just as in his day Dr Adhikari had felt it his duty to return to practise in the area where he had been born and brought up, thirty years later another orthodox practitioner whose roots belonged in Borli settled there.

In 1934 when the Kolaba peninsula was still ruled over by the nawab of Jungira, opportunities for educated Hindus were mostly limited to clerical jobs in the nawab's administrative offices. But from an early age, Nilkanth Joshi aspired to greater things.

I was born and raised in Diwaga, which in those days was a very poor place. When I was six, I attended the primary school in Borli and used to walk the one mile there and back each day. But during the rainy season, the road across the paddyfields always turned to mud and although I tried to go, I kept losing my *chappals*. As my parents couldn't afford always to be buying me new footwear, I had to stop at home. In this way I missed a lot of schooling and had to work very hard to catch up with my classmates.

In my childhood there was no doctor in Diwaga and I remember how my mother suffered, because she was often ill with some kind of gynaecological problem. When she needed Dr Adhikari, it was sometimes two or three days before he could visit because he was the only doctor all the way from Borli to Shriverdhan. So I made a vow that when I grew up I would become a doctor, even though I didn't know how this could happen. When I was nearing the end of my schooling, a good Muslim neighbour put in a word for me with the nawab and he made it possible for me to go to Pune and sit the entrance examination to medical school. To my joy, I was accepted.

I received my medical degree in 1960 when I was twenty-six. At this time all my fellow graduates were deciding to set up in big towns and cities. When they heard I intended to go back to my home village to work amongst my own people, they laid bets that I would never achieve this ideal. But I was determined. There was only one unexpected difficulty to my plan. During my last year in college I met a lady student from Ratnagiri, who was a year junior to me. We liked each other a lot. When we talked, we shared the same hopes for the future. Vasudha also wanted to help country people when she qualified. But of course, our parents had already arranged marriage partners for us. So what could we do?

Well, Vasudha had an uncle who was a doctor. She felt he might be sympathetic to how we felt and willing to engage in a little subterfuge in order to help us. Luckily, he agreed. This uncle went to Vasudha's parents and said just by chance he'd heard about a very promising young doctor who was anxious to find a wife who was also a medical graduate wanting to go into rural practice. Was there a remote possibility that his niece Vasudha might be interested in such a suitor? Needless to say, Vasudha was careful not to be too enthusiastic when she condescended to meet this 'unknown person'. So that is how we got our way without upsetting the family!

Government regulations for newly-qualified doctors insisted that before going into private practice they spend two years in a hospital appointment. Nilkanth Joshi was sent as medical officer to a small government dispensary west of Shriverdhan. Before taking up this position he and Vasudha got married. Then Vasudha Joshi went off to a post-graduate internship at a rural infirmary at Satar. But while they served their separate two-year government appointments, they were making plans for their married life together.

Dr Joshi instructed his brother-in-law at Diwaga to supervise the construction of two small double-storey buildings on a piece of ground not a stone's throw from Dr Adhikari, one to be the Joshis' family home, the other to house an out-patient clinic, dispensary and, upstairs, a six-bed hospital. Towards the end of 1962, the young couple arrived in Borli to begin their medical careers.

Nilkanth Joshi was no stranger to the people, but he had been away for seven years. The villagers remembered the boy but did not know the man. In the way of country people, they gave their new doctor a luke-warm reception. They did not quite know what to make of his wife. Although a large painted sign outside the clinic proclaimed both their qualifications, none of the villagers had any experience of women as medical practitioners and for a long time they did not believe that Vasudha was a doctor.

We set up a table in our new clinic, and from eight in the morning until ten or eleven at night, my husband and I used to sit waiting for patients. Some came to the door, stared at us for a while and then went away. A few came to consult us, but only about very trivial complaints. We knew they were watching us—and especially watching me.

Then one of our servants told us that everybody thought I was the doctor's nurse. So after that we sat in different rooms. I expected the village women surely to prefer to have me examine and treat them and the male patients to go to my husband, but this wasn't so. Everyone went to Nilkanth, even our maternity cases. Nobody believed a woman could be a good doctor!

When the Joshis had been in the village for almost a month, they had still not been called to attend to any serious cases. One morning a man came running to the dispensary with an urgent message. 'Come quickly, doctor,' he cried, pulling at Dr Joshi's sleeve. 'My father is having very bad pains in his chest.'

Nilkanth fetched his bag and hurried after the man, down the back lane which led to the market-garden on the other side of the big mosque. Behind a farmer's *bungala* he found an old man calmly spreading rice-straw for his oxen. 'Are you the patient? You don't look very ill to me,' Nilkanth challenged, struggling to catch his breath. The old man spat on the ground and, fixing Dr Joshi with a penetrating gaze, replied: 'You are quite right, Sahib. I enjoy excellent health. But now I know and my neighbours also know, that if ever we want you in a hurry, you won't let us down.'

Vasudha Joshi's acceptance by the villagers was a more gradual process. As the months passed, she was occasionally called to maternity cases, but all too frequently found that inexpert attention had already jeopardised the infant's life.

When we first came to Borli the main problem was infant mortality. Out of every three babies born, one used to die at birth. So I wanted to see why this happened. Normal deliveries always took place in the house, and in this village there was just one old woman who used to attend the mother. So I went into some houses to observe what she was doing. This woman would come straight from her work in the fields to help with the birth. Without even washing her hands, she would cut the umbilical cord with rusty scissors and tie it off with dirty string. No wonder half these babies succumbed to tetanus.

Now we had one young girl at the dispensary learning to be our nurse. Whenever I sent her to help with a home confinement, there was no problem because she'd been instructed to use clean scissors and string which had first been disinfected. So we called the old midwife and explained to her that dirt was the cause of so many babies dying when she attended their births. She got so angry with us. She said such deaths were the will of the gods.

Sometimes we managed to save these babies with anti-tetanus vaccine, but usually by the time the mothers brought their sick infants to our clinic they'd stopped suckling and were much too ill to be innoculated. In any case, I dare not give injections because then the people would say my needle had killed the child! So what I had to do was insist that, if a woman wanted me to deliver her baby, she must come to our hospital. Well, after that I got no calls at all. People didn't trust me as a doctor and preferred to trust that old woman.

But just before the first rainy season after our arrival in Borli, everything changed. It happened like this.

One day, after sitting the whole time at my table and only treating one man with a cut hand, Nilkanth and I finally locked the clinic and went to bed. We hadn't been asleep long before there was this tremendous banging on the door and outside in the pouring rain stood a *tonga* (horse-drawn carriage). I could see steam coming off the horse's neck so knew the driver had been forcing it to hurry.

Well, it had brought that old midwife, and although I'd told her we wanted nothing more to do with her, she begged me to help. Her granddaughter was having her first labour and although the baby's head had been presented for many hours, it would not be born. She feared the young mother was going to die. Nilkanth told me to get the flashlight and go ahead in the *tonga*. He'd rouse our house-boy and follow in the ox-cart, because in those days we didn't have our jeep.

By the time my husband arrived at the woman's house, I had delivered the baby with forceps and was putting stitches in the mother. That was the first time people came to understand I was a proper doctor, not just a nurse!

When the mains electricity supply was brought to Borli late in 1963, the Joshi Clinic was one of the first to be connected to the village grid, an ugly structure not unlike a guillotine erected just below the municipal well.

The villagers now had two modern amenities intended to improve the quality of their lives; piped water and electricity. But just as the water taps were invariably broken, so also the new electricity supply was notoriously unreliable. Nevertheless, it was brought in the name of rural progress, even though to begin with few could afford the privilege. The actual electricity was cheap enough. It was the installation of the meters which was expensive. Initially, only government buildings in Borli, some of the larger shops and a dozen or so private houses were connected. A decade later, most homes had electric lighting, but another five years passed before village homes had both lighting and power points.

The advent of electricity revolutionised the treatments that village doctors were able to give. At last they could refrigerate vaccines and other perishable medicaments, instead of having to send to Shriverdhan for them—a journey of several hours, which, in some instances, turned into a life-or-death mission when vaccines for rabies or snake-bites were urgently needed. Power for refrigerators meant that a small reserve of these antidotes was always available.

Assured of a supply of anti-tetanus serum, the Joshis decided to offer immunisation to all the pregnant women in Borli, in the hope of reducing the appallingly high incidence of neo-natal deaths. In theory, this was an excellent move; in practice, it was doomed to failure for reasons which soon became apparent.

In order to protect the unborn from the ravages of an un-hygienic delivery, women needed three injections spaced across the first three months of pregnancy. But in point of fact, few women actually realised their condition until well into the second trimester, when it was too late for immunisation to begin.

The second drawback to any form of mass immunisation, whether for tetanus or for the other major diseases, such as polio, cholera and typhoid, hinged upon the problem of malnutrition. People suffering from undernourishment did not react to im-munisation by producing the expected antibodies. What they needed was food, not medicine. Malnutrition was frequently caused by intestinal worms caught by drinking polluted water; to alleviate the symptoms without providing a clean water supply was not the solution.

Of course, people had been told to boil their water before drinking it. Once again, the social problems compounded the medical ones. Boiling water required extra fuel and, as wood became increasingly scarce, and expensive, people economised by saving wood to cook food not water—and suffered the con-sequences. In truth, it was impossible to isolate medical problems from social, economic and even ecological ones, as the judicious practitioners of Ayurvedic medicine had always known.

* * *

Towards the end of the monsoon period, cases of cholera and typhoid often occurred in the village, and occasionally there were more serious outbreaks. The doctors had the preventive vaccines, but the message of innoculation had little meaning for people who could not grasp the connection between an injection given when they were healthy and the possibility of sickness in the future. This lack of understanding was parti-cularly true of polio, a disease which started to appear in Borli as soon as there was a free exchange of traffic between the village and inland cities.

The disease mostly affected children and especially young babies. But the doctors could get supplies of Salk vaccine from Bombay and did their best to explain to village parents that in order to protect their children from this disease, they must be given the immunisation at the age of six weeks.

Because infant diarrhoea and slight fevers were an accepted part of normal development, village parents did not connect an episode of infant fever with the paralysis which only showed months later when the child began to walk. And because they could not relate the first event to the second, their response to the idea of infant immunisation was less than enthusiastic. Then an incident occurred which changed their minds, and which brought tragedy to the lives of the very people trying to help them.

Three years after they arrived in Borli, the Joshis' first child—a daughter—was born, followed two years later by a son. At the time, Nilkanth's widowed mother lived with them, competently taking charge of all the household affairs in order that the two doctors were free to attend to their patients.

In 1968, the year their son was born, there was a serious outbreak of polio in Borli and, with scarcely time to eat or sleep, the two doctors did their best to cope with an inundation of house calls, soon exhausting their supplies of Salk vaccine. When the Joshis' small son developed a slight fever and diarrhoea, his parents thought it was nothing serious. Their son's condition seemed so mild and there were so many calls on their time that in the end they decided not to undertake the three-day round journey to Bombay for further supplies of the vaccine. It was a decision they lived to regret. Within the week their small son's fever had subsided, and they congratulated themselves that all was well. Months afterwards, when the boy started to take his first steps, they saw that his right foot was paralysed.

Ironically, it was this personal tragedy which finally brought home to the villagers the message which no amount of propaganda had managed to achieve. Thereafter they started coming forward for innoculations—for polio and for the other infectious diseases which modern drugs could prevent.

But there was a much more persistent health problem in Borli which the doctors were powerless to prevent. Amongst the Muslim community, especially the women, tuberculosis was a widespread complaint. Not only did the custom of *purdah* mean that Muslim women were confined to the house for long periods, but whenever they ventured out, cloaked from head to foot in their long black *bourkas*, they were prevented from getting exposure to health-giving sunlight. Other Muslim habits also increased vulnerability to consumption. They liked to sleep rolled up in blankets and several to one bed; when one member of the family got the disease, it invariably spread to others. The habit of expectorating and blowing the nose on to the floor greatly aggravated the risk of respiratory infection.

With early diagnosis, tuberculosis could be successfully treated with modern sulphur drugs. To persuade an infected family to adopt a lifestyle which would prevent the disease recurring was, however, virtually impossible. Such advice inevitably encroached upon religious beliefs. Older and un-educated Muslims strenuously resisted change. All the village doctors could hope for was the eventual co-operation of a more liberal-minded younger generation.

For the doctors of Borli, there never was a quick and easy way to overcome ignorance, superstition and poverty. Certainly, after several years in the village, the crusading ideals which had brought Nilkanth and Vasudha Joshi to Borli often faltered.

> Sometimes we felt that however hard we tried to teach the simple lessons of basic hygiene and sanitation, we were banging our heads against a brick wall. Then, by and by, we ourselves had to learn to accept that it wasn't a question of the people being stubborn to new ideas. The villagers had lived the same way for hundreds of years. How could we expect to come along and change all this in five minutes?

The one disease which above all linked the villagers to their ancient past still occurred in Borli. When a patient came to her consulting room displaying suspicious white skin blotches, Vasudha Joshi had to consider the possibility that the diagnosis might be leprosy. There was a simple, but reliable, little test she used to decide one way or another. After extinguishing a lighted match, she touched the hot match-head against the blemish. If the patient flinched, she felt reasonably certain that he had not got the disease.

> The leprosy virus creates areas which are quite insensitive to pain. That is why I use my match-stick test. The person who has the disease never feels when he is being hurt or damaged, even when he suffers knocks or burns or crushing accidents. Therefore he neglects to protect himself, then infections occur on the skin and that is how the well-known disfigurements are caused. If the disease has settled in the extremities, which it often does, the patient cannot feel pain in those parts. Some-times I've known patients lose fingers and toes because at night, when they were asleep in their huts, they never knew if rats or mice were eating them!

Nowadays a team of specialists travels to rural areas treating lepers who refuse to go into sanatoria with new drugs, like Dapsone. So perhaps one day leprosy, like smallpox, will become a disease of the past. Meantime, people here are very harsh with somebody who gets this disease. They still believe leprosy is catching, although we tell them that this is not true. The sick person is always turned out of his home—maybe out of the village. He must live alone and beg for his bread, and there is nothing we can do to stop this cruel practice.

Rabies was another age-old disease which had been with the peninsular people for as long as they could remember. All carnivores were potential carriers of hydrophobia. Despite the risk, Borli had a large population of pye dogs, mainly because it also had a large population of rats. Indeed, with no other means of sustenance, the pye dogs had to catch and eat rats in order to survive. The dogs were utterly miserable creatures, with barrel-shaped bodies on thin legs, with large erect ears, long skinny tails and bulbous yellow eyes. Only a scant covering of sandy-coloured hair grew on their leathery hides which were invariably covered with open sores.

Pye dogs were everywhere, skulking in the lanes, stretched out in the shade of buildings, their tongues lolling and infested by flies. Usually they were ignored, but sometimes—and for no apparent reason—people subjected the dogs to bouts of stone-throwing and stick-beating, as if part of their usefulness was to provide entertainment or convenient targets for the venting of human frustrations. If, as occasionally happened, a dog turned and bit someone, it was immediately killed. Even if the dogs did not thrive, they certainly multiplied to such an extent that periodically the village elders had to send to Shriverdhan for the trappers, occasions which Ummie recalled with disgust.

These men go about the village and, when they see a dog, they throw it a piece of poisoned bread. Dogs are always hungry, so they eat this bread. Then they go away to sleep. When they wake their legs is paralysed and they can't hardly walk. They stagger this way and that. Then we see them lie down and shiver. Then they die.

Many dogs are killed in this way. Last time the trappers came to Borli, three dead dogs was in the lane outside my house. Those municipality men should have dug a big hole in a field and buried the dogs, but they were too lazy to do that. Instead, they got an ox-cart and tied ropes round the necks of the dead dogs and dragged them off down the Karlia road to the countryside. Then they threw them in a gully and left them there. Then people wonder why they get sick so often.

It is those flies which get on the rotting animals and then come into the village to sit on our food. But that is the way those trappers go on. They don't seem to have much good sense.

But still with the choice of being infested by either dogs or rats, the people chose the former, accepting that the occasional case of hydrophobia was the price they had to pay. Confronted with patients who had been bitten, Nilkanth Joshi had no alternative but to give a course of rabies vaccine.

As the dog was always killed when it bit someone, we could not check to see if it was indeed infected. So to be on the safe side, I always gave HDC vaccine. The treatment lasts for thirteen or fourteen weeks with weekly injections under the abdominal wall. It is very painful for the patient. But we have to give it. Otherwise, if the patient has been infected, it is a death sentence.

I was called to a lady in the village who had pneumonia and, when I examined her, I saw there was a small scar on her leg. When I asked the family for the story, they told me about twenty days back the woman was bitten by a dog. So then I knew there was nothing I could do except give her supportive treatment. In a few more days the woman could not swallow anything, so I put her on intravenous glucose. She was trying to bite those who were looking after her so she had to be strapped to the bed. If she had injured any of them, they too would have been infected. For about five days she made a howling noise, just like a dog. Then she had a very bad death.

Now there's an improved vaccine. Only three injections are required, but unfortunately this is too expensive to use in the village. Just recently one of my relations was bitten by a rabid dog and I sent him to Bombay to get this new treatment. Each injection cost him Rs 350 whereas the old vaccine only costs Rs 30 for the whole course.

If people co-operate with us, we can save them, but still when they get bitten by a mad dog, they go to the country medicine man instead of coming straight to us. The *fakir* takes some earth and hair from the animal that caused the bite. Then he says some prayers and binds this mixture on the patient's wound. People believe that the hair of the dog will cure them. And of course, if that dog didn't have rabies, then it certainly will!

What we are always trying to tell people is that if they want to keep a dog they should give it anti-rabies injections. But nobody troubles to follow this advice. They don't want the expense.

* * *

In Borli illegitimate children are unknown and unwanted babies a rarity. With large extended families and plenty of good neighbours, the sound of a child crying means one of two things. Either it is hurt or it is ill, and the first is unlikely due to the care lavished on all small children. Children are considered to be a blessing and the childless woman one who must have been bewitched at her wedding.

When a Hindu girl got her first period, it used to be the custom for her to go into the woods, pick a bundle of leaves and then walk home with it balanced on her hip, as if it were a baby. It was supposed that this simple magical formula guaranteed the girl's future fertility. In some Hindu homes a menstruating woman, referred to as 'a woman in flower' (the fruit to follow at its appointed time) was barred from certain duties. She was not permitted to fetch water or prepare and serve food to her family. And she had to keep away from fields where crops were growing for fear she might poison them. Lastly, because a menstruating woman was considered to be extremely toxic, coitus was taboo in case the contact poisoned her husband.

Hindu peasants were reputed to practise sexual intercourse at least twice if not three times each day, an act considered to be 'the sowing of the seed in its proper place'. According to popular belief, it was one way to limit conception on the grounds that 'grass that is well trodden doesn't grow'!

Although the women produced a fair number of children, a large proportion did not survive more than a few years; six children in a peasant family was fairly average. Nor were parents altogether unmindful of the need to use some form of contraception. In the old days, a preparation from the roots of a plant called *katai* was used as a fertility barrier; very conveniently, flowers from the same source also formed the basis for an elixir highly valued as an aphrodisiac.

If the birth of a Hindu peasant baby left much to be desired in matters of hygiene, the mother's labour was competently stage-managed by those who knew exactly what had to be done to give her every physical and moral support. When the mother's pains began, one of the two assistants would dip a hand in oil and press it against the wall of the hut. If five fingers were clearly imprinted, the mother was assured that she was going to have an easy labour. Thus, psychologically fortified, the woman settled herself on the floor and relaxed while the assistants massaged her all over with coconut oil, occasionally interrupting this soothing task to thump the mother's back each time contractions came.

When it was judged that the birth was imminent, one assistant kneeled behind to support the mother's shoulders while the other, after placing a cloth on the floor to receive the baby, sat opposite the mother and placing her feet on the insides of the woman's thighs, forced her legs apart. Once the baby was born, if the placenta did not quickly follow, the assistant behind stuffed the mother's mouth with her own hair. As she struggled to spit it out, the placenta was also ejected. Before scissors became available, the umbilical cord was severed with a piece of bamboo or a shard of pottery. Then a hole was dug in the floor on the spot the baby was born, the afterbirth buried in it and a fire set over the top.

When a woman experienced a difficult labour, the Hindu people had a remedy. A hole was cut in the roof directly above where the mother sat and a virgin girl dispatched to the well to fetch a *hunda* of water. Then a man climbed on the roof and carefully poured it through the opening into the woman's upturned mouth. After three mouthfuls her labour was supposed to continue without further trouble. If this failed, another person went to the nearest lightning tree to bring back a piece of dead wood. Once set fire to and held close to the pregnant woman so she could feel its warmth, her labour was said to proceed immediately to its natural conclusion.

The love and attention which villagers bestowed upon the youngest members of their families made them, naturally, unwilling candidates for the national birth control campaigns which began in 1956. Reducing the size of a family in order to raise the standard of living for future generations was the ideal behind the concerted efforts of para-medical teams, which toured the country for the next two decades.

With the aid of simple posters and film-slides, the use of artificial birth control techniques was explained to the Hindu people. But, in homes where standards of hygiene were minimal, it was found that the risk of infections resulting from the use of condoms and interuterine devices made these impracticable.

Contraceptive pills also proved unreliable in the hands of the illiterate because, although illustrated packaging helped the woman keep track of the daily dosage, it did not help her keep track of when, in her own menstrual cycle, doses were supposed to be suspended. Furthermore, when a country woman ran out of supplies, unless there was a local government dispensary, she had no means of replenishing them. Such methods were much too complicated for the average Hindu peasant woman. They were also totally alien to her strong maternal instincts.

So campaigners switched the emphasis to sterilisation, offering financial incentives to encourage 'volunteers'. Again, it was a scheme which ran into difficulties. Word soon got about that vasectomy not only destroyed a man's virility, but it also sapped his physical strength with the result that he could no longer earn a living. In a nutshell, sterilisation was a slow form of suicide. So government doctors resorted to less direct tactics. Nilkanth Joshi recalled the stratagem used by a colleague anxious to boost attendance at his vasectomy camp clinic in Diswali.

He let it be known that if a man agreed to come for a simple injection, he would pay Rs 20 to that person. In no time he had a line of men waiting outside his tent. So one by one he got them to lie on his surgery table. Then he counted out the money and gave the injection. But it was really a local anaesthetic, which enabled him to perform the small vasectomy incision without the patients being any the wiser!

Nowadays when a woman accepts voluntary sterilisation, the health authorities pay her Rs 135, which is quite a lot of money. But few come forward for this operation. If the woman has no children, or loses those she already has, will the state look after this woman and her husband when they grow old? I think not.

Indian birth control propaganda programmes have largely failed to halt the population explosion and by 1984 the population had reached 700 million. Had these ventures been conducted hand-in-hand with widespread social reforms such as the creation of employment opportunities and pension schemes, they might have succeeded in at least stabilising the population growth. In fact, what happened was a lengthy episode of a somewhat confused bureaucracy. As improved medical services were put to work on reducing the national incidence of neo-natal morbidity—and largely succeeded—birth control campaigners laboured to reduce the size of families—and largely failed! The Hindu peasant continued to 'sow his seeds in the proper place', and every birth in the village was greeted with uninhibited joy.

Muslims also ignored the gospel of the birth control missionaries who from time to time arrived in the village and set up their 'camps' with explicit anatomical diagrams and rubber goods. The Muslim reaction expressed by Noor Pangaka, a Borli timber merchant, represented the views of all orthodox followers of Islam.

How can we listen to talk of limiting the number of children we have? Must I be responsible for the destruction of other souls so only two of my children may have life? Children come from God. God created everything in this world for us, and he will also provide for the children he sends, however many that may be.

Look at me! I'm here with a chance in life because my father did not use contraceptives. We can only obey God's laws. Our destiny is already written by God. We never question this.

However, certain extenuating circumstances did entitle a Muslim woman to break the Islamic groundrules. Should her health be threatened by continual pregnancies, she could (with her husband's consent) seek contraceptive advice. The possibility that this might lead to relegation as wife number two was a chance she had to take. But, as already mentioned, absentee husbands working overseas achieved family limitations which no amount of government propaganda could induce.

* * *

There was, in Borli, a Muslim farmer who undoubtedly regretted—for purely financial reasons—his fourth son's remarkable fecundity which could not be solved by sending him abroad to work. The young man in question was a well-known personality in the village. Although a childhood illness robbed him of both speech and hearing, Hassan grew up to be an intelligent, cheerful and well-liked young man who managed to communicate by expansive gestures and yelping noises. He also became a proficient lip-reader.

Once Hassan was old enough to handle his father's ox-cart he took on the task of village water-carrier. Each year, when water supplies ran dry, Hassan went to the river to fill two large oil-drums, his piercing birdlike calls a familiar sound on the lanes as he peddled the water to householders for Rs 2 a gallon.

After his three elder brothers had married and gone overseas, Hassan waited to see what his father would do about finding him a wife. In due course a poor family in Dighi were persuaded to give their youngest daughter in marriage. The young couple settled down to live with Hassan's parents and three other daughters-in-law. As year succeeded year, Hassan's progeny increased apace so not only did the family home become over-crowded, but Hassan's father also began to resent the responsibility of so many new mouths to feed. After the arrival of the seventh grandchild, the old man decided the time had come to intervene.

He told Hassan he knew of a Bombay doctor who might be

able to cure his disability with a small operation. Only too anxious to co-operate, Hassan accompanied his father to the city for the required medical examination. Leaving his son to wait outside, the old man went alone to the doctor's consulting room and, after explaining that his grandchildren were proving too much of a financial burden, asked if the doctor could do something to help. The doctor agreed that this was possible, providing he had Hassan's consent. So Hassan was called in and told to climb on the examination couch. When the doctor mouthed the words: 'Do you agree to this small operation?' the young man eagerly nodded his head.

When Hassan eventually realised his father's trickery, his indignation knew no bounds. Needless to say, all attempts to gain the sympathy of his village neighbours involved gesticulations which kept their cheeks running with tears of laughter for many moons afterwards.

* * *

As their practice became established, the Joshis purchased a jeep, the first of its kind in the district. On rough hilly roads it was the ideal vehicle and, should house-calls reveal someone in need of more intensive attention, the jeep provided rapid transport back to the Joshi hospital.

During the monsoon, Nilkanth Joshi's jeep fared little better than any other form of wheeled vehicle.

One day in the rainy season I was called to a patient's home in Karlia. When I reached the river's edge, the bridge was submerged. Usually the river was about two feet deep but that day it was nipple-high with strong currents. So I had to be carried across by a Katkari.

When the river is running deep, these people act as ferrymen. They are small, but very sturdy and can lift more than their own weight. A Katkari man weighing 50 kilos could easily carry someone of 60 kilos on his shoulders through the water.

When roads were made impassable by mud and flooding, the old-fashioned curtained litters also came into their own for bringing sick people to the Joshi hospital, which in those early days provided somewhat rudimentary facilities. Upstairs, a low-raftered room with board floors was furnished with half a dozen iron bedsteads with thin cotton mattresses, an equal number of iron cribs for the newborn and metal folding chairs. Behind this main room two small cells, with examination couches and glass-fronted instrument cupboards on the damp-stained walls, served as delivery rooms. Dust, stirred by passing traffic, covered every surface with a silken patina, and flies and even the occasional venturesome crow enjoyed easy access through the iron-barred windows.

Patients wore ordinary clothes in bed (this being the custom in homes also) and, although the doctors had several Hindu girls to act as nurses, the bed-bound relied on relatives to feed and wash them. There were always large numbers in attendance, infecting the atmosphere of disinfectant with smells of hot spiced foods and sweat.

In the out-patient clinic below, the doctors seemed totally unperturbed by the constant presence of people jostling in the open doorways to their respective consulting rooms. Privacy (a very un-Indian word) played no part in the public drama of ill-health. When, as often occurred, a patient received an injection, with one accord the audience gasped and grimaced with graphic empathy!

Medicines were dispensed on the premises by young assistants in khaki jackets, who had also been trained by the doctors. Working behind a high wooden counter plastered with posters for dried milk and vitamin supplements, they presided over shelves crowded with dusty bottles and tins. Pills were counted out by hand and deftly parcelled in pages torn from old school exercise books, ointments scooped from large containers into smaller ones and liquid concoctions decanted into bottles, which were then corked and shaken vigorously before being handed over in exchange for cash.

A substantial number of the Joshis' patients were both illiterate and impecunious; treatment was given on a strict cash basis. Accordingly, both doctors had on their tables a cash-box and ledger. However, whenever they came up against a case of genuine hardship, the only payment they received was often some rice or fruit or the promise of a service to be rendered at a future date. In this way, a bond of mutual trust and respect was gradually forged between the village people and their new doctors.

Without so many of the modern facilities enjoyed by their city equivalents, the Joshis were nonetheless constantly reminded of their professional limitations.

> Nilkanth used to day-dream about having an X-ray unit and ready access to a blood-bank; even the possibility of putting glass in the clinic windows to keep out the dust.
>
> I had another dream. Whenever I lost a patient who needed a Caesarean section I felt terribly frustrated because I didn't have the qualification to perform what is really quite a simple

operation. One day I vowed to return to college and take a post-graduate degree in obstetric surgery.

One episode above all reinforced this resolve in the mind of young Vasudha Joshi.

* * *

On each occasion that her four daughters became pregnant for the first time, they gravitated back to Ummie's old house in the village, wanting their confinements to take place under the same roof that had sheltered them during the many privations they had once endured together. The cavernous roof and unplastered walls seemed to emanate a tangible sense of strength and security, which each of them found exceedingly comforting at the moment of parturition. And, of course, there was also the presence of Ummie, providing the same indomitable fortitude which had sustained them throughout their childhood.

A month before her first child was due, Aisha asked her husband's permission to travel to Borli for her confinement. As she stepped off the bus to be reunited with Ummie and Halima, the three Muslim women shed tears of happiness. That same night, Aisha woke in the big *palang* in Ummie's bedroom and nudged her mother awake, begging her to go and fetch a light. In the flame of the *buttee*, where Aisha had been lying there was a pool of blood.

It was late May 1965; the rainy season had made a brief appearance and then disappeared. When the emerald squares of rice seedlings in the corners of every paddyfield began to turn a sickly yellow, it was time to call out the local rainmakers. Like carol singers from the Western world, the Muslim children put on long white dresses and carrying saucers of burning incense, trouped from house to house, pausing at each to sing prayers begging the heavens for deliverance. A day later it was the turn of a group of lusty Hindu men and boys from Diwaga. Stripped to the waist, they performed gyrations on the lanes of Borli, stamping their feet in the dust and shouting noisy incantations to the accompaniment of bells and drums.

Not three days afterwards, as Ummie made her way up through the village to the Joshi Clinic, a brisk breeze stirred the humid night air and suddenly the beam of her 'battery' was fractured by spears of driving rain. Undeterred, she hurried on, following the long farmworkers' lane, until just below the village compound it forked right to pass directly in front of the little hospital.

Half an hour later, after examining Aisha, Vasudha Joshi took Ummie aside. 'Your daughter is unfortunate. The afterbirth has grown in the wrong place and is causing this bleeding. Let her sleep now, and tomorrow we must discuss the best thing to do.'

By next afternoon, despite treatment to try and staunch the haemorrhage, Aisha's condition suddenly worsened. As Ummie repeatedly changed the blood-drenched towels, she whispered prayers for her daughter. Halima was sent to Diwaga to fetch Amina, who arrived with her husband. After an urgent consultation with both the Joshis, it was decided that Aisha's only chance was to be taken back to Bombay with all possible haste.

At that time the route inland was in a very bad state and the rains made it even more treacherous. I told Ummie to ask her son-in-law to find a lorry and half fill it with coconuts to prevent it bouncing about too much on the way, but it was evening before this truck came to the door. We put a *charpoy* on top of the nuts for Aisha and covered her over with a tarpaulin. Ummie and Amina sat beside her and, after I'd given the girl a sedative, I climbed up beside the driver to make sure he drove as carefully as possible.

In darkness and rain, the truck jolted slowly along, often skidding on roads edged by nothing more than a sheer drop to the valley. Every so often Vasudha Joshi called a halt in order to examine her patient who, for the most part, was mercifully unconscious.

A full ten hours later, the truck pulled up outside a Bombay hospital. Willing hands quickly lifted down the *charpoy* and carried the woman inside. In an empty corridor dimly lit by a single dangling bulb, Ummie, Amina and Vasudha Joshi waited outside the operating theatre. They did not have long to wait. Within half an hour, a gowned nurse appeared briefly at the door, carrying a tightly-swaddled infant loudly proclaiming his indignation at such an untimely arrival!

It was dawn when Vasudha Joshi left Ummie and her daughters at the hospital to travel back to Borli on the coconut lorry. This time the journey was accomplished at speed, the driver reverting to a more customary and reckless style of driving, which involved hugging the crown of the road and only swerving at the last moment to avoid head-on collisions with approaching traffic.

After an absence of twenty hours, the truck reached the village and dropped Vasudha back at the clinic. Although soaked to the skin and exhausted, the young doctor felt strangely elated. Certainly this was partly due to the happy outcome of the night's events which could so easily have ended in tragedy, but there was also a more personal reason. In less than two months the Joshi doctors were expecting their first baby. And as she looked forward to motherhood, Vasudha Joshi felt positive that the birth of this child would mark an important turning-point in her medical career. Henceforth she knew that her commitment as a doctor in the village would be concentrated upon the health and welfare of the children—the next generation of hillside citizens.

❦ CHAPTER TEN ❦

ONCE A YEAR, on the village compound, the bicycle *yogi* performed his marathon ride. In a roped-off area lit by fluorescent tubes, for seven days and seven nights he pedalled round and round, simultaneously defying the laws of gravity, sleep and inertia.

Every so often assistants passed amongst the audience to make collections. Then, without once losing momentum, the young man added entertainment to this feat of endurance. Twisting his body, he rode backwards sitting on the handlebars or—to the evident delight of the onlookers—balanced his stomach on the saddle and pedalled with his hands. As the ride neared completion, hundreds turned out to witness the last dramatic moments as, in a state of trance, the *yogi* circled the arena, his bloodshot eyes fixed in an unseeing stare, his body caked with dust. On the seventh day, at the stroke of midnight, the assistants rushed forward to hold the bicycle. Slowly the *yogi* dismounted and instantly crumpled in a senseless heap. In awed silence the crowds parted to make way for stretcher-bearers. The still figure was hurried to the small government hospital at the opposite end of the compound, where a doctor waited to administer oxygen.

Next morning, attired in well-tailored slacks and slim-fit shirts, the *yogi* and his entourage caught the noon-day bus for Mahsla to set up their next performance.

But in the early 1980s the spectacle of the bicycle *yogi* was no competition for more sophisticated entertainments; by then both television and videos had reached the village.

At a glance there was nothing to advertise the fact that video shows were a feature of the Borli bazaar. Only tall aerials protruding from the rooftops of boarded-up shops revealed their 'secret' location as each evening, and with all the furtiveness of young men making their first visit to a brothel, patrons could be seen pushing open unmarked doors and disappearing into the darkness, to watch not 'blue' movies, but very probably a showing of Charlie Chaplin classics.

The cost of importing colour television equipment was phenomenal. Extremely heavy duty was levied on all foreign goods. However, this did not prevent village entrepreneurs from making a substantial profit on their investments even after paying a percentage to the local guardians of law and order. In India, as elsewhere, public video shows were illegal.

A scattering of privately-owned television sets also existed in Borli and Diwaga. Spindly aerials were an incongruous sight on raggedy pipe-tiled roofs; and the sound of test-match commentaries filtering out on to lanes where wooden-wheeled carts trundled past and women sat shaping cow-dung cakes to dry in the sun was similarly incongruous. Perhaps, on the other hand, it was the incongruity itself which had become a familiar feature of village life as the paraphernalia of Western cultures created bizarre contrasts between the old and the new, the natural and the patently artificial. The evidence was everywhere.

Opposite the *paan* stall in the bazaar was a sweet-shop selling bubble-gum. The sight of young children blowing lurid pink bubbles alongside someone squirting betel juice into the dust was not uncommon. Nor was the sight of Hindu peasants, perhaps with baskets of dung on their heads, wearing spectacles with heavy black 'executive'-type frames; or the local *saddu*, with saffron robes and flowing hair, buying indigestion tablets at the corner chemist; or the sound of a telephone ringing in the middle of the coconut gardens; or a new house, with real glass windows, built on a ricefield. These were some of the trivial, and not so trivial, signs that the peasant community had been sucked into the artificial trappings of a 'consumer society', and not by any means always to its best advantage.

In the bazaar where once only local produce was sold, people could now purchase a whole range of manufactured merchandise which nobody even realised they needed until it was there! Detergent washing powders, tinned goods, Typhoo Tips, packets of factory-made biscuits, fluoride toothpaste, plastic toys, aluminium kitchenware, fizzy drinks and cordials, white bread and sugar—at a glance, innocent enough commodities, but in quite unexpected ways capable of changing the intrinsic quality of village life. For instance, kitchen utensils made from aluminium or plastic undoubtedly deprived local potters and metalsmiths of trade. They also created another, less obvious difficulty. Without any organised system of refuse collection, broken plastic containers, bottles and worn-out aluminium ware were discarded in back lanes and ditches and created unsightly accumulations of litter which nobody did anything about.

The repercussions from the deleterious effect manufactured foodstuffs had on health were, however, even more serious. Sweets, fizzy drinks and ice-cream heavily laced with refined sugars caused widespread tooth decay amongst village children. Before, if this complaint was seen at all, it was almost exclusively associated with the old. The nearest dentist, at Mahsla, charged for treatment; he was also the only dental practitioner in an area of about 10,000 people.

The protracted effects of manufactured and processed foods did not stop at teeth. Once the craving for sugar was acquired it was followed by the villagers' preference for white flour and 'polished' rice, which gradually caused vitamin deficiencies requiring correction with expensive vitamin supplements.

Mahatma Gandhi had endeavoured to emphasise the importance of a diet which included the natural rice grain and to warn of the long-term dangers of refined foods introduced to India by Europeans. In a 1935 booklet called *Key To Health* he wrote: 'Machine-polished rice removes an overcoat rich in vitamins, especially B_1. Lacking these vitamins, Indians—for most of whom rice is the chief staple food—are subject to numerous debilitating diseases, notably beriberi. Hand-pounded rice retains this vitamin-rich coating.'

Gandhi also expatiated on the nutritional value of milk, bananas, fresh-leaf salads and the mango kernel, which he urged people to eat with the fruit to get the maximum nourishment from this widely available food. But the association between refined foods and the enviable lifestyle of the affluent was the indelible picture imprinted on the minds of the majority, as they struggled to achieve a better standard of living for themselves.

In Borli, money to spend on shop-bought luxuries, combined with a liking for foods cooked in *ghee* (clarified butter) and, for some, a largely sedentary life, brought health problems which doctors had not encountered before. Illnesses directly attributable to obesity, such as arthritis, diabetes and bronchitis, were common complaints; more serious was the increasing incidence of coronary heart disease, especially amongst Muslim people.

Paradoxically, the achievement of improved living standards turned out to have as many drawbacks as so-called deprivation! Certainly, the idea of going to rural areas such as Borli to practise private medicine was no longer regarded as an unrewarding proposition.

*　*　*

By 1984 Borli had six resident physicians, as well as specialist surgeons who regularly visited the village. Up on the main compound, the government free hospital, built in the mid-1960s and staffed by one medical officer, had recently been extended to provide a maternity wing. Dr Adhikari, although in his eighty-fourth year, still spent a few hours daily seeing patients. Out on the main bazaar road, two young Muslim doctors had recently set up in private practice.

Nilkanth and Vasudha Joshi, both now in their fifties, continued in their small private hospital to work as hard as ever for the people of Borli, some—if not all—of their youthful dreams having indeed materialised. First of these was the X-ray unit, which was installed in 1975 after Nilkanth had spent some time in Bombay studying the techniques with a friend who was a radiologist.

When I had my new jeep, I had to learn to drive it. So also did I have to learn to drive my X-ray machine. The difficult part was learning to read X-ray plates. This took several months of study. Every day I used to sit examining plates at my friend's clinic, and with the help of books also, I gradually obtained the information I needed.

After the machine was installed at Borli, for a while an X-ray technician from Bombay came to help me get accustomed to using it. Developing the plates was another skill I had to learn. A small storage room was converted into a dark room and that's how we managed.

As I'd always thought, having this X-ray facility was a valuable addition to our work in the village. Formerly patients had to go to Alibarg or Bombay for X-rays. With our machine we could get an immediate diagnosis, which was very important with cases of tuberculosis. Then we could start early treatment. The first day we used our X-ray equipment we had a grand opening ceremony. About eight hundred people gathered outside our hospital and the elders made speeches. Sad to say, it was the month of September. It rained all day and everybody got very wet!

In 1977, at the age of forty-six, Vasudha Joshi also realised her ambition to take a course in obstetric surgery, although she was reluctant to leave her husband to cope alone with the practice and their third, and youngest, child who was just starting school in the village. However, Nilkanth urged her to go, even though this meant she would be away from the village for two whole years. The two eldest Joshi children already shared an apartment in Pune, where they were attending college. Vasudha joined them for the duration of her studies.

All the post-graduate students were so much younger than me. It felt very strange to be back in the classroom, and even stranger to be living in a noisy city after so many years in Borli. And being a student again wasn't easy for me. I found the theoretical work extremely difficult, but luckily had no trouble with the practical side. In fact, my professors gave me many opportunities to assist with operations, so even before I got my degree I gained a wealth of valuable experience.

I came back to Borli in 1980, keen to practise my new skills, and quite soon a young woman with a pregnancy complication arrived at the hospital. Nilkanth X-rayed her and it was then quite obvious that the patient's pelvis was too small for a natural birth. I explained this to the girl's parents and said I would operate. To my disappointment, they refused to allow me to do this myself. Instead I had to agree to drive my patient to a senior obstetrician at Murud, a long way from here. Of course, this man knew I was qualified. When the girl was under the anaesthetic he said to me: 'Come on, you perform the operation and I'll assist.'

This surgeon was accustomed to performing classical Caesareans, not the lower segment method I'd been taught. He was much impressed with the new technique and the operation was quite successful. The young woman had beautiful twin girls. Of course, I told the grandparents I'd done the operation and they were quite happy. This way news got round that I was now a proper surgeon. Since then I've performed nearly fifty Caesareans here in the village, saving babies who might otherwise have died. So, no more long rides in coconut lorries, I'm glad to say!

After more than twenty years in the village, the Joshis were unable to live in any kind of professional isolation or indeed even confine their outside interests to their own circle of family and friends. By attending to the most intimate needs of so many villagers, the nature of their commitment ranged well beyond the consulting room.

There was one area of village life in particular which Vasudha Joshi's crusading spirit would not allow her to ignore.

We had so many educated women in Borli who, once their children were at school, sat at home all day with nothing much to do. To me this seemed such a dreadful waste of talents. So some of us got together and formed a committee to organise social occasions for these housewives and sometimes coach trips to places of special interest.

At first, my intention was to get house-bound women accustomed to going out and about on their own. Then we started to appeal to their social consciences and point out how valuable they could be to the community if they helped their less fortunate sisters by spreading the message of hygiene and discussing simple health matters. Changing the habits of older uneducated people has always been such an uphill task. I felt sure our women would be ideally suited for this kind of welfare work. We have an Indian saying that when you teach something to a husband, you teach one man; when you teach something to a wife, you teach a whole family. So you see, it was just a case of organising our own village feminine movement!

In other ways, also, future health care for the villagers gathered momentum, backed by the tireless enthusiasm of the Joshis. In the late 1970s they introduced regular medical checks for schoolchildren in order to identify and give early treatment to cases of diet deficiency, eye complaints and, especially, tuberculosis. On every alternate weekend the Joshis turned their clinic over to an eye surgeon from Pune who arrived late on Friday night. Beginning at daybreak on Saturday morning he carried out eye tests. Through the afternoon and evening he performed cataract operations using local anaesthesia. On Sunday morning, after packing up his instrument bag, he departed on the early bus.

In 1983, work started on a large extension to the Joshis' hospital. The two small buildings, which had existed side by side since their marriage, disappeared behind a spacious concrete façade, the upper level of the new wing, with its long tiled balcony, providing a ward of twenty beds and modern bathroom facilities. Below, a similar space enabled the doctors to increase the size of their consulting rooms and create a more comfortable waiting area for patients. Then, shortly before the 1984 monsoon set in, a lorry from Bombay brought a very precious straw-wrapped load to Borli; it carried sheets of glass to glaze the windows of the new Joshi hospital.

Once the new building was completed, Nilkanth Joshi went ahead with plans to stir community spirit amongst the un-educated men of Borli; the introduction of cess-pit sanitation and piped drains was long overdue in the homes of the workers.

> I began by asking some of these men to drop in during the evening for a chat about this and that. Then, whenever I saw my chance, I'd drop in a little item about health and hygiene, so in this way they could slowly absorb new ideas. Country people have always been afraid of change. This appears to be a threat to their security. But they understand common sense when they hear it. And once a village man grasps a new idea, he becomes a faithful convert. My concern is to make sure it is the right idea which is grasped, not the wrong one!

There is still no blood bank in the village and BCG vaccination, which could protect the villagers from tuberculosis, is too expensive to use in mass immunisation programmes. The unreliability of the local electricity supply has forced the doctors to buy their own portable generator and, whenever they need certain medicaments in a hurry, one or other of them has to make the arduous two-day round trip to the city, bringing back what is needed stored in chilled thermos flasks.

Today, as they have done for the past two decades or more, the Joshi couple work round the clock, perpetuating a commit-ment which, for Nilkanth Joshi, began in his youth.

> My life has been an ascending and descending graph. I began as a poor boy in Diwaga, went to school in Borli and, after matriculation, to medical college in Pune. When I qualified I began the return journey, so to speak, working first in Pune, then Diswali, then Borli.
>
> Now my one wish is to complete the graph by returning to live in Diwaga, where I will give my medical services free of charge to my people. In this way, my life will have come full circle.

* * *

Each evening, during the fine months, people like to promenade in the bazaar, using last-minute shopping as a pretext to catch up on local news and small talk. Fluorescent tubes besieged by flying insects illuminate the interiors of the little open-fronted shops, which also serve as convenient meeting-places for cups of tea and a gossip. Or small groups congregate on the crossroads which form the hub of the market, the buzz of conversation marking the end of another village day.

In February 1984, one particular topic was causing chins to wag. Yet another ricefield had been sold off for private building, this time just beyond the bridge on the northern side of Borli. And it was not so much the sale of the field which caused such intense interest, but the price paid for it by the Muslim brothers who owned the corner chemist next to the metal-worker's hovel. The sum involved was so exorbitant that nobody could mention it without an incredulous roll of the eyes.

The field in question fetched one and a half laks (about £9,000), and the construction of the dwelling planned for this site (according to the wife of one of the chemist brothers) would cost at least another three laks. Who would have thought, marvelled the loquacious, that so much wealth could be earned by selling laxatives, pills and bottles of iron tonic? Not that malice or indeed envy entered into this chatter. People respected anyone able to achieve prosperity in such unlikely surroundings. It reassured them to know that the possibility existed. The owner of this ricefield was a poor farmer who never had two paisas to rub together, and the village gossips were delighted at his good fortune. In an entire lifetime of toil this man and his family would never have been able to make so much money growing rice.

While private enterprise saw the gradual spread of village homes out beyond the tree-covered hillside on to the flat arable lands below Borli, by the 1980s there were also two government-sponsored housing projects for poor people in the area. One was the Katkari settlement on the Karlia road; the other was on the seashore side of the coconut gardens at the northern end of Diwaga, where, with a gesture of short-sighted magnanimity, a few acres of sand had been set aside to provide housing for the homeless. In a clearing surrounded by saw-edged *kiora* cactus, about a dozen two-roomed *bungala* had been sloppily erected on a strip of dunes with a glorious view of the bay. Except that each dwelling had been built with its back to the ocean—and for very good reasons.

From October to April the sea was deceptively blue and calm, with scarcely enough momentum to fulfil its appointed tides. During the rainy months these same waters became transformed into an expanse of boiling activity which was crowned by perpetual clouds of spray coloured by indiscriminate rainbows whenever the sun appeared. After only one monsoon, unpredictably high tides inundated the new Hindu housing estate, forcing the occupants to seek shelter elsewhere.

The Katkari settlement, however, was perched inland on a choice piece of hillside, facing west and protected from prevailing winds by the curving embrace of higher ground. But apart from these two government concerns, local property development remained in the hands of private enterprise; and once rumours, which had for some time been circulating in the bazaar, congealed into hard facts, land prices started to rise. The first rumours that the area was to become the focal point for industrial development began in 1980. By 1984 preliminary construction work had already started at the Dighi end of the peninsula. After centuries of virtual isolation, the people were suddenly confronted by the kind of changes which, even in their wildest dreams, they could never have envisaged.

Bombay, only eighty kilometres away by sea, had always been India's premier port. The port facilities, however, proved increasingly inadequate for the huge volume of traffic it needed to handle. So the authorities prospected for another suitable coastal location to develop and soon pinpointed the deep sheltered waters of the Rajpuri creek at Jungira-Murud.

By 1984 work had already begun on jetties, which would begin to turn the creek into a major port by the end of the decade. Inevitably, this expansion was only the beginning. Other industrial concerns, to support and exploit the new shipping centre, would follow. Plans for a new road system were part of the government blueprint for the area, also a rail link, even an airstrip on a flat hilltop near Dighi. Foundries, workshops, factories, cold-storage, trucking and container terminals—the list of developments was endless, as massive government and private investments transformed the lives of farmers and fishermen.

The proposed railway link with inland India meant that Borli would at last have an excellent outlet for local produce. Ravi Kulkarni predicted the construction of canning factories to deal with fruit crops, such as mangoes and jackfruit, as well as fish, and other incentives to give a fresh impetus to local farming.

People here must turn their attention to cash crops to send to the cities instead of just growing for their own needs. When we get improved water supplies to the district, then properly constructed irrigation systems will enable two crops of rice a year. This has been done elsewhere in India and the yield from irrigated rice crops is always better than from monsoon rice.

We must also work hard on conservancy programmes to put the trees back on our hills—trees like cashew, jackfruit, *ber* and mango, which give valuable cash crops. Also bigger trees for timber uses. We are starting a planting programme in our high school. The children will plant small trees in the hills and keep a watch on them. That is our hope.

But farmers around here will only have a good future if they accept modern methods to improve the fertility of their land. And they must hold on to their land, not sell out for big prices to those who wish to exploit it for other purposes. When the money the farmer gets is gone, then what is left? His children have lost their rightful heritage.

But while reafforestation, chemical fertilisers, pesticides and high-yield grains formed an integral part of India's national agricultural policies, the question of mechanisation on the land was always discouraged. One tractor, it was maintained, took away the livelihoods of ten workers. Older agriculturalists still agreed with this embargo. According to Noor Pangaka, the young Muslim timber merchant and farmer, this was an altogether short-sighted policy.

My belief is that preoccupation with hard manual labouring on the land will become counter-productive. Proper irrigation giving two crops of rice a year will lower the market price, so for twice as much work the farmer will only earn the same amount of money. If mechanisation makes farmworkers redundant, it seems to me these people would be better employed working on municipal jobs to improve the appearance and sanitation of our village. They could lay drains, dispose of rubbish and construct hard road surfaces to get rid of this dreadful dust. But as things are now, a fieldworker who starts work at six in the morning and doesn't return home until six at night, cares nothing for the appearance of his neighbourhood. He works, he eats and he sleeps. Mechanisation on the land would break this hand-to-mouth existence. And I'll tell you something else. With a regular job away from the land, the worker wouldn't have to keep his children away from school to make them work in the fields. Instead he could give them a better chance in life because they would not have to follow in his footsteps.

But, as always in this place, the biggest problem is rousing people to have a sense of social responsibility, to look ahead. I myself feel the future for this village will belong to those who can accept the changes that are coming for all of us. If we want to live well in the future, we must put aside the past.

And as always, it was the younger generation that welcomed

206

the future. The older people, still very much occupied with the gentle rhythms of their agricultural surroundings, were less enthusiastic. They did not trust the future, especially when in 1983 the threatened arrival of a piece of it—so to speak—in their very midst.

One day a private plane flew over the village and spent some time circling low over the coconut gardens before disappearing to the north. Some weeks afterwards, the throbbing sound of a helicopter was heard, and eventually the machine was sighted as it emerged from between the hills and dropped down to land on the beach at Diwaga. That evening the bazaar buzzed with rumours. Men in city clothes had been seen walking on the beach, making notes and taking photographs before climbing back in the whirly-bird and taking off again. What could they possibly be looking for on a deserted seashore?

It was some months before the purpose of that visit became common knowledge. Then reaction in Borli and Diwaga was sharply divided between those who welcomed the prospect of a big hotel on the beach and those who violently opposed it. The village elders, both Muslim and Hindu, saw this plan as one which would have untold corrupting influences on local people. Would there not be heavy drinking and white women walking about half naked? Who wanted speedboats and sailboats in the bay, getting in the way of the fishermen? Who could possibly welcome the fornicating and even drug-taking that would take place in such a building?

The elders gathered to compose a letter of protest to the appropriate officials and, when no more planes came to the hillside, the matter of the beach hotel faded from their minds. It was hoped that the speculators had gone elsewhere, although nobody knew for sure.

In their hearts, the elders knew they would have to accept the disadvantages of so-called progress in order to enjoy the benefits. As sophisticated strangers brought to the village their own social and moral values, amenities to accommodate them would be provided; hotels, drinking bars, cinemas and garages. Sooner or later all this was bound to come as the winds of change, which had already inflated local land prices, blew the seeds of a new society on to the little peninsula.

Ummie owned several small pieces of land which she had always thought to be worthless. Below the kindergarten school was a piece of waste land which had always been part and parcel of the ground on which her old house and that of Halima's

stood. She also owned a smaller triangle of land below Halima's
back yard, as well as the single ricefield which her late
husband had left her all those years ago when she first came
to Borli.

Ummie's first intimation that she might be sitting on a
gold-mine came with a letter from the municipal offices at
Shriverdhan. Like everyone else, she had heard the kind of
prices land was fetching in and around Borli and, with the
arrival of this letter, the old lady thought that perhaps at long
last fortune was about to smile upon her.

> The letter was calling me to the land office because there
> was a compulsory purchase order on that little corner of land
> below my Halima's house. The letter said it was needed to
> widen the place where the lane behind my house joins the one
> from the *agri* quarter. Well, I got very excited. I thought at
> last I'm going to be a wealthy woman. I got all dressed up to
> go to that district land office and then, when they paid me the
> money, what a shock! My bus fare cost half of what they put
> in my hand; thirteen rupees!

That was in 1981. Three years later, with land prices still
rising, the large piece of ground opposite Ummie's house was
also taken from her—this time not by the authorities, but by
the descendants of her late husband's other wives. Confident
that Ummie could not afford to take legal action, they com-
mandeered this land to sell for building. Ummie also lost the
ricefield, which during her early years of hardship had represented her only certain source of sustenance.

> My husband's relations came to me and said they intended
> to claim this field because otherwise in one year's time the old
> couple who worked the ground for me would be legally en-
> titled to secure it for themselves.
> Although I have title deeds to this field and to the ground
> opposite my house, I say nothing. I'd rather see those old
> workers get my field than those greedy relations who already
> have so much. But what can I do? I never could argue with
> these hard-headed people, and now—at my age—all I want is
> peace. I'm too old for family fights.

However, in terms of property, both Ummie and Halima
had become wealthy. Built in 1945 and still structurally sound,
if not structurally complete, Ummie's half of the old family
house was worth two laks (£12,000). Halima's house, built to
more modern specifications in 1972 at a cost of Rs 40,000
(£2,500), was worth at least eight times as much in a housing

market which reflected one thing—the peninsula people were on the threshold of a new era of prosperity.

*　*　*

According to the Hindu calendar, the Festival of Sankrant on the fifteenth of January marks the shortest day of the year. On this day, Hindu mythology relates, the god Diva rides on the back of an animal casting her evil eye either north, south, east or west. Wherever she fixes her gaze, misfortune will follow.

In 1984, the astrological almanack stated that Diva was on horseback riding from the south with her eyes fixed firmly on northern India. After a troubled period with Sikh separatists, Mrs Indira Gandhi, prime minister of India, was assassinated by her Sikh guards on 1 November 1984 at Delhi, in northern India. In December two and a half thousand people in Bhopal were killed by gas leaking from the American-owned Union Carbide plant.

In the village some Hindus regarded the Festival of Sankrant as an occasion to remain close to home and thus avoid the risk of an accident. Anyone hurt on this particular day was supposedly destined to suffer a series of mishaps throughout the coming year. Among less superstitious villages, Sankrant was an occasion for young married women to dress up in pretty paper crowns crusted with 'jewels' and entertain their women friends. Little sweetmeats covered with sesame seeds were distributed, the tiny seeds representing the number of new friendships the recipient hoped to make in the coming year.

Up on the village compound, Sankrant also marked the culmination of the academic year at the high school, when the results of state examinations became known and preparations for the grand end-of-year school concert were nearing completion.

The high school was the pride and joy of Nana Kulkarni. He was largely responsible for its inception back in 1956, when his farm out-buildings housed the first classrooms.

Before we had a high school here in the village, children from well-off homes had to be sent away to Bombay or Pune for their education. But our big concern was always for the poor children of the village. Unless they received an education, we felt the living standards in this place would never improve.

In 1964 the Janata Shikshan Saristha High School received official recognition and financial support from the national government. Children from families whose annual income was below Rs 2,500 were to get free schooling. But still we found many families that only sent their boys to the high school. They said girls had no use for further education; they only needed to know about household matters. And these poor people were also concerned that girls of twelve and thirteen must not mix with boys as this would compromise their future chances of a good marriage. Then two things happened.

We arranged to have separate classrooms for girls and the government notified us that they would pay a poor family Rs 25 a week for every girl sent to the high school. But we elders soon realised that if this money went directly to the parents it would be spent on drink or other things. And even if it wasn't that girl would not be able to study at home. She would be made to fetch water, wash clothes and so forth. So we asked well-to-do people in the village to agree to sponsor the education of poor girls; and poor boys also whom we considered would benefit from a high school training.

My friend Dr Adhikari sponsored the son of his maid-servant. At this boy's home there was no electricity, and he had so many brothers and sisters that he could never do his schoolwork in peace. So for all his years at the high school, he lived with the good doctor's family, where he got his food and school uniform. Eventually, this peasant boy matriculated with distinction. Now he is away at college studying for his B.Sc.

But of course education probably means children from peasant homes will never again be satisfied with the living conditions endured by their parents. Many will move away, looking for an easy life in the cities. But this has to be. Education is the only way to break the endless circle of rural backwardness.

The Muslim community in Borli was never entirely satisfied with the high school as a suitable place of learning for their children. Staffed by Hindu teachers who encouraged academic achievement in the name of patriotism, it lacked the religious discipline Muslims wanted for their teenage sons, who were required to turn towards Mecca five times each day and render homage to Allah, the one and only God. Muslims disdained the Hindu view of a more liberal-minded creator who—in the words of the *Gita*—favoured less formal patterns of worship: 'How-so-ever men approach me, so do I accept them; for on all sides the path they choose leads them to Me.' They also frowned upon an educational system which gave equal opportunities to both girls and boys and, worse still, under the same roof.

So Muslims in Borli founded an association called 'The Royal Educational Society' (the word 'royal' referring to 'worthiness' not regal patronage!) with a brief to establish independent schools influenced by their own religious in-doctrination. Equally important, the society planned to make English a curricular priority, since so many young Muslim men would eventually go abroad to work in countries where English was needed.

The society already had a primary school near the bazaar to cater for their youngest children; it also had ambitious plans for a senior school, where their sons could receive a standard of education so far denied them at the high school.

In 1984 the foundations for the new Muslim high school were excavated in a ricefield just below the village on the Diwaga road, the first stage of a building which had been designed by an architect in Manchester. It was hardly going to be a building which would merge gently with its mellow surroundings. The blueprint elevations depicted a double-storey hexagonal structure with large glazed windows and a flat roof, a conical spire at its centre. Inside, the facilities in-cluded science laboratories, a library and—wonder of wonders —the first modern washrooms and toilets seen in the village.

Much of the cost of this venture, set at £35,000, was being raised by contributions from members of the Muslim Society who had connections with Borli. When completed, the new school was intended to take 1,200 pupils who would each pay a monthly fee of Rs 35. Muslim families who could not afford such an exclusive education could still send their teenage sons up the hill to the free high school.

However, Noor Pangaka, secretary of the Royal Edu-cational Society, envisaged that they might have difficulty recruiting suitable staff for their new school.

Making English the spoken language in our high school may take time. At the moment our smallest Muslim children learn English from Indian teachers, who have never practised speaking English with English people. So they speak with what I must call a heavy accent and often use incorrect grammar, which is passed on to the pupils. Our ambition is to employ at least one teacher from England. This person need not have high qualifications. A provincial student-teacher from Man-chester, where we have many Muslim friends, would suit us very well.

So the bizarre prospect that one day Borli's Muslim children might end up speaking English with a Mancunian accent, is not beyond the bounds of possibility!

* * *

On the night of the Hindu high school concert, an immense moon sailed from behind the darkened hills and flooded the countryside with its softly luminous glow. On the compound, where the gentle slope of ground made a natural amphitheatre, long before the appointed hour people began trudging up the lanes which converged at the hilltop clearing, intent on getting a good seat.

At the lower end of the slope a covered stage, framed by coloured lights, had been erected; the proscenium was concealed by curtains on drawstrings operated by pupils hidden in the wings. Radiating from this focal point, a multiplicity of threads hung with hundreds of little paper flags had been secured to poles at the top of the auditorium to form a fluttering canopy over rows and rows of children sitting cross-legged and very close together.

Behind and on both sides of the children, an assortment of chairs and benches had been set out for the paying public, ushered to their seats by khaki-clad boys brandishing flashlamps.

Shortly before ten, the loudspeaker music abruptly ceased and the deafening chatter of the children slowly subsided, as the stage curtains jerked apart to reveal the sedately-seated figures of all the most respected Hindu citizens of Borli Panchatan. In the centre sat Dr Adhikari and Nana Kulkarni, wearing white *dhoti*, black *barathea* (fine wool) coats buttoned up to the throat and black Gandhi caps. Dr Adhikari's hands rested on a silver-knobbed ebony stick firmly planted between his knees, the footlights transforming his horn-rimmed *chessma* into orbs of light.

Nana Kulkarni, grand patriarch of Borli, sitting with ramrod straight back, had a stern expression etched into his sharp-boned features. To his right sat Dr Vasudha Joshi, prominent member of the school board, and next to her, Mrs Morey, principal of the high school, the glint of gold thread in these women's opulent silk saris eclipsing the mundane printed shirts and trousers worn by the other three people on the stage, Ravi Kulkarni and two senior teachers.

Each of the elders stood up to make lengthy speeches, which the audience received with customary polite silence. Only when their head teacher announced, her voice ringing with pride, that every student had successfully passed the state examinations, did a flutter of head-wagging and smiling ruffle the packed assembly. Then, as hesitantly as they had parted, the curtains slowly screened the dignitaries from sight, and immediately a tidal wave of human chatter surged across the compound.

The entertainment, composed of meticulously rehearsed songs and dances, performed to the music of *tabla* drums and harmonium, continued for several hours. Traditional dances, gracefully executed by children attired in exotic traditional costumes, were interspersed by pupils attired in T-shirts, jeans and dark glasses giving their interpretation of Western 'disco' dancing. A diminutive but audible stand-up comic was followed by a long recitation, followed by two lanky boys performing a comedy sketch which reduced the audience to howls of appreciative laughter—and so it went on, quickly passing the time until the early hours of the morning and the grand finale.

Two senior Hindu students and one Muslim took the stage, clothed in simple white *dhoti*, *kurta* and with coloured bands tied round their foreheads. Squatting down on their hunkers near the footlights, the two Hindu boys softly drummed an accompaniment as the Muslim boy sang, the thrilling cadences of his deep and confident voice rising up, up through the paper flags and the leaves of the ancient banyans to be lost in the blackness of the night.

* * *

In a climate which was either all rain or no rain at all, cultivating gardens had no appeal for the villagers. They were quite content to have a dusty back yard in which to do their cooking and spread out their washing to dry.

As a girl in Cape Town, Ummie remembered the beautifully tended grounds which surrounded the McKenzie household where she was employed as a servant. So, in her old age, Ummie made a garden alongside her house in the village. Roughly fencing off a square of ground with sticks and cactus, she fixed a palm-leaf gate on a post to keep out chickens and goats, and inside this small enclosure laid out some brick-edged flowerbeds. Each spring the old lady weeded back the ground-greedy periwinkle, pruned her rose bushes and carefully sprinkled marigold and forget-me-not seeds in the dusty soil.

Whenever he came from Bombay to spend time with his grandmother, nineteen-year-old Wazir enjoyed working in Ummie's garden. He cleared debris off the little pathways, reinforced the cactus fence to prevent passing children pilfering flowers and brought buckets and buckets of water to irrigate the beds.

By 1984 Ummie had twenty-eight grandchildren in India and four in South Africa. She also had four great-grandchildren. But of them all, Wazir—the grandchild whose birth was preluded by that frantic ride in a coconut lorry—was the grandson who had the greatest affection for the village and its surroundings. Wazir took long walks into the countryside knowing every bird and plant by name. He also went to the seashore, happy as a child to paddle in the shallows of the estuary searching for sea-silk and other shells. In this way, he tried to forget his future had already been decided by his father. Once he had learned to type, Wazir was to apply for clerical employment in a Saudi-Arabian city. The one hope remained that his request for a work permit would not be granted. By now, the demand for unskilled or semi-skilled migrant labour was subsiding; new cities, roads and airports were completed and indigenous citizens were trained to do the work which once only the imported labourers could do. And having no further use for Indian workers, the Arabs started to send them home.

Fortuitously perhaps, the end of the Saudi-Arabian boom-time for village men coincided with plans for the industrial developments on the peninsula. Wise migrant workers had saved to set themselves up in businesses, ready for the arrival of technological prosperity. For centuries, Hindu and Muslim villagers had lived out their lives linked to the soil, the seasons and religious traditions. The civilisation virus, which had already landed at Dighi, was destined to spread up the tiny peninsula, driving a wedge of artificial dependency between the people of Borli Panchatan and their natural heritage.

The last of India's 'little republics' was poised on the edge of cultural extinction.

* * *

At sunset, Tilak the Katkari boy hurriedly left the hut where his family lived and scrambled up the goat path behind the settlement. He climbed without stopping until he reached a promontory of bare rock. There he squatted down to brood on the unfairness of the blow which had driven him from his home.

Most evenings when Tilak's parents returned from work, they were drunk. Quarrels materialised out of thin air and any of the children who got in the way caught the backlash of this anger. With eight in a single room, it was seldom possible to escape it. When he could, Tilak grabbed his share of the meal and took the food with him to his favourite vantage point.

From up there he could look across the salt ricefields, where the cutchera pond gleamed like a purple eye in the setting sunlight and between the coconut gardens and the estuary a sea-eagle swooped on evening breezes to forage on the beach.

As the last call to prayer from the Borli mosque thinned on the still air, the boy watched flocks of fruit bats rise from the banyans on the village compound and, stretching spiked wings against a vivid orange sky, flap slowly towards Diwaga.

Then for a fleeting moment, the scene he was gazing at melted and re-formed into another and totally unfamiliar sight. Below on the rice-fields, Tilak glimpsed the bright lights of a large town on the edge of which were buildings with tall smoking chimneys. He saw the flare stacks of an oil refinery where the coconut gardens once were, heard the rattle of couplings in a marshalling yard . . . the sad wail of a train whistle . . . and out to sea, watched a procession of tankers steam for the shore, leaving trails of rainbow luminescence in the waters of the bay.

The chill night air roused the Katkari boy from his dreaming. It was dark as he left the rock to go home. He never knew he had been sitting where once Kabutari, his tribal ancestor, had sat on a day long, long ago when two small sailing ships brought five holy men from Arabia to rest their bones on a far hillside.